THE ROUGH GUIDE to
Ethical Living

by
Duncan Clark

with contributions from
Kevin Lindegaard

Credits

The Rough Guide to Ethical Living

Editor: Ruth Tidball
Design & layout: Duncan Clark
Proofreading: Anita Sach
Production: Aimee Hampson
& Katherine Owers

Rough Guides Reference

Series editor: Mark Ellingham
Editors: Peter Buckley, Duncan Clark,
Matthew Milton, Ruth Tidball, Tracy Hopkins,
Joe Staines, Sean Mahoney
Director: Andrew Lockett

Publishing information

This first edition (an updated and expanded version of *The Rough Guide to Ethical
Shopping*) published November 2006 by Rough Guides Ltd,
80 Strand, London WC2R 0RL
375 Hudson Street, New York 10014
Email: mail@roughguides.co.uk

Distributed by the Penguin Group
Penguin Books Ltd, 80 Strand, London WC2R 0RL
Penguin Putnam, Inc., 375 Hudson Street, NY 10014, USA
Penguin Group (Australia), 250 Camberwell Road, Camberwell, Victoria 3124, Australia
Penguin Books Canada Ltd, 90 Eglinton Avenue East, Toronto, Ontario, Canada M4P 2YE
Penguin Group (New Zealand), 67 Apollo Drive, Mairongi Bay, Auckland 1310, New Zealand

Printed in Italy by LegoPrint S.p.A

Typeset in Din, Minion and Myriad

The publishers and author have done their best to ensure the accuracy and currency
of all information in *The Rough Guide to Ethical Living*; however, they can accept no
responsibility for any loss or inconvenience sustained by any reader as a result of its
information or advice.

336 pages; includes index

A catalogue record for this book is available from the British Library

ISBN 13: 9-781-84353-792-2
ISBN 10: 1-84353-792-3

1 3 5 7 9 8 6 4 2

Contents

About this book

In the last few years, ethical living has gone mainstream. From politicians installing wind turbines on their roofs to Marks & Spencer selling Fairtrade-certified jeans, it's clear that the environmental and social impacts of our lifestyles are no longer a niche concern. Despite this growing awareness, however, it can still be difficult for concerned individuals to find concise, balanced information about the relevant issues – from low-emission cars to garment sweatshops.

The purpose of *The Rough Guide to Ethical Living* is to provide this kind of information. The book aims to enlighten rather than preach, and to give both sides of the story whenever a debate exists (which is most of the time). It won't answer every question, but it should prove a useful starting point for anyone who wants to lead a greener and fairer lifestyle.

Part I begins with **Ethical Living: A Primer**, which outlines what ethical living means and examines how many ethical consumers there are. The following chapter, **Reducing Your Carbon Footprint**, spells out in brief why climate change is such a pressing concern and explains how to take stock of the greenhouse gases you're personally responsible for. Finally, **Responsible Shopping** looks at the issues surrounding ethical purchasing – such as boycotts, fair trade and the ethical claims of big businesses.

Part II focuses on more specific areas, kicking off with the household arena: **Home Energy** provides tips on reducing the carbon emissions caused by your heating and electricity use; **Waste & Recycling** explains how to minimize the amount you send to landfill; and **House & Garden Products** looks at everything from washing-up liquid to timber and paint. Then comes **Food & Drink**, which covers issues such as food transport and organic farming before moving on to individual foods and where to buy them. **Clothes, Cosmetics & Jewellery** should help you dress without sacrificing style *or* ethics, while **Money Matters** gives the low-down on ethical banks, pensions and investments. Finally, **Transport & Travel** explains how to be a greener driver and looks at the impacts of our air travel and holidays.

Of course, there's a limit to the amount of information that can be squeezed into a book of this size. For that reason, you'll find pointers in each chapter to websites where you can read about the relevant topics in greater depth. For more general further reading, turn to **Find Out More**, which lists some of the best sites for researching the ethics of individual companies and gives details of some useful books and magazines.

Acknowledgements

This book – and *The Rough Guide to Ethical Shopping*, which it grew out of – has benefited from interviews, emails, images and advice from scores of people. These have included, in no particular order: Harriet Lamb, Diana Gayle, Abi Murray and Dave Goodyear at the Fairtrade Foundation; Mike Brady at Baby Milk Action; Beverly Mirando at Nestlé; Becky Price at Genewatch; Professor Michael Wilson from Horticulture Research International; Nina Smith at the Rugmark Foundation; Anne Lally at the Fair Labor Association; Mil Niepold at Verité; Wendy Higgins at BUAV; Bernadette Clark at the Marine Conservation Society; The UK Social Investment Forum; Jon Entine; Shelley Simmons at The Body Shop; Oliver Knowles at Greenpeace; Matthew Criddle at Naturesave Insurance; Paul Garrod at Chandni Chowk; Meagan Tudge at Ethically Me; Richard Young at the Soil Association; Sam Maher from Labour Behind the Label; Frances Galvanoni from the Energy Saving Trust; Greg Valerio at Cred; Scott McAusland at EIRIS; Rob Harrison and Elanor Gordon at *Ethical Consumer*; Wendy Martin at *New Consumer*; Kat Alexander at the Ethical Company Organization; Daniel Blackburn at VegOilMotoring; Christine Miles at *The Chichester Observer*; the *Garstang Courier*; Regina Dinkla and Chrissie Bestley at Fair Flowers Fair Plants; Craig Simmons at Best Foot Forward; Heather Gorringe at Wiggly Wigglers; Ellie Williams at Valpak; Anna Addison at Electrisave; and Rick Mills.

Thanks also to everyone at Rough Guides and Penguin: Jonathan Buckley and Mark Ellingham for signing such an off-the-wall title as *Ethical Shopping*; John Duhigg and Andrew Lockett for ushering through *Ethical Living* with great haste; Joe Staines for three years of press cuttings; Pete Buckley for picking up the slack on other books; and, especially, Ruth Tidball and Matt Milton for fantastic editorial input under tight time restraints.

Part I

The big picture

Ethical living: a primer

"Ethical living" is quite a blurry term, which could easily refer to everyday moral issues such as donating to charity or giving up a seat on a bus to make way for an elderly person. But in the last few years, the phrase has come to mean something more specific: adapting our lifestyles and shopping habits with the aim of reducing our negative impact (and increasing our positive impact) on the world's environments, people and animals.

These adaptations don't have to be extreme. Ethical living doesn't have to mean installing a £20,000 solar roof. And it doesn't have to mean following a prescriptive list of evil companies that need to be boycotted. It simply means taking the time to learn a little about how your lifestyle affects the wider world, and making your own decisions about what constitutes an ethical or unethical lifestyle.

The case for making the effort is strong. After all, the energy we consume and the goods we buy involve us in many of the most pressing issues in the world: from the potentially catastrophic impacts of climate change to the oceans' dwindling fish stocks; from sweatshop labour to the funding of US presidential election campaigns; from the long-term sustainability of our farming systems to oppressive governments benefiting from foreign trade. That's not to say all these problems are the *fault* of consumers, or that consumers are in a position to solve them. But we live in an increasingly integrated world, and the implications of our lifestyles reach far further than we might think.

Getting started

There are two main approaches to ethical living. The first involves aiming to reduce our direct impact on the environment – and climate change in particular – by becoming more efficient in our use of electricity, gas, petrol and other fuels. This isn't easy but at least the aim is clear – and you may even save some money in the process. For an introduction to reducing your so-called carbon footprint, turn to chapter two.

The second approach is ethical shopping, which involves considering social and environmental matters when deciding which products and services to buy. This can be complex, since there's no one-size-fits-all approach – no simple list of moral ticks and crosses. Is it better, for instance, to support the local independent café round the corner, or buy a fairly traded cup from the global chain across the road? Is it "ethical" to favour local products – doing your bit to limit environmentally harmful transportation – or does that mean harming impoverished countries that are keen to export? These kinds of questions are discussed in chapter three: Responsible Shopping.

From fringe to mainstream

The impact of ethical living depends partly on the number of people who get involved. But this is actually something that's very difficult to measure. We can keep tabs on how much people are spending on explicitly "ethical" goods, such as those carrying the Fairtrade Mark (more than £195 million each year in the UK and rising fast). But it's not so easy to work out what people *aren't* buying on ethical grounds, through boycotts. It's also difficult to analyse people's motives. For instance, consumers may be choosing energy-efficient fridges to save money rather than to save the planet, or favouring local stores because they're nearer, rather than because they want to take a stand against the supermarkets' control of the food chain.

The only way to gauge people's commitment and motives is to ask them. And, as social scientists tend to agree, people often give answers they feel their questioner wants to hear – or ones which reflect their ideals, even though they might rarely act on those ideals. In one poll commissioned jointly by *The Guardian* and Toyota, for example, two-thirds of consumers claimed to make ethical purchasing decisions. Yet sales of ethical goods simply don't bear such claims out. Similarly, countless reports have suggested that consumers are adamantly against animal testing for cosmetics, but products bearing the Humane Cosmetics Standard (see p.254) account for less than 2% of the UK market.

Words can speak louder than actions

One basic premise of ethical living is the idea that, if you're concerned about issues such as social and environmental justice, then you have a responsibility to actually *do* something about it – be it buying fair trade products or opting for a lower-emissions car. There's no point in getting het up about the world's problems, the argument goes, if you can't be bothered to take personal action to improve the situation. Taking action not only has a direct effect but can also influence others. For instance, someone who determines to give up travelling by plane not only directly reduces the demand for plane tickets but is also likely to get their friends thinking about climate change in a way that a news article or government leaflet could never achieve.

It is, however, worth remembering the alternative approach: registering our concern or demanding change through words. For instance, though reducing your house-hold energy use is a valid way to tackle the threat of climate change, you may be able to have an even bigger effect by writing to your MP and encouraging them to lean on the government to pass legislation which requires *everyone* to reduce their greenhouse emissions.

When it comes to ethical shopping decisions, communicating your message may be even more important. For instance, it's all well and good to favour one high-street brand over another due to their respective ethical standards. But unless you go to the trouble of *telling* one or both of the brands involved that ethical issues influenced your decision, then your choice will have less of an effect than it otherwise might – or it may even have the opposite effect.

Take the example of a clothes shop which notices that sales are down. The shop's owners will probably assume (correctly) that this is mainly because consumers were unhappy with the season's styles or prices. Without a comprehensive market-research campaign, they may never realize that a small percentage of that loss might have been people going elsewhere on ethical grounds. As one commentator put it, the signal the ethical shoppers are trying to send may become "lost in the general market noise". And if that market noise is demanding, say, lower prices, the quiet ethical shopper may be unwittingly contributing towards a price-slashing drive, in which the shop leans even more heavily on its suppliers to produce more goods for less money: not good news for workers' rights.

Ironically, then, you may make a bigger difference expressing concerns to a shop's manager as you hand over your credit card than you would by simply not going in. However, perhaps the ideal approach is to act and to communicate in other ways – cutting your carbon emissions *and* writing to your MP, for instance.

The Internet makes it easier than ever to contact companies and political representatives alike. These days, there's no need to mess around with stamps or faxes or to spend ages tracking down contact details. Simply drop into a company's website and look for the Contact Us link. Or, in the case of writing to your MP, go to one of the following websites, enter your postcode and away you go.

They Work for You www.theyworkforyou.com
Write to Them www.writetothem.com

But if there's one thing we can say for certain, it's that ethical living as a whole just keeps on growing. The best guide is the **Ethical Consumerism Report**. This annual report, published by the Co-operative Bank and New Economics Foundation, keeps tabs on the whole movement, from boycotts to people opting for public transport over their car on ethical grounds. Since its launch in 1999, the report has charted the steady rise in individuals attempting to be green and fair in their consumer choices, as the graph below shows.

Another report, *Shopping With Attitude*, commissioned by the Co-operative Group supermarkets, found that 60% of respondents were more concerned with ethical issues in 2004 than they were ten years ago, with

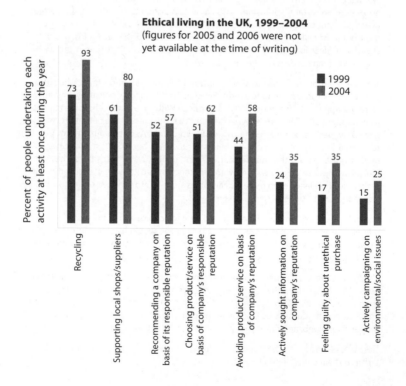

Ethical living in the UK, 1999–2004
(figures for 2005 and 2006 were not yet available at the time of writing)

Percent of people undertaking each activity at least once during the year

■ 1999
■ 2004

Activity	1999	2004
Recycling	73	93
Supporting local shops/suppliers	61	80
Recommending a company on basis of its responsible reputation	52	57
Choosing product/service on basis of company's responsible reputation	51	62
Avoiding product/service on basis of company's reputation	44	58
Actively sought information on company's reputation	24	35
Feeling guilty about unethical purchase	17	35
Actively campaigning on environmental/social issues	15	25

84% prepared to pay more for ethically produced products (up from 62% in 1994).

None of these statistics should be treated as concrete – the Co-operative Bank accepts that "the full extent of ethical consumerism will always be difficult to gauge, given that it is about the motivation behind a particular

UK ethical living in figures

£25.8 billion ▶	total value of "ethical consumption" in the UK, including donations to charity
£10.6 billion ▶	spent by consumers on ethical financial services
£5.5 billion ▶	invested in ethical or green funds
£4.7 billion ▶	deposited in banks with ethical policies
£2.3 billion ▶	personal charitable donations
£1.9 billion ▶	cost to companies of ethically driven boycotts of food and drink products
£1.5 billion ▶	cost to companies of other ethically driven boycotts
£1.4 billion ▶	spent on energy-efficient appliances
£1.1 billion ▶	spent on organic food
£173 million ▶	the total spent on cosmetics certified as not tested on animals (less than 2% of total)
£195 million ▶	spent on food bearing the Fairtrade label
£132 million ▶	the total spent on responsible tourism
2/3 ▶	the proportion of people who would never return to a product once they have boycotted it
52% ▶	the proportion of people who claimed to have avoided at least one product on ethical grounds in the last year
50% ▶	the proportion of shoppers who recognise the Fairtrade Mark (see p.26)
41% ▶	the proportion of eggs sold that are free range
5% ▶	the proportion of consumers in the "global watchdogs" category, according to MORI
1–2% ▶	the total market share of ethical goods and services

Sources: Co-operative Bank (Ethical Consumerism Report 2005)*; MORI; EIRIS; Fairtrade Foundation*

// In order to make an ethical choice, consumers wanted the full facts about the make-up of the different products on offer. But three quarters (76%) said they were being kept in the dark ... they were hungry for information. //

Co-operative Group, *Shopping With Attitude*

purchase as much as the product or service itself". But they do provide a broad-brush impression of ethical consumerism's rise.

Another observation made by just about every relevant survey and poll is that people would *like* to be more actively ethical than they are, but feel held back by a lack of information. As more information is becoming available each year, this suggests a possible snowball-effect growth for ethical living in the not-too-distant future.

Reducing your carbon footprint

Environmentalists have long campaigned for people in rich countries to scale back our consumption levels in an attempt to reduce our collective impact on the planet. Back in the 1980s and before, these aims, though laudable enough, were also somewhat vague. But human-induced climate change has changed that. We now know that the gases emitted directly or indirectly by almost every human activity – from agriculture and manufacturing to driving cars and heating homes – have the potential to change the planet's climate in potentially catastrophic ways.

There isn't space here for a full discussion of the science and potential impacts of climate change, but it's worth quickly spelling out a few key facts. Despite a handful of remaining sceptics in the scientific community (their voices amplified by corporate-funded think tanks), there is now a solid scientific consensus that humans have measurably changed the climate in the last century. We've done this by releasing huge volumes of so-called **greenhouse gases** into the atmosphere. The most important greenhouse gas – carbon dioxide or CO_2 – is released primarily by the burning of fossil fuels such as coal, oil and natural gas to create electricity, power vehicles and machines or heat buildings. Others, such as methane and nitrous oxides, are released mainly by farming and industrial processes.

As sunlight reaches Earth, it's converted into infrared energy and emitted back through the atmosphere and into space. Greenhouse gases absorb some of this energy, reducing the amount that is lost to space and hence warming the atmosphere. There have always been greenhouse gases in the air (if there were none, our planet would be a freezing, lifeless chunk of rock), but in the last century and a half, we've increased their levels with remarkable speed.

It's true, of course, that the world's climate has always been in a state of flux: ice ages have come and gone, and in the really long run the Sun will grow to 250 times its current size, boil the oceans, kill all life and cause "iron rain and silicon snow" to fall on Earth, in the words of *New Scientist*. Unlike this unavoidable, natural climate change, however, our emissions of greenhouse gases threaten humans and other species now – rather than at some unimaginably distant point in the future.

Indeed, some serious impacts are already observable. The World Health Organization estimates that in 2000 alone, more than 150,000 people died as a result of direct and indirect climate-change impacts such as the widening reach of **malaria** and **dengue fever**, the seemingly paradoxical increase in both **drought and flooding**, and a rise in the intensity of **heat waves** and **hurricanes**.

Looking forward, the potential changes are terrifying. A study published in science journal *Nature* in January 2004 concluded that, if mid-range predictions for greenhouse emissions and the climate's sensitivity to them prove correct, 15–37% of the world's plant and animal species will be "committed to extinction" by 2050. By the end of the century, a combination of warming oceans and melting Arctic and Antarctic ice could raise sea levels by as much as a metre, devastating low-lying regions such as Bangladesh through loss of land and higher-reaching storm surges. A couple of centuries further on, the sea-level rise could be many times greater, displacing billions of people and destroying many of the world's great cities, London and New York included.

Of course, a different climate may also have some benefits, but the costs are likely to be incomparably greater and will be felt most acutely by people who are least financially able to adapt (the same people who are least responsible for the problem in the first place). As for the UK, climate change may take the edge off our cold winters, but it looks set to bring increased rainfall and flooding too. It may even partially shut down the Gulf Stream and North Atlantic Drift – the ocean-based cycles that bring warmth to Northern Europe from the tropics. If this happened, Britain would end up as cold as equivalent latitudes in Russia or Canada.

For a comprehensive overview of climate change science, see *The Rough Guide to Climate Change*.

One way to reduce your carbon footprint is simply to try and buy less stuff. This approach to ethical consumerism is embodied by Buy Nothing Day, which has been running since 1993. The challenge is to go 24 hours without buying anything. It's a commitment to consuming less, recycling more and challenging corporations to clean up and be fair. "Culture jammers" stage pranks and protests in shopping malls, make puppets (see www.consumermonster.com), start a Saturday job timed specifically to get fired from it (for refusing to sell anything on Buy Nothing Day, of course) and generally raise awareness of our ecological footprints.

Solutions great and small

As individuals, we can attempt to tackle climate change both directly – by seeking to reduce the greenhouse-gas emissions that we're personally responsible for – and by lobbying our political representatives to put the issue towards the top of the national and international agendas (see p.5 for information about contacting your MP). We can also consider paying a carbon offset company to invest in projects that will counteract some or all of our emissions (see overleaf).

When focusing on the personal level, the first step is to take stock of your personal **carbon footprint** – the total amount of CO_2 emissions that you are directly or indirectly responsible for. A good start is to play with a carbon calculator. These simple online tools allow you to calculate how much carbon each activity in your life generates and how your total compares to those of the people around you and elsewhere in the world. The carbon-offset companies all offer calculators for specific activities, but to quickly assess your overall carbon footprint, visit:

Ecological Footprint Quiz www.myfootprint.org
BP www.bp.com/environment

These sites, though useful, tend to focus on our most obvious carbon-intensive activities, such as flying and driving. A more comprehensive analysis should include less obvious emissions sources such as the production and transport of all the goods we buy. The following charts, based on figures from Best Foot Forward (www.bestfootforward.com), break down

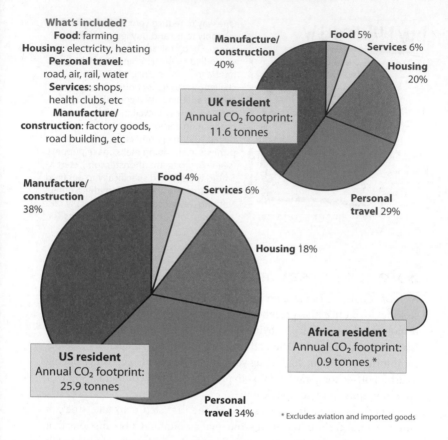

What's included?
Food: farming
Housing: electricity, heating
Personal travel:
road, air, rail, water
Services: shops,
health clubs, etc
**Manufacture/
construction**: factory goods,
road building, etc

Manufacture/
construction
40%

Food 5%
Services 6%
Housing
20%

UK resident
Annual CO_2 footprint:
11.6 tonnes

Personal
travel 29%

Manufacture/
construction
38%

Food 4%
Services 6%

Housing 18%

US resident
Annual CO_2 footprint:
25.9 tonnes

Africa resident
Annual CO_2 footprint:
0.9 tonnes *

Personal
travel 34%

* Excludes aviation and imported goods

the carbon footprint of the average UK and US residents, with an average figure for Africa provided for comparison. They include aviation and the manufacture of imported goods, both of which are usually excluded from official per-capita emissions statistics.

As the charts show, about half of the average UK citizen's emissions are accounted for by home energy (heating and electricity) and travel (road, air and sea). So these are sensible areas to focus on. Later in this book you'll find lots of tips to get started – see p.69 for household energy and p.287 for travel. But what about the other half of our emissions? These are caused by the production and transportation of the food and goods we buy, the construction of our homes, offices and roads, and the services we use. Some of these emissions are completely beyond our control. But we

Carbon offset schemes

Anyone who wants to neutralize their effect on climate change will be interested in the various schemes that allow you to "offset" your carbon footprint. Whether you want to cancel the CO_2 of a single long-haul flight, a year of car journeys or your entire existence, the process is the same. First, you visit the website of an offsetting organization and use their **carbon calculators** to work out the emissions related to whatever activity you want to offset. This will be translated into a fee which the offsetting organization will use to soak up a matching amount of CO_2 from the air. To do this, they fund projects such as the replanting of damaged rainforest or the distribution of long-life, low-energy light bulbs in developing countries. As a guide, it usually costs around £7/$12 to offset a tonne of CO_2. At this price, a seat on a round trip from London to New York costs around £12/$20 to neutralize, while a typical year of driving in an averagely efficient car clocks in at around £20/$35.

Offset schemes have proved popular not just with individuals, but also with global corporations (HSBC and other office-based giants are going "climate neutral"), celebrities (Pink Floyd, Pulp and the Pet Shop Boys have all neutralized their tours), and even publishers (the production of the book you are reading was offset by Rough Guides).

However, offset schemes are not without their critics – as evidenced by *New Internationalist* magazine's July 2006 special edition, which had "Do Not Sponsor This Tree!" emblazoned across its cover. One argument levelled against offsetting is that it's just a plaster on the wound, hiding the inherent unsustainability of carbon-intensive Western lifestyles. There's some truth in this point – offsetting isn't as good as not emitting the carbon in the first place. But it's certainly better than doing nothing, and there's no reason why people can't buy offsets *and* make efforts to reduce their emissions directly.

Another criticism sometimes made is that offset projects may not make the swift, long-term carbon savings that are claimed of them. It's true that some of the projects – most notably tree planting – may take decades to soak up the carbon you've paid to offset, which is one reason why many offsetting groups are moving towards sustainable energy projects instead of trees. As for whether the carbon savings are real, the major offsetting services are externally audited to address just this question. They include:

CarbonNeutral Company www.carbonneutral.com (01932 828 882)
Climate Care www.climatecare.org (01865 207 000)

can reduce them somewhat by recycling, avoiding unnecessary purchases and favouring local (preferably organic) food.

Another approach is to favour brands, shops and services that have sought to reduce their own emissions, and avoid those which have lobbied against mandated cuts in greenhouse-gas emissions. Until fairly recently, the latter category included most of the mainstream business community, especially in the US. In May 2001, for example, Thomas J Donohue, CEO of the Chamber of Commerce of the United States of America, which speaks on behalf of "three million businesses", wrote a letter to President George W Bush claiming that "global warming is an important issue that must be addressed – but the Kyoto Protocol is a flawed treaty that is not in the US interest". Today, however, many companies have managed to reduce their emissions considerably – or have at least ended their membership of industry lobby groups such as the Global Climate Coalition (see p.298), which was once enormously influential in derailing climate protection measures.

Given President Bush's rejection of the Kyoto Protocol, there's also a decent case for avoiding any company that has bankrolled his election campaigns (see p.64).

Beyond climate change

Climate change may be the single greatest threat to the world's environments but our consumer choices can harm the planet in more specific, localised ways. **Rainforest clearance**, for example, is driven mainly by demand for wood and the desire for land to grow crops such as soya (mainly used as feed for the meat and milk industries) and palm oil (which is found in everything from soap to biscuits). Such clearances have been responsible for many of the estimated 300,000 species that have been rendered extinct in the last fifty years.

But it's not just animals and plants that feel the effect of local-level ecological destruction: when the environment suffers, people also tend to suffer, and that usually means the poor. There are countless manifestations of this fact, from the persecution of indigenous people that goes hand in hand with deforestation, to the cancer and blindness that result when industrial effluent is pumped untreated into rivers used for water supplies, such as has happened around Bangladeshi leather tanneries (see p.233). Local-level environmental problems have also forced millions of people from their homes. Though **environmental refugees** are not spe-

Ecological footprints

The concept of a carbon footprint grew out of a longer-established and broader idea: the **ecological footprint**. This is a measure of our consumption levels in terms of the total area of the Earth's surface needed to support our individual existence. This area – measured in hectares of average productivity – includes the space for growing crops, grazing animals, harvesting timber, catching fish, accommodating infrastructure and absorbing carbon dioxide emissions. The icons below give some sense of the inequality in the footprints of people around the world. The global average is 2.28 hectares.

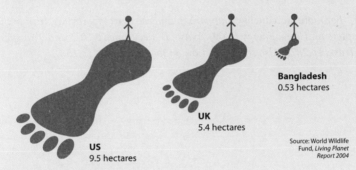

Bangladesh
0.53 hectares

UK
5.4 hectares

US
9.5 hectares

Source: World Wildlife
Fund, *Living Planet
Report 2004*

To calculate your own ecological footprint (and find out how many planets we'd need if everyone lived just like you) see:

Earth Day Footprint Quiz www.myfootprint.org

Or for more information about the ecological footprint system, visit:

Redefining Progress www.redefiningprogress.org

cifically recognized by the Geneva Convention, there may now be more of them than political refugees: 25 million compared with 22 million, according to analysis by the environmental ecologist Norman Myers. And this figure is set to rocket as climate change kicks in.

The typical response of environmentalists to all this is to advocate buying and consuming as little as possible, but many exponents of globalization have a different view. They claim that people only start to care for their local environment when they reach a certain level of material wealth (two academics from Princeton University put the threshold at an annual average income of $5000). That explains, the argument goes, why air and water quality are generally going up in rich countries and down in poor countries. Since many poor countries rely on exporting goods to Western markets, then cutting back on consumerism could end up harming developing economies. The only way people there are likely to become rich enough to be able to pay heed to environmental issues, we're told, is through more trade – which necessarily involves people buying and consuming more.

But, even if it's true, there's at least one serious problem with this line of reasoning. Rich countries may have fewer local environmental problems, but they are incomparably worse when it comes to global warming.

☛ *For more on reducing your carbon and ecological footprints, turn to the chapters on Home Energy (p.69), Waste & Recycling (p.101) and Transport & Travel (p.287). Also see the section on food transport (p.156).*

Responsible shopping

Much of this book is concerned with the social and environmental implications of specific products and companies, and the choices faced by ethically minded shoppers. But first it's worth taking a step back and thinking about "ethical" or "responsible" shopping in more general terms. This chapter does just that, exploring the key tools of the ethical consumer – such as buying fair trade and participating in boycotts – and examining some of the broader issues, such as sweatshop labour and oppressive regimes. First of all, though, it's worth asking something even more fundamental: is ethical shopping a good idea?

World changer or waste of time?
The cases for and against ethical shopping

This may sound like a silly question. But while very few people suggest we should deliberately *ignore* ethical issues when choosing what to buy, some do claim that focusing on them too much is a waste of time – or even counterproductive. Here, then, are the main arguments for and against ethical shopping.

Arguments for

The basic case for ethically minded shopping is very simple – that, now more than ever, the things we buy link us to a huge range of environmental, social, economic and political issues. We can choose to ignore this fact

> **❚❚** We have to accept that we're born consumers, and the only rational course open to us is responsible, accountable consumerism. **❚❚**
>
> Anita Roddick

> **❚❚** Buying ethical products sends support directly to progressive companies ... while at the same time depriving others that abuse for profit. **❚❚**
>
> *Ethical Consumer* magazine

if we like, but there's really no denying it. It's not that you have to be vindictive to shop "unethically". After all, it won't say on the label if an item of clothing has been made in a factory that denies workers the basic right to join a union and bargain for decent pay and conditions. Nor will it say if a piece of furniture is made from wood logged from Indonesia's swiftly disappearing rainforests. But the fact remains: if we buy such products, we support the companies in question and the way they produce their goods. Likewise, if we buy products from the firms that fund politicians – which many of them do (see p.63) – we give our vote to whichever party they're bankrolling.

However, it's not all about the *negative* impacts we make on the world. As many people in the ethical consumerism "movement" are keen to point out, responsible consumers can make a *positive* difference, too. By supporting progressive businesses, or products bearing labels that testify to their social and environmental credentials, we may help bring about deeper change. Cred jewellery, for example, are a small fair trade supplier, but they've been integral to the slow ethical awakening of the whole jewellery industry. Similarly, companies specializing in renewable electricity, "green" paints or electric cars are likely to be actively involved in the research and development of eco-friendly products and practices that may gradually enter the mainstream.

Or think of the **Fairtrade** labelling scheme, which aims to ensure that marginalized producers in poor countries – cocoa farmers in West Africa, say – get a bigger proportion of the price we pay for their goods, as well as up-front payments and other benefits. The scheme is entirely consumer-driven, yet many of its principles are starting to crop up in the policy ideas of parliaments, companies and radical political writers alike. This doesn't mean that ideals of equity and partnership will soon come to be embedded in all global trade (and some people doubt whether that would be a good idea anyway – more on that later), but it does show that ethical consumers have influenced thinkers of all kinds.

Furthermore, buying socially or environmentally focused products can **raise the profile of issues** that might otherwise be ignored. The very availability of an "ethical" option inevitably gets people thinking, whether it's about the real costs of fossil fuels (in the case of a domestic wind turbine) or the environmental and animal-rights impacts of intensive agriculture (in the case of organic food).

Finally, on a less ambitious level, considering the implications of what we buy may simply allow us to align our beliefs with our actions – a purely personal aim, but there's nothing wrong with that.

Arguments against
(and the arguments against them)

Arguments against the "moralization" of consumerism come from both the reactionary right and the radical left, as well as from semantic pedants and those who simply grumble that it's all just "political correctness gone mad". Following are some of the most common objections.

A distraction from the real problems

Ethical consumerism has a love-hate relationship with the extreme left. Though many radicals dutifully buy their fairly traded bananas, others worry that the whole idea of ethical consumerism is potentially danger-ous. After all, though it's usually seen as a progressive, essentially left-wing movement, ethical consumerism is still a form of **consumer power** – something once described by *The Guardian*'s Larry Elliott as "one of the unintended consequences of the Thatcherite revolution". As such, some argue, it may act as a distraction from engagement with national and international politics. Journalist and author George Monbiot, for example, claims that this problem has been apparent for years. The greatest failure of the green movement in the 1980s, he once wrote, was the misconcep-tion that "we could buy our way out of trouble".

That's a fair point, but it's not as if anyone who thinks about ethical shopping is somehow using up all their intellectual energy and will give up engaging in real politics – especially when you consider that many organizations involved in ethical consumerism spend considerable effort raising awareness of broader political issues and campaigning for global, structural change. Fair trade companies, for example, have long cam-paigned for a reduction in the European farm subsidies which make it hard for developing-world farmers to compete (see p.26).

That said, some of ethical shopping's advocates do like to hint at the goal of a new **consumer democracy** that can deliver where the state and

> **// Because ethical consumerism is based *wholly* on market solutions ... it is incapable even of recognising the *root* cause of that crisis, namely the atomising nature of market society. //**
>
> Anarchist FAQ webpage

> **// 'Light' green business tends to merely perpetuate the colonisation of the mind, sapping our visions of an alternative and giving the idea that our salvation can be gained through shopping rather than through social struggle. //**
>
> Christopher and Judith Plant, *Green Business: Hope or Hoax*

social activism have failed. In this model, the checkout is the new ballot box and "commercial disobedience" the new civil disobedience. Noreena Hertz, for example, wrote that "In a world in which power increasingly lies in the hands of corporations rather than governments, the most effective way to be political is not to cast one's vote at the ballot box but to do so at the supermarket or at a shareholders meeting."

Such statements (which, it should be said, do not fully reflect Hertz's views) are unhelpful – not just because they might discourage political engagement, but also because they're based on a skewed concept of democracy that's heavily weighted in favour of the wealthy. Political democracy is based on the principle of one person one vote, but in a consumer democracy you vote in hard currency.

For all this, the sensible response is not to dismiss ethical shopping; rather, we should simply make sure that we're always aware of its limits and not let it take the place of politics. Some have put it like this: be ethical citizens first, and ethical consumers second. Bear that in mind as you read this book, and in addition to making any changes to your lifestyle and shopping habits, consider writing to your MP (see p.5).

Letting governments off the hook

Another view from the left is that, by pressuring companies rather than politicians, ethical shoppers make it easier for governments to avoid legislating for legally enforceable, across-the-board change. This doesn't apply to fair trade companies and other "ethical specialists", but if consumers manage to persuade big firms to introduce **voluntary codes of conduct**, for example, or join **ethical trade bodies**, then politicians can say "we don't need to introduce any new laws or regulations ... the corporate sector is already dealing with the problems".

This argument is entirely valid (politicians have indeed sometimes taken this line) but not entirely persuasive. For one thing, it's just as logical to suppose that progressive, responsible companies will catalyze new laws and new regulations – by showing that good corporate practice is achievable – as to assume that they will deter them. After all, once a company has committed, say, to only selling wood from sustainable sources, then a law making this a general requirement would actually be in its interest, since the company's competitors would then be forced to play catch-up. So supporting big companies that make voluntary improvements may weaken, rather than strengthen, anti-regulation corporate lobbying.

Furthermore, in reality, laws can often only go so far. Much, perhaps most, of the world's labour abuse and environmental damage is already illegal but goes ahead regardless. That's why an increasing number of charities and non-governmental organizations (NGOs) now agree that problems ranging from safety in diamond mines to working hours in clothes factories can only be really solved when governments, NGOs *and* companies are all genuinely committed to change. And companies will never become committed without pressure from consumers.

// The purpose of corporate social responsibility is to avoid regulation. It permits governments and the public to believe that compulsory rules are unnecessary, as the same objectives are being met by other means. Of course, the great advantage of voluntary rules is that you can break them whenever they turn out to be inconvenient. **//**

George Monbiot

Hurting the poor

From the opposite side of the political spectrum comes the opposite criticism: not that ethical consumerism may deter new laws and regulations, but that it might in itself be almost *too much* of a regulation. This argument is based on a strong belief in the **free market** – that if you let supply and demand do their thing, it will be in everyone's interest, and anti-market ethical meddling, however well meaning, will simply get in the way.

For example, if coffee prices are low due to oversupply, then we must let the market do its work and force down the number of coffee growers: propping up an unsustainable system via the Fairtrade label is just dragging the problem out. Likewise, if Western consumers demand higher labour standards for workers in poor countries, this will force up the cost of producing in the developing world, reducing the number of companies

// **The adoption of Western standards would mean that the cost of production in the developing countries increases manifold; this would take away their entire competitive edge.** *//*

Ranvir Nayar,
The Indian Express

moving their facilities there, and denying people naively described as "exploited" the very jobs they desperately want and need.

Furthermore, the argument goes, if we have patience, the invisible hand of the market will eventually improve working conditions: once enough sweatshops and export farms open up in a country, unemployment will drop, the workforce will get better off, and employers will have to compete with each other to raise standards and attract staff.

There is certainly some truth in all this but, again, it's not a wholly convincing case. For one thing, it makes little sense to criticize ethical consumerism as being "anti-market". It is, after all, about people making free choices about what they do and don't want, and using their spending power in the marketplace to implement those decisions – practically a textbook definition of how a free market should work. Second, there's quite clearly no such thing as a genuinely free market anyway: all markets exist within a framework of laws (covering everything from monopolies and the minimum wage to slavery and toxic dumping) and ethical shopping, like voting, is a perfectly valid way of taking a stand about what these laws should be. Third, on the ground level, and especially in poor countries, "free" markets are often in practice hugely distorted, with political corruption and violent threats having far more sway than supply and demand. In many cases, ethical consumerism is helping to limit, not add to, these market distortions – by giving us the option to buy direct from producers, for example.

Despite all this theory, however, it's still a valid question to ask whether well-meaning ethical shoppers may end up doing more harm than good in relation to specific issues, such as third-world labour standards (see p.48) and Fairtrade coffee (see p.206).

There are more valid ways to spend your money

Many ethical consumer choices – such as buying an efficient, low-emissions car instead of a gas-guzzler – can end up saving us money, in the long term at least. But in other cases, the apparently obvious ethical choice costs extra money that could be spent in other ways. For instance, buying organic food lets us support a more responsible farming system that is better for wildlife, soil fertility and animal welfare – undoubtedly worthy causes. But the problems it addresses arc arguably far less acute than – to pick a random example – the lack of essential medicines at any number of the world's refugee camps. As such, how can we justify spending an extra £20 or so each week buying organic food "on ethical grounds", instead of hunting down bargains and giving the money saved to Oxfam or Médecins Sans Frontières? Can conventional agriculture really be so bad that we'll prioritize it over appalling human misery?

Some would say that the answer is that ethical consumerism allows us to deal with structural problems rather than just symptoms. And that's a fair point – the world needs social and environmental justice as well as charity. But could it also be partly that conscientious consumerism gives us greater guilt relief than charity, as it makes us feel at ease with our comparative wealth?

Nothing's truly "ethical", so why bother?

The argument that no individual – let alone a producer or product – can be truly, categorically "ethical" is often given as a reason for not bothering with ethically minded shopping. After all, if it's ethical to, say, choose a car with lower greenhouse emissions, it must be even more ethical to walk instead of drive, to take the stairs rather than the lift, or to only eat raw food to save wasting the energy used in cooking. The logical conclusion, sceptics sometimes revel in pointing out, would be to minimize your negative impact on the world by stopping breathing altogether.

The "e" word is without a shadow of a doubt **subjective**, morally loaded and often problematic. But, while you could spend hours arguing over the subjectivity of it all, semantic nit-picking is not really very good grounds for ignoring our impacts on the world. And, while we all have our own specific ideas of what should and shouldn't count as "ethical standards", it's probably fair to say that we all aspire to some common ideals. For example: *no* to unnecessary harm to people or the environment; *yes* to the provision of safe, dignified conditions for workers; *no* to hiding the social and environmental implications of a product from the person buying it. It's surely more constructive to ask how these standards can be achieved than to argue over whether or not ethical consumerism is an oxymoron.

That said, it's true that you should treat ethical claims with a certain degree of caution until you know exactly what it is they refer to – especially when someone's trying to make money out of them.

Fair trade

How does it work? How "fair" is it?

There are many approaches to fair trade and just as many terms to describe them. For instance, "fair" is sometimes substituted with **alternative**, **responsible** or **ethical** – perhaps on the grounds that no business arrangement between rich consumers and poor producers can ever be entirely fair. Other organizations prefer the term "community trade", to emphasize how their version of the idea aims to support local communities. And, as we'll see, there are different levels of formality, from officially certified products bearing the **Fairtrade Mark** to uncertified goods whose ethical credentials are based mainly on trust.

For all this, however, the basic idea remains the same: a business model that aims to improve the livelihoods of poor and marginalized workers in the developing world. As most consumers understand it, this simply means paying producers – whether they be farmers, plantation workers, manufacturers or craftspeople – more money for their goods than they would usually receive. And it's true that dealing directly with suppliers and paying them a decent price for their work is a key fair trade principle. But this isn't the end of the story. Fair trade also aims to **empower producers** by – among other things – encouraging them to form democratically run co-operatives. And it involves making **up-front payments** and committing to **long-term trading** arrangements, to save producers relying on potentially crippling loans and to enable them to plan ahead.

In return, the suppliers are expected to produce goods of a very high quality and ensure that the environment is properly cared for. All in all, the exchange is based on partnership and co-operation, rather than straightforward buying power.

// Proper economic prices should be fixed not at the lowest possible level, but at a level sufficient to provide producers with proper nutritional and other standards. //

John Maynard
Keynes, 1944

As well as making a direct difference to producers, the fair trade movement also aims to improve things beyond its immediate sphere of influence. It seems reasonable to wonder, for example, whether company-specific initiatives – such as Chiquita's "Better Banana" scheme and Starbucks' "Commitment to Origins" – however imperfect they may be, would ever have happened without the benchmark of the Fairtrade label.

What's wrong with "normal trade"?

The fair trade movement aims to re-connect producers with consumers and to ensure a fairer deal for the former. There are a whole host of reasons why this is necessary, but one of them is that under current world trade rules, things often seem distinctly skewed in favour of rich countries. This is what organizations such as Oxfam (with their "Make Trade Fair" campaign) have been trying to publicize over the last few years.

Fair trade defined

The closest thing to an official definition of fair trade has come from FINE, an association of four international organizations:

F ▶ **Fairtrade Labelling Organizations International** www.fairtrade.net

I ▶ **International Federation for Alternative Trade** www.ifat.org

N ▶ **Network of European World Shops** www.worldshops.org

E ▶ **European Fair Trade Association** www.eftafairtrades.org

The definition

"Fair trade is a trading partnership, based on dialogue, transparency and respect, which seeks greater equity in international trade. It contributes to sustainable development by offering better trading conditions to, and securing the rights of, marginalised producers and workers – especially in the South. Fair trade organisations (backed by consumers) are engaged actively in supporting producers, awareness raising and in campaigning for changes in the rules and practices of conventional international trade."

The goals

▶ **To improve the livelihoods** and well being of producers by improving market access, strengthening producer organisations, paying a better price and providing continuity in the trading relationship.

▶ **To promote development** opportunities for disadvantaged producers, especially women and indigenous people, and to protect children from exploitation in the production process.

▶ **To raise awareness** among consumers of the negative effects on producers of international trade so that they exercise their purchasing power positively.

▶ **To set an example** of partnership in trade through dialogue, transparency and respect.

▶ **To campaign for changes** in the rules and practice of conventional international trade.

▶ **To protect human rights** by promoting social justice, sound environmental practices and economic security.

One issue is **import tariffs**. At the moment, for a poor producer to sell their goods in Europe or North America, they often face duties that are four times higher than those paid by producers in rich countries. This is estimated by trade justice campaigners to cost poor nations around twice as much as they receive in aid: $100 billion annually. And, in the agricultural sector, the tariffs are usually higher on processed goods (tinned fruit, say, rather than fresh fruit), which locks poor producers into selling raw commodities while the West benefits from processing, where most of the profit is made.

Another issue is **Western farm subsidies**. The EU spends around half its total budget – tens of billions of pounds – subsidizing its own farmers to produce and export agricultural goods, making it very difficult for poor countries to compete. Take sugar: though the subsidies were reduced in 2006, British farmers are still paid to grow sugar beet in Yorkshire and East Anglia at the expense of more efficient farmers in Africa and the Caribbean. After numerous wranglings at the World Trade Organization, EU farm subsidies are slowly being reduced, but it will be years – or even decades – before they're completely eradicated.

One aim of fair trade, then, is to help producers in the developing world overcome these kinds of barriers.

The Fairtrade Mark

The concept of fair trade has been around much longer than the formal labelling and certification system. But today, this "official" system – which first emerged in Holland in the 1980s, in response to plummeting international coffee prices – dominates the fair trade world. So how does it

Guarantees a **better deal** for Third World Producers

FAIRTRADE

Administered in the UK by the Fairtrade Foundation, the Fairtrade Mark depicts a person waving (a producer to a consumer, or vice versa), but also suggests a road going forward through a landscape and someone holding up an arm in solidarity.

work? In short, any product bearing the label, or Mark, has been traded according to a set of **internationally agreed standards** (more on these below) and the supply chain has been **audited** to make sure that the rules are being stuck to. It's important to note that Fairtrade is not a brand or a company, but a certification system.

Unlike many comparable schemes, the Fairtrade system isn't primarily funded by the producers. Other than a small percentage, the cost of administration and certification is passed on to the licensee of the Mark – the specific coffee brand, for instance – which ultimately passes it on to the consumer or absorbs it in reduced profits. This system allows the economically marginalized to get involved without large sums of up-front capital.

From its niche origins, the Fairtrade Mark has become part of mainstream British culture, with half of adults now familiar with the label. Since the first product bearing the Mark was launched in the UK – Green & Black's Maya Gold organic chocolate, in 1994 – sales of Fairtrade-labelled retail products have climbed to £195 million a year, and continue to rise steeply. In the case of roast and ground **coffee**, they account for around 20% of the total market.

At the other end of the chain, nearly a million producers and their dependants, in more than fifty countries, are benefiting from the system, and (though food and drink is still the focus) there is an ever-growing range of products available. There are now even "**Fairtrade Towns**" proudly being declared all over the UK (see overleaf).

The standards

Unlike with organic foods, say, where the "rules" are very general, each new product certified under the Fairtrade system gets its own specific criteria, since each raises a different mix of problems and priorities. But there are certain core ideas that apply to all products. Fairtrade traders must:

▶ Pay a price to producers that covers the costs of **sustainable production and living**

▶ **Pay a premium** that producers can invest in development

▶ Make **partial advance payments** when requested by producers

▶ Sign contracts that allow for long-term **planning and sustainable production** practices

Behind these core ideas are two underlying sets of standards. One covers crops such as coffee and cocoa, mostly grown by **small-scale independent producers**, and is primarily concerned with ensuring that farmers in "democratic and participative" co-operatives receive a decent and stable minimum price for their crops, rather than being left to ruthless middlemen and the fluctuating prices of the world commodity markets. The

Fairtrade Towns

The small town of **Garstang**, near Lancaster, may not be a familiar name. But in 2000, it created a place for itself in the history books by becoming the world's first Fairtrade Town. Right back in 1995, just a year after the Fairtrade Mark was launched in the UK, the tireless Garstang Oxfam Group were out on the streets doing their own version of the Pepsi Challenge – the Cafédirect Challenge – showing punters that Fairtrade coffee was good for the tastebuds as well as social justice. Five years of campaigning later, the town was thoroughly converted, and the council, the government and the Fairtrade Foundation all agreed that it should become "the world's first Fairtrade Town".

Soon after, the Fairtrade Foundation drew up a set of goals for anyone wanting to achieve **Fairtrade status** for their local town, city or zone. These include the local council committing itself to promoting awareness of the Fairtrade Mark, and a range of Fairtrade products being readily available in local shops and cafés. Scores of regions, towns and zones are now on the list, which takes in major cities such as Liverpool (London is in the process of getting there) as well as islands (including the aptly named Fair Isle). And a similar scheme has also been established for **schools, universities** and **churches**. But no one can match the tireless folks of Garstang, who are now twinned with a cocoa-producing town in Ghana, and organize regular exchanges for adults and children.

If you fancy attempting to convert your own town or zone, download the relevant Goals and Action Guide from: www.fairtrade.org.uk

other set of standards is for crops such as tea, which are largely produced on estates; it focuses mainly on issues such as the **pay and conditions** of the workers, the right to form unions, health and safety, child labour, and so on.

As well as these minimum trading requirements, Fairtrade bodies also have a set of so-called **progress requirements**, which are implemented if and when a producer receives enough Fairtrade revenues. Through this system, producers are encouraged to invest continuously in improving environmental sustainability, social provision, working conditions and business efficiency.

Who's in charge?

After having grown independently in different countries, the Fairtrade certification system became internationally unified in the late 1990s, with the establishment of **Fairtrade Labelling Organizations International** (FLO). This body is now responsible for defining the standards and certifying that accredited products really are produced in accordance with them. To do this, it works "with a network of independent inspectors that regularly visit all producer organisations", and implements a trade auditing system which "checks that every Fairtrade-labelled product sold to a consumer has indeed been produced by a certified producer organisation".

Based in Bonn (Germany is very much at the heart of ethical consumerism), FLO comprises a membership of so-called National Initiatives – twenty at the time of writing – which implement the FLO system at the country level. The UK's body is the London-based **Fairtrade Foundation**, originally set up by CAFOD, Christian Aid, Oxfam, Traidcraft Exchange and the World Development Movement, with a little help later on from the Women's Institute.

For more information on the organizations, standards and so on, see:

FLO International www.fairtrade.net
Fairtrade Foundation www.fairtrade.org.uk

Food and beyond

Though "unofficial" fair trade covers a wide range of goods, the Fairtrade Mark still appears primarily on **food and drink** (see p.209 to get an idea of the range of products available). The reasons for this focus are partly historical – as already mentioned, the labelling scheme was set up as a response to the coffee crisis. But they're also partly practical: compared to many manufactured goods, food and drink products have a comparatively simple supply chain from raw commodity to consumer, which makes it practical to audit each step along the way.

In the last couple of years, however, the Mark has started appearing on a wider range of goods. First came **footballs** and **roses**, and then cotton products – both **clothes** (see p.244) and **cotton wool**. Handicrafts and precious metals and stones are future possibilities. And considering the problems that exist in the rubber industry, the head of the Fairtrade Foundation told Rough Guides, we might even see the Fairtrade Mark on condoms at some stage.

Beyond the third world?

Despite the fact that the Fairtrade Mark is appearing on an ever-wider selection of goods, one parameter likely to remain is the focus on products from the developing world. The organizers recognize that some small-scale producers and farmers in **rich countries** suffer many of the same problems as those in the third world, but they have decided – after consultation with Fairtrade stakeholders – that the system should focus on poverty in developing countries rather than in the wealthier countries of the global North. This is why the idea – floated back in 2003 – of marketing Fairtrade **organic food** grown in the UK never finally took off. Instead, the UK organics movement has set up its own "ethically traded" label (see p.201).

Fair trade without the label

Fair trade goods that don't bear the official Fairtrade Mark are not necessarily certified or traded according to any single set of standards. So anyone can theoretically slap "fairly traded" on their products without adhering to any specific international code. As such, it sometimes all seems to be entirely based on trust. The VeganLine website, for example, at the time of writing describes its T-shirts as "said to be made in fair working conditions by the Nepalese exporter". Such statements, though admirably honest, don't wholeheartedly inspire confidence in the integrity of unlabelled fair trade. Indeed, they seem oddly similar to the ethical assertions of most transnational companies such as Nike – which, though never calling itself a fair trade company, claims to ensure all its workers receive a "fair wage". So can we trust a self-declared "fairly traded" item to be what it says it is?

IFAT and BAFTS

Speak to those in the fair trade movement, and they'll tell you that we shouldn't worry too much about people trying to pull the fairly traded wool over our eyes. For one thing, the majority of unlabelled fair trade goods are produced, imported and sold by groups who are members of respected fair trade organizations, the most important being **IFAT**: the **International Fair Trade Association**.

To join IFAT, producer groups have to undertake a self-assessment programme comparing their business practices to the core IFAT principles;

once signed up, they have to be open to random spot-checks to ensure they are sticking to their plan. Importers undergo a similar process and must have fair trade as their primary focus. Similarly, shops specializing in fair trade goods are usually members of the **British Association for Fair Trade Shops** (see p.139), which keeps a carefully vetted directory of approved importers and is itself a member of IFAT.

In any case, much of the importing and selling is done by trusted groups who have been around for longer than the Fairtrade Mark and were, in fact, central to its establishment. Perhaps the best-known example is **Traidcraft**, a faith-based (Christian) organization set up in 1979 with the sole aim of combating poverty through trade.

Unfortunately, however, there's still no way for shoppers to tell what is and what isn't produced by an IFAT member. The Association recently launched the **FTO (Fair Trade Organizations) logo**, which member groups can use on their promotional material. But there's nothing that appears on the actual products. Discussion is now underway about the introduction of a product label, but it remains to be seen whether this will happen and, if it does, whether it will be a completely separate one from the Fairtrade Mark we're already familiar with.

Either way, it would certainly help introduce a new level of trustability to the system. In the meantime, if you do wonder about the legitimacy of a "fairly traded" product that doesn't bear the Mark, try asking the retailer whether it comes from an IFAT-approved supplier, or whether the shop is a member of BAFTS. If they can give you an informed response, then there's no need to worry. After all, fair trade "scams" are pretty well unheard of – there are easier ways to make a fast buck than trying to con ethical consumers.

For more on IFAT or BAFTS, see:

IFAT www.ifat.org
BAFTS www.bafts.org.uk

Boycotts
Bashing the bad guys

The idea of punitively refusing to do business with a particular person, company or country is nothing new. The term dates from the late nineteenth century (**Charles C Boycott** was a land agent in Ireland who, after ignoring calls for lower rents, found himself shunned by mailmen, servants, shopkeepers and others) and boycott organizers since then have included the likes of **Mahatma Gandhi**, whose *swadeshi* campaign encouraged the rejection of British goods in favour of local self-sufficiency. However, the idea of con-

sumers taking part in national or worldwide boycotts in response to problems which don't affect them directly is a more recent phenomenon. It first really took off in the 1970s and 80s with calls for consumers to avoid companies doing business in **apartheid South Africa**, and **Nestlé**, for its irresponsible promotion of baby milk products in the developing world.

Today, boycotts are perhaps the most widely understood approach to ethical consumerism, aimed not just at companies and countries but also at types of products, such as tiger prawns, mahogany and GM food (all discussed later in this book). Though it's impossible to measure accurately, it is estimated that the value of goods boycotted on ethical grounds – by UK shoppers alone – is more than a billion pounds per year.

Do boycotts work?

Many people would doubtless want to boycott companies and products they find morally reprehensible even if they didn't think it would have any effect. But, in theory at least, a boycott can be a powerful force for change if enough people get involved: the moment a company thinks that improving its behaviour is more profitable than not doing so, it will opt for reform. After all, directors have a legal duty to their shareholders to take the path of maximum profits, even if it means swallowing their pride. And, in an era of "brand value", companies are so keen to avoid negative publicity that they might capitulate even if a boycott isn't currently making much difference to their bottom line.

In practice, of course, it's actually very difficult to tell how effective boycotts are. For one thing, rather like the wildly contrasting attendance numbers given by police and organizers after a political demonstration, the targets and practitioners of consumer boycotts tend to have very different views on their impact. A case in point is the **StopEsso** campaign (see p.298). The organizers have claimed that more than a million people don't buy Esso petrol on ethical grounds, but, as *The Observer* reported, the oil giant disagrees: "The Stop Esso campaign … has not affected our fuel sales." The company does seem to have gradually shifted its position on global warming since the boycott kicked in, though it denies this has had anything to do with the boycott.

Likewise with **Nestlé**, which for more than a quarter of a century has suffered a high-profile international boycott on the grounds of its alleged advertising of formula milk in the developing world (see p.214 for more details on this particular case). While the campaigners claim that the

Corbis

Greenpeace activists at Shell's Brent Spa oil platform, the subject of a high-profile consumer boycott in 1995 that forced Shell to abandon plans to sink the disused rig into the North Sea

company has still not cleaned up its act, they acknowledge that things have improved. But the extent to which this has anything to do with the boycott is debated. Nestlé claims that any changes in its behaviour are due entirely to it proactively responding to new regulation and health research. But then it also told Rough Guides that the boycott has had no effect on its sales, which – since it's clear that some people do avoid Nestlé goods – simply cannot be true. The company's evidence was simply that sales have kept rising rather than falling: not the same point at all. That said, if Nestlé thought the boycott was costing it as much in lost sales as its developing-world formula milk brings in – and that's reported to be less than 1% of its total turnover – you might think it would have stopped selling formula milk in poor countries, which it hasn't done.

The campaigners, for their part, claim that the boycott *has* hit sales, with some product lines down by 3% when the Church of England started advocating avoiding Nestlé, forcing the company to up its advertising budget. Moreover, the negative publicity has hurt Nestlé in other ways, making it hard for the company to get stand space at graduate recruitment fairs, for instance.

Of course, boycotts are usually only one part of a wider campaign, so even when a company does capitulate, it's very difficult to work out how much of this is down to consumers withholding their custom and how much is down to the inconvenience and embarrassment of having hardcore **activists** invading and picketing their stores, offices or petrol forecourts. Activists and ethical consumers may be two sides of the same coin, but we shouldn't credit responsible shoppers for all the hard work of committed campaigners.

Still, consumer boycotts, and the public debate they help generate, can certainly be effective at times. One case often given as an example is the international boycott of Shell in 1995 against the proposed dumping of the **Brent Spar** oil platform into the North Sea. Many people now think that the environmental arguments against the dumping were factually flawed – and hence describe the result as a mixed success – but the boycott certainly seemed to work. Sales were reported to drop below half in some stations and Shell eventually backed down (though here, too, pressure didn't only come from consumers: the issue became so high-profile that German chancellor Helmut Kohl is said to have personally requested prime minister John Major to do something about it).

Another good example is the numerous companies that stopped doing business in South Africa after consumer boycotts of their products. **Barclays Bank**, for example, pulled out soon after its share of the student

Barcodes: the future of ethical shopping?

Books, magazines and websites are OK for getting the ethical lowdown on companies. But with supermarkets stocking more than 30,000 products, and companies endlessly changing ownership and practices, you'd need a great deal of time to check every item you might want to buy. The future of conscientious shopping, then, will surely include some means by which we can get information about any product at any time.

Enter the **Corporate Fallout Detector** (CFD). Created by American "interaction designer" James Patten, the CFD combines a barcode scanner with the ECRA Corporate Critic database (see p.318), and another database of US polluters. When a product is swiped, the device makes a geigercounter-style clicking in proportion to the nastiness of the company in question. Just "swipe and gripe".

OK, it's early days. The CFD is a big, cumbersome box with limited information inside it – as Mr Patten is well aware. But the idea is a good one. There's no reason why, in a few years, we shouldn't have barcode scanners in our mobile phones, say, which would be able to provide all sorts of product info, including the ethical standards of the company in question. They might even be able to send an email to each company that has been scanned but not passed the test, to let them know that they've "just been boycotted".

Obviously, any system of ranking companies automatically is rife with problems of methodology and standards. But there's no reason why we couldn't each set out our own "ethical criteria".

The devil's in the barcode: James Patten armed with his Corporate Fallout Detector, ready to "swipe and gripe" in the supermarket aisle

Some current boycotts

Following are some of the high-profile boycotts under way at the time of writing – some serious, some less so. Please note that inclusion of a campaign here doesn't suggest endorsement from Rough Guides.

Bacardi www.ratb.org.uk
For allegedly attempting to have Fidel Castro overthrown while continuing to use Cuban imagery to promote its products.

Drugs www.huumeboikotti.org/en
We might rail about oil firms and trainers companies, but, according to this Finnish campaign, the illicit drugs industry is probably the least ethical of all. Cocaine, especially, has led to countless deaths in Colombia, but all drug production and distribution is "firmly in the hands of organized crime [and] goes hand in hand with corruption and money-laundering".

Companies that donate money to George W Bush www.boycottbush.net
You'd be amazed who bankrolls the US's simplest-ever president. See the box on p.65 for a list of companies.

Companies based in the US
Calls to boycott the US – in response to everything from the invasion of Iraq to the financing of the Turkish military – are nothing new. But George W Bush's tearing up of international initiatives on climate change and the International Criminal Court has provoked more bad feeling than ever. There are many groups suggesting US boycotts, though about the only website that provides a decent-sized list of US companies and the brand names they own in the UK is KryssTal: www.krysstal.com/democracy_whyusa_boycott.html

Companies doing business in Burma www.burmacampaign.org.uk
This campaign appeals to UK consumers to boycott all the companies who still do business in Burma, despite calls from the pro-democracy groups within the country for them to pull out (for more on the situation in Burma, see p.310). A more comprehensive list, including many foreign companies you've probably never heard of, can be found at: www.global-unions.org/burma

Companies doing business in Israel www.bigcampaign.org
More controversial than most consumer campaigns are the calls – now relatively widespread – for consumers to boycott goods produced in Israel. The pressure subsided a little after Israel bowed to EU requests to stop labelling items which have been grown or manufactured in the Occupied Territories as "produce of" or "made in" Israel. But the bombardment of Lebanon and Gaza in 2006 will doubtless offset this development. This particular campaign and product list is maintained

by the Palestine Solidarity Campaign, which targets "Israel's refusal to abide by UN Resolutions, International Humanitarian law and the Fourth Geneva Convention". The controversy is heightened by the Israeli claim that if people stop importing Israeli produce, then their goods will be consumed domestically, which will ultimately hurt the Palestinian producers who rely primarily on export to the Israeli market.

Companies doing business in China

www.boycottmadeinchina.org

A collection of "loose-knit groups and individuals" are behind this campaign to boycott Chinese goods. The campaign is a response to the full range of human rights abuses by the Chinese government and its refusal to recognize independent trade unions, but it focuses primarily on the occupation of Tibet. Note that not all human rights activists think that a China boycott is a good idea, for the reasons discussed from p.40.

Esso www.stopesso.com

A major campaign to encourage consumers to avoid the oil company doing the most to "sabotage international action on global warming". For more on the Esso boycott, see p.298.

Gillette

www.boycottgillette.com

For using "spy chips" to stop shoplifters making off with their Mach 3 razorblades.

Nestlé

www.babymilkaction.org

The International Baby Food Action Network promotes the ongoing boycott of Nestlé's armada of products for the company's allegedly irresponsible marketing of breast-milk substitutes in the developing world. For more on this issue and a list of Nestlé brands, see pp.213–215.

There are scores of other boycotts under way, from **tropical timber** (see p.127) and **tiger prawns** (see p.191) to **Janet Jackson** (for duetting with Beenie Man, a ragga DJ whose lyrics, some maintain, advocate the murder of homosexuals). Also on lists are **Canada**, for the mass slaughter of seals (see www.boycott-canada.com), and **Adidas**, for using kangaroo skin in its football boots (www.viva.org.uk). To stay up to speed with boycott news, visit:

Ethical Consumer Boycotts List www.ethicalconsumer.org/boycotts/boycotts.htm

market starting falling. Similarly, the Burma Campaign UK (see p.310) has successfully used consumer boycotts, or the threat of them, to persuade companies to stop dealing with Burma's ruling junta. Victims have included **Kappa**, **JJB Sports** and the underwear company **Triumph**, who couldn't fail to capitulate after the "support breasts not dictators" campaign. The tuna fishing industry taking measures to stop killing dolphins is another success. For more examples, see:

Successful boycotts www.ethicalconsumer.org/boycotts/successfulboycotts.htm

Regardless of their *direct* impact, boycotts – like fair trade – can also be useful in raising the profile of important issues. Even if you believe the Nestlé line on the ineffectiveness of the boycott against them, it's difficult to deny that it has massively raised people's awareness of a problem linked to tens of thousands of unnecessary deaths each year. The same goes for the Esso boycott and what it has revealed to people of the corporate response to global warming. And while boycotts of high-profile clothes and footwear brands have been contentious – since non-name-brand clothes are arguably at least as bad (see p.58) – the consumer debate has pushed the issue of sweatshops into the public eye like never before.

Regardless of the direct or indirect impact of consumer boycotts waged so far, one thing that can be said for sure is that they are less effective than they could be. That's because, as discussed in chapter one, most boycotters don't take the time to tell the company in question, which in many cases renders their action ineffectual.

What about the workers?

When it comes to developing-world factories, some commentators – including many of the most vocal trade unions and campaign groups – take the line that boycotting companies may be counterproductive. If workers are being treated badly, we should demand better treatment for them, but if we actually boycott their employer, we'll **reduce demand** for the goods they're producing, putting their jobs at risk and hurting the very people we're trying to help.

It's certainly true that an uninformed, knee-jerk reaction from the public might have a negative effect: a big Western company pulling out of a factory or region after child labour is discovered may mean catastrophic loss of jobs in a poor area. However, a few things are worth bearing in mind here. For one thing, most boycotts relating to sweatshops and child labour are called when a Western company *pulls out* of a factory rather than staying put and cleaning up its act.

Second, it's unlikely that a company will change its ways unless "requests" for it to reform are backed up by a credible threat of force – in this case reduced sales. Indeed, for a company's director to follow his or her moral instincts without a financial motive could be interpreted as a breach of their legally binding fiduciary duty. So, even if it's possible that a boycott might harm workers now, this has to be weighed up against the potential for creating long-term change. And that's not necessarily unattainable: even the commentators (such as Philippe Legrain, author of *Open World*) who write about Nike being far more ethically progressive than unbranded clothes producers admit that actual or threatened boycotts have been integral in raising Nike's standards.

Third, while there's a theoretical possibility that we might be jeopardizing the jobs of the people we're trying to support, this has to be balanced against **supporting decent jobs elsewhere**. Unless boycotting a company means that you're actually going to stop buying something full stop – which usually isn't the case – then, by taking your custom somewhere else, you're probably going to be supporting the same number of jobs, only decent ones rather than exploitative ones. True, we each need to decide where to draw the line about what constitutes "decent": boycotting any company that pays low wages by Western standards, for example, would mean shunning all companies who produce in the developing world, which would hardly be constructive. But boycotting sweatshops in favour of ethically sourced goods from the same countries can hardly be a bad thing overall for workers there.

As for boycotting whole countries due to their repressive governments, that's a different, and rather more complex, matter...

> **//** When you threaten to boycott a company that buys stock from a shady supplier, the company's immediate reaction is to cancel orders and turn to another supplier who is not necessarily any better. This attitude does not help to improve the conditions of those working for the first supplier, who are likely to be laid off, whilst other workers are faced with the same problem elsewhere. So boycotts should only be used as a last resort. **//**
>
> Neil Kearney, General International Textile, Garment and Leather Workers' Federation

Oppressive regimes
Should we boycott them?

As mentioned earlier in this chapter, some of the first boycotts of companies were really a means of boycotting a government – that of South Africa, in protest at the apartheid regime. People still debate the degree to which Western consumers contributed towards apartheid's eventual fall (they were just one of many political and economic pressures applied), but most agree that they did help. That success triggered other similar attempts to avoid products – and services, in the case of holidays – from countries with oppressive governments.

The logic is straightforward. A government always benefits from its country's exports – via corporation tax, export tariffs and the like. So when we buy goods imported from a country where the regime in power is oppressing its own people, we may be adding to the government's coffers and tightening its grip on power. Likewise if we give our custom to any multinational company that does business in the country in question.

If, on the other hand, we avoid all goods from oppressed countries (and the big businesses operating in them), consumers can help to isolate the

Corbis

governments economically, cutting off their much-needed cash supplies, weakening their grip on power and giving their people a better chance to rid themselves of their tyrants. Even Western governments seem to acknowledge the potential power of such a tactic. The US Department of Commerce Bureau of Industry and Security operates the Office of Antiboycott Compliance, which

Activists of the Tibetan Youth Congress shout anti-China slogans during a rally in New Delhi on December 8, 2002. Campaigners such as these call on Western consumers to avoid Chinese goods until China stops human rights abuses among its own people and the people of Tibet

aims to "encourage, and in specified cases, require US firms to refuse to participate in foreign boycotts that the United States does not sanction".

But boycotting countries is always going to be a thorny issue. For one thing, it's difficult to know which countries to avoid. There is, after all, no single and uncontroversial measure of the "oppressiveness" of a regime. And where should we draw the line? If we're going to boycott oppressive regimes, then shouldn't we really also be boycotting the Western countries that fund, or otherwise support, such regimes? This would certainly seem the logical conclusion, but if we're taking foreign policy into account (not to mention crimes against the global environment), then not many countries would be left on the thumbs-up list. What about the UK, for instance? Considering that the current government has, among other things, waged an illegal war in Iraq and maintained a special relationship with a US administration hell-bent on derailing the international response to climate change, should ethically minded Brits boycott goods from their own country?

Unintended consequences

Besides these conundrums about moral consistency, there's also the risk that boycotting oppressive regimes may actually be counterproductive. While hitting a government where it hurts is fine in principle, inevitably it could also mean harming the population – at least in the short term. Indeed, oppressed countries are usually also poor, and with terribly unequal distribution of wealth, so if Western consumers refuse to buy goods from such countries, it may well hit factory and agricultural workers much harder than the government itself. If so, the effect could be a double whammy: the poor will go hungry and also find themselves *even more* reliant on the regime in question than before, leaving them less able to do anything about it.

No single boycott of a country has ever been big enough (and independent of other international pressures) for us to know whether this argument stands up. But we can perhaps get a sense of the effects of a boycott on a country's people by looking at what happens when states impose trade sanctions on each other. Take Iraq, which was subject to around a decade of international sanctions (imposed by the UN but driven by the US and UK) to "contain" the military capabilities of Saddam Hussein. This case was unusual in that it involved an "Oil for Food" programme (through which Iraqi oil could be exchanged for humanitarian goods), in theory ensuring that the poor of the country didn't feel the brunt of the sanctions.

And yet by all accounts the results were still a humanitarian catastrophe. Denis Halliday, former UN humanitarian co-ordinator in Iraq, described the sanctions as "genocidal", pointing to "the death of some 5000–6000 children a month" through malnutrition, disease resulting from damaged water infrastructure, and so on. It seems that the sanctions were bad for nearly the whole population, except perhaps Hussein, whose government seemed only to tighten its grip.

Oppressive regimes lists

There is no definitive list of oppressive regimes, but there is a huge amount of research available as to how the various countries of the world compare on **human rights** issues, political openness and other such criteria. Much of this research is carried out by non-governmental organizations such as Amnesty International, Human Rights Watch and Freedom House. Governments also sometimes release surveys of this kind of information.

A number of organizations concerned with ethical consumerism use all this data to maintain their own lists of oppressive regimes, which shoppers and investors can choose to take into account if they so desire. Following are two examples of lists from respected groups: the Ethical Investment Research Service (see p.268) and ECRA – the research body behind *Ethical Consumer* magazine (see p.320).

Such lists are always **controversial** – not just inherently, but because, in practice, they're very prone to going out of date, since they're time-consuming to compile and rely on third-party on-the-ground research. The following may have been updated by the time you read this.

Ethical Investment Research Service oppressive regimes list

Category A (the worst offenders)

▶ Afghanistan	▶ Congo (DRC)	▶ North Korea	▶ Tunisia
▶ Algeria	▶ Egypt	▶ Oman	▶ United Arab
▶ Angola	▶ Iran	▶ Pakistan	Emirates
▶ Brunei	▶ Iraq	▶ Rwanda	▶ Vietnam
▶ Burma	▶ Ivory Coast	▶ Saudi Arabia	▶ Zimbabwe
▶ Cameroon	▶ Kazakhstan	▶ Somalia	
▶ China	▶ Lebanon	▶ Sudan	
▶ Colombia	▶ Libya	▶ Syria	

Category B

▶ Azerbaijan	▶ Central African	▶ Eritrea	▶ Indonesia
▶ Bahrain	Republic	▶ Ethiopia	▶ Israel
▶ Belarus	▶ Chad	▶ Guinea	▶ Kenya
▶ Bhutan	▶ Cuba	▶ Guinea-Bissau	▶ Kyrgyzstan
▶ Burundi	▶ Equatorial	▶ Haiti	▶ Laos
▶ Cambodia	Guinea	▶ India	▶ Liberia

True, this is an extreme case. And it's worth remembering that a similar argument was once used by Margaret Thatcher and Ronald Reagan to discourage people from boycotting South Africa. But it demonstrates that the effects of economic isolation can be negative. A very different example is Cuba, which since October 1960 has faced a trade embargo from the US. Critics of the embargo regularly and rightly point to the fact that the negative effects are felt not by the government but by the Cuban people.

▶ Maldives	Republic of)	▶ Sri Lanka	▶ Turkmenistan
▶ Mauritania	▶ Qatar	▶ Swaziland	▶ Uganda
▶ Morocco	▶ Russia	▶ Tajikistan	▶ Uzbekistan
▶ Nepal	▶ Serbia and	▶ Tanzania	▶ Venezuela
▶ Nigeria	Montenegro	▶ Togo	▶ Yemen
▶ Congo (People's	▶ Sierra Leone	▶ Turkey	

ECRA Oppressive Regimes Category

ECRA make no distinction between bad and *really* bad. For the most up-to-date version see: www.ethicalconsumer.org/magazine/buyers/categories.htm

▶ Afghanistan	Guinea	▶ Lebanon	▶ Sudan
▶ Algeria	▶ Eritrea	▶ Liberia	▶ Swaziland
▶ Belarus	▶ Ethiopia	▶ Libya	▶ Tanzania
▶ Brazil	▶ Fiji	▶ Malaysia	▶ Thailand
▶ Burma	▶ Guatemala	▶ Mexico	▶ Togo
▶ Burundi	▶ Indonesia	▶ Nigeria	▶ Tunisia
▶ Central African	▶ Iran	▶ Pakistan	▶ Turkey
Republic	▶ Iraq	▶ Qatar	▶ United Arab
▶ Chad	▶ Israel	▶ Russian	Emirates
▶ China	▶ Jordan	Federation	▶ Uzbekistan
▶ Congo (DRC)	▶ Kazakhstan	▶ Rwanda	▶ Vietnam
▶ Cote d'Ivoire	▶ Kenya	▶ Saudi Arabia	▶ Zimbabwe
▶ Egypt	▶ Kuwait	▶ Senegal	
▶ Equatorial	▶ Laos	▶ Somalia	

If you'd rather go straight to the source and get information about specific countries, try:

Amnesty International Library www.amnesty.org/library
Human Rights Watch www.hrw.org
Freedom House www.freedomhouse.org

Or read the out-of-date but nonetheless informative *Observer Human Rights Index 1999*, available online at www.guardian.co.uk

Trade as Trojan horse?

A more controversial argument against consumers shunning oppressive regimes and the companies doing business in them is the claim that even if international trade may help a bad government in the short term, it may ultimately be the best way to "open up" a repressed country – especially when big foreign businesses are involved. After all, global trade can encourage communication, transparency, clear property laws and other factors which those on the right tend to see as likely to bring about democracy and respect for human rights.

On one level, such an argument is patently absurd; there have been countless examples of oppressive and corrupt governments feeding off international trade while their people get nothing except pollution, further oppression and increasing inequality. Just think of **Nigeria**, where infamous dictator General Abacha stole a staggering amount of public money (an estimated $4 billion) in the 1990s, almost all of it from oil sales to the West.

And yet, despite a few notable exceptions, measures of economic "openness" – such as the Index of Economic Freedom compiled by the right-wing combo of the Heritage Foundation think-tank and *The Wall Street Journal* – do tend to equate roughly with measures of political freedom. And foreign trade often encourages this kind of economic openness.

This is a wide and heated debate. Take **China**, for example, which is swiftly becoming the "factory of the world", and which features high up on every list of oppressive states thanks to its appalling record on torture, deaths in custody, prisoners of conscience, unfair trials, detention without charge or trial, and executions, among other things. Some human rights campaigners claim that increased foreign trade is gradually helping to make China's government more open, less oppressive and more

// The rise of democracy in South Korea and Taiwan attests to the power of the market in generating political liberalization. Both countries have moved from closed, authoritarian regimes to open-market democracies without bloody revolutions and without the threat of economic sanctions ... will China follow? **//**

James A Dorn, *The Cato Journal*

// We have reached the point where the most ardent defenders of Chinese communism are US capitalists. **//**

Trade unionist Mark Anderson in 1996, on the US's decision not to make China's "most favoured nation" trade status conditional on human rights improvements vulnerable to pressure from the rest of the world (for example through the World Trade Organization, which China recently joined). But the regime's human rights standards are still extremely bad, and many critics, not least those in the Free Tibet movement, are calling for the international community – consumers included – to use a trade boycott as a way of putting pressure on the Chinese government to make much more radical improvements.

So what can you do?

There's no golden rule that says whether trade will be a blessing or a curse for the people living under an oppressive government. It depends on the specific regime, and the specific circumstances, such as the products being exported (natural resources, for example, seem to spell much more trouble than manufacturing). And it depends on the speed with which an economy opens up to international trade: a recent study by Israeli academics suggested that the faster the transition, the greater the amount of corruption it creates.

If a boycott is called for from within the country itself, by opposition groups which represent the majority of the population, then there can be little question that it's the right thing to do. This was the case in South Africa, and at the time of writing is the case with **Burma** (Myanmar). There, pro-democracy leaders won free elections by a landslide more than fifteen years ago but have been prevented from taking office by a brutal military regime. They are calling on the world's companies, shoppers and travellers to boycott the country (see p.310).

But in most other cases the picture is less clear, and citizens of the countries in question are sometimes shocked and offended to find their homeland – including all the companies their friends and families work for – on an international boycott list. Ask people from Venezuela, say, whether they support Western consumers boycotting all big companies that operate in their country, and you're unlikely to get a very positive response.

So once again it's a matter of making your own decisions, and once again it's true that making your views known politically is likely to be far more effective than simply buying or not buying. If you do decide that shunning certain countries is the way to go, the box on pp.42–43 shows the governments that certain organizations define as being oppressive; the box on pp.36–37 lists a few current high-profile country boycotts.

Local versus global
World trade: for better or for worse?

The idea of "buying local" whenever possible is often thought of as a core tenet of ethical shopping. Proponents of this strategy accept that trade is an essential and potentially beneficial part of life, but claim that it's more of a force for good if trading networks are local, creating accountability (people are less likely to rip off or exploit their neighbours) and collaboration (everyone sharing the goal of furthering the wellbeing of the community). On an international scale, they argue, vast distances and powerful financial interests come between the parties engaged in the "real" exchange – the producers and the consumers – and wealthy countries and companies have the political and economic clout to determine the terms of trade. Hence poor countries end up being robbed of their natural resources, and their workers are exploited in sweatshop-style factories.

Furthermore, localizers claim, global trade is inherently eco-unfriendly, both directly – as it relies on the burning of a vast quantity of transport fuel, contributing to **climate change** – and indirectly, since it separates consumers from the mess their goods are making, removing any pressure on them to act accordingly. The environmental impact is compounded by the fact that world trade is inherently tied up with a corporate-driven consumerism which encourages us all to buy and use as much as possible. And there's the question of **food security**: our long-term ability to feed ourselves. As we become ever-more reliant on transporting food from abroad, the oil that facilitates that transport gets closer to being exhausted.

For all these reasons, the argument goes, as well as numerous others, the best way forward is a new era of **localization**, which consumers can help realize by favouring local goods and services wherever possible. Obviously, there will always be some national trade (it wouldn't make sense for every town to make its own buses, say) and some international trade (not every country has the minerals and metals necessary to make buses, nor the climate to grow coffee). But whenever home-produced is available – in agriculture, clothes production, or whatever – that's what ethical consumers should go for.

Overall, localization might mean that we'd end up **producing and consuming less**, the argument continues, but that's not a bad thing, since the world simply cannot sustain the West's ever-rising consumption levels. Moreover, our food would be fresher; local engagement with politics and environmental problems would be stimulated; perhaps we'd even be happier. Poor countries would in theory also benefit: no longer reliant on cash-crop and manufacturing exports, they'd be able to grow their own food, protect their environments, shape their own development and benefit from processing and using their own natural resources.

One step forward or three steps back?

Most progressive commentators agree that a move towards localization for fresh foods would be a good idea on the environmental level. This may not *always* be the case – sometimes the energy efficiency of foreign growers may more than offset the environmental costs of transportation. But few deny that air-freighting out-of-season strawberries or mangetout from the southern hemisphere to a UK supermarket is a heavy and unnecessary burden on the environment; or that locally farmed vegetables are a better option, in terms of minimizing climate change, than those trucked from the other side of Europe. (For more on food transport, see p.156.)

But when it comes to favouring locally produced dried foods, clothes, wines and other goods with an aim to winding down global trade as much as possible, it's not quite so simple. For a start, these kinds of goods are usually shipped, not flown, so the environmental costs, though not negligible, are as much as fifty times lower per kilogram than the aforementioned mangetout. But the real crux of the matter is whether a reduction in international trade would be good for the developing world. Will it really help Bangladesh if we produce our clothes in Birmingham?

Not according to anti-poverty groups such as Oxfam, which have spent the last few years campaigning hard to get *more* access to world markets for producers in poor countries. They claim that without trade, poor

// Localisation ... has the potential to increase community cohesion, reduce poverty and inequality, improve livelihoods, social provision and environmental protection and provide the all important sense of security. **//**

Colin Hines, author of *Localization: A Global Manifesto*

// The problem with localisation is that it would trap the poorest economies in their current subordinate relationship to the rest of the world, and would require a whole new coercive apparatus to impose it. It is a backward looking and reactionary reformism. **//**

Paul Hampton, Workers' Liberty

countries can only get hard cash via aid – which is not only insufficient, but puts recipient countries under the thumbs of the donors and is no kind of long-term solution anyway.

Of course, trade in itself is no immediate answer to poverty. For example, a 2004 report by the United Nations Conference on Trade and Development (UNCTAD) pointed out that the world's least developed countries have opened their markets to external trade during the last few years but have gained very little – or even lost out. But there are many cases of countries gaining high standards of living through embracing international trade – such as the "Tiger" economies of East Asia. This applies not just to manufacturing but also to agriculture. As Oxfam's senior policy advisor Kevin Watkins wrote in a debate for *The Ecologist* magazine, in countries such as "Uganda and Vietnam, where smallholder production dominates, agricultural export growth in the 1990s contributed to rapid rural poverty reduction".

Watkins acknowledges that increased global food trade can cause environmental damage and, in some cases, raise inequality, and that these problems "have to be addressed". But he believes that "making common cause with protectionist lobbies and right-wing populists to exclude poor countries from rich country markets in the interests of 'self-reliance' is a prescription for mass poverty and inequality".

Sweatshops and export farms

Regardless of the potential benefits of global trade described by groups such as Oxfam there are, however, very clearly some downsides. Over the last decade Western consumers have read, heard and watched reports of all kinds of abuses in developing-world export sectors – from sweatshop working conditions to the appropriation of water and land for the growing of cash crops.

Trainers, toys and footballs have garnered most of the media attention in the area of worker exploitation and child labour, but really this issue covers everything from cut flowers to car parts, bananas to silk, tobacco to electronic equipment. A report by the New York-based National Labor Committee, for example, found serious abuses in Chinese export factories manufacturing products ranging from bicycles (fifteen-hour shifts, seven days a week with no overtime pay) to handbags (guards beating the workers for being late).

Countless other reports – from investigative exposés to studies commissioned by the very Western companies that use developing-world suppliers – have documented manufacturers in Asia and Latin America paying wages as low as 10p per hour. Whether or not it's true (as some activists recently calculated) that it would take a Bangladeshi garment worker sewing Disney clothes more than 200 years to earn what the company's CEO gets each hour, there's no question that the inequality built into most global trade is extreme.

Another well-documented issue is that workers in export factories are often not paid on time, or have wages deducted for making mistakes or for being a few minutes late. A recent study by the Department of Labor and Employment in the Philippines, for instance, showed that nearly half the companies inspected failed to pay workers properly – and those are just the official figures. Moreover, job security is scarce, with workers commonly dismissed for being ill, late or pregnant – or simply because a factory has become financially unsustainable after a big company has placed its orders elsewhere.

Just as important as wages and terms are **health and safety**. A staggering number of workers – more than two million – die every year due to work-related accidents or illnesses, according to the UN's International Labour Organization (ILO). This is an international problem, but poor countries bear the brunt of it: the rate of fatal workplace accidents in developing countries in Asia, for example, is four times higher than in the industrialized world. The same can presumably be said for the hundreds of millions more affected annually by non-fatal health problems, such as the three million farmers around the world who (according to World Health Organization estimates) suffer acute agrochemical poisoning each year.

Various less dangerous but equally demeaning conditions have cropped up again and again in official and unofficial reports: unsanitary toilets available only at certain times of day, round-the-clock surveillance and crowded dormitories to give just three examples. Sometimes humiliation tactics appear to be a deliberate policy: according to Oxfam Community Aid Abroad, for example, Indonesian women working in some export factories don't take their entitlement of two unpaid days of menstrual leave per month, since to qualify they have to remove their underwear in front of (female) factory doctors to prove that they are indeed menstruating. Even more seriously, **verbal and physical abuse** is widely reported, from minor offences to serious sexual assault.

Perhaps most significant of all, however, is the fact that collective bargaining for better terms and conditions through **unions** and other groups – something recognized by the ILO as a fundamental right of all workers

– is often impossible. In some countries only a state-controlled union is allowed (such as the All-China Federation of Trade Unions, which is so much a tool of the state that it has reportedly turned down offers of increased wages from foreign companies in order to help keep China cheap and business-friendly). In others, free unions are legal but rarely tolerated: organizers are usually simply fired, but in many cases they're harassed, beaten, jailed or even killed. According to the International Confederation of Free Trade Unions (ICFTU), 213 trade unionists were assassinated or "disappeared" worldwide in 2002 alone.

Child labour

With more than 350 million children aged 5–17 classed as "economically active" by the International Labour Organization, children account for a substantial proportion of the global workforce. Around half of this total is considered to be "acceptable": 15- and 16-year-olds working full time in safe conditions, or younger children doing a few hours after school. But much of the rest, in the ILO's words, "is not jobs for kids … it is adults exploiting the young, naive, innocent, weak, vulnerable and insecure for personal profit".

While the issue is widely associated in the West with stitching footballs and sports shoes, in reality the problem is much more diverse, the most widely affected industries including **silk**, **carpet weaving**, **brassware** and **glassware**, **precious stone cutting**, **mining**, **leather tanneries** and **farming**. A frightening 170 million children are involved in work classified as hazardous, and more than a third of these – roughly an equivalent number to the entire population of the UK – are aged eleven and under. At the most shocking end of the spectrum, at least eight million children are stuck in what the ILO describes as the "unconditional worst forms of child labour": armed conflict, forced and bonded labour, prostitution, pornography and illegal activities.

While (nearly) everyone agrees that it's imperative to end all dangerous and degrading forms of child labour, there's no consensus on the best response to the hundreds of millions who are working in safe, or at least relatively safe, conditions. Studies by the ILO have shown that if all child workers were put through **education** instead of working, the result would be an enormous boost not only to the children's quality of life, but also to the economy of their countries. However, in most cases, no one is offering to pay for these children to be educated and, until someone does, a clampdown may simply exacerbate the problems, forcing it underground and further marginalizing and impoverishing the children involved. After all, child labour tends to be primarily a **symptom of poverty** (though interestingly it appears to be more common in households which own land), and enforcing a ban is unlikely to help reduce this poverty.

So where does all this leave the concerned consumer? One thing worth noting is that the vast majority – probably around 95% – of child labourers are not working

Made in the developing world: ethical or unethical?

How should ethically minded consumers respond to all this? For people who feel that benefiting materially from such harsh conditions is unacceptable, the obvious conclusion is that we should where possible support "decent" jobs by favouring goods produced in, say, Europe or America. But the idea of helping developing-world workers by simply shunning their products is obviously problematic, since jobs in export factories are clearly in big demand. True, even some of the more ethically aware Western brands have found themselves in court for using sweatshops

in the formal economy creating goods for export to the West. They're working largely for a local or domestic market – on **subsistence farms** or producing silk, bricks, cigarettes or matches. A large number are also working in domestic service. As such, some people say that the best way forward is to encourage more global trade – since child labour is a symptom of poverty, and world trade, they argue, is the best way to make countries richer. Others claim that it's none of the West's business – it's a cultural issue and we shouldn't meddle. This debate is bound to run and run.

But what about the 5% of children – still a number in the millions – who *are* producing goods for the West, making clothes, carpets, shoes and furniture, tanning leather and mining and polishing gems? Should we demand that all our goods are "child labour free"?

For **factory-produced goods**, at least, the obvious answer is yes. If global trade, as its advocates claim, is providing valuable and in-demand jobs in the poor world, then surely it would make sense for these jobs to go to poor adults rather than poor children (not least as the adults may then be able to afford to send their children to school). But in other areas, such as more **craft-based industries**, there's an argument to say that an unqualified demand for child-labour-free goods may add up to refusing to do business with the poorest people, hence worsening their position.

Partly, it all depends on who's in charge and what other opportunities – if any – will be offered to children who currently are working. A faceless directive from a corporate headquarters to stamp out all child labour – or to pull out from regions where child labour is widespread – may do more harm than good, with desperate children left with no option but to turn to dangerous work, crime or even prostitution. According to Oxfam, this is exactly what happened in Pakistan after large numbers of child labourers were found to be making Western footballs.

Local schemes set up specifically to deal with the problem – such as the Rugmark label for South Asian rugs (see p.136) – have shown that it's possible to reduce child labour constructively, using a labelling scheme both to inform Western consumers and fund education for ex-child labourers.

that exploit **indentured labour** (whereby workers are conned into signing away a large proportion of their wages in return for securing the job, putting them in a vicious cycle of debt and making it impossible to leave). But this is the exception rather than the rule – the vast majority of workers are taking these jobs by choice.

And no wonder, globalization advocates argue, since jobs in the export sector are usually the best thing going. According to right-leaning think-tanks such as the Institute for International Economics, American and European firms in poor countries pay on average around twice what equivalent local firms offer. Of course, these wages still sound shockingly low to those in the West, the argument goes, but the alternative for a worker is either even worse pay from a domestic firm, or rural work. The latter, despite Western middle-class idealization of countryside living, usually involves grinding poverty and hard labour – hence the tens of millions of subsistence farmers voluntarily leaving home each year to head for the cities and factories. (Furthermore, converting third-world wages into Western currency can slightly exaggerate the inequality, because in countries where, say, 25p per hour is a standard wage, 25p tends to buy a lot more than it would do in the UK, a fact that backpackers on six-month trips around Asia are all too aware of.) And it's not just wages that are better in export jobs, pro-globalizers claim. Other problems such as health and safety risks and child labour – widely associated in Western eyes with, say, Nike factories – are actually most problematic in areas where Western companies aren't involved, such as artisan mining and small-scale farming.

// 30 years ago, South Korea was as poor as Ghana. Today, thanks to trade led growth, it is as rich as Portugal. **//**

Mike Moore, ex-Director of the World Trade Organization

// Trade is the fuel for growth but not the engine ... we need development-led trade policies. **//**

Michael Herrmann, UNCTAD specialist in least developed countries

The same people also argue that sweatshop-style jobs can be an important part of **economic development**, pointing out that in the 1960s the West's shoe sweatshops were in **Japan**, which is now a bigger economic power than the UK and has strict labour and environmental legislation. In the 1970s and 80s, they were in **Taiwan** and **South Korea**, which have since become specialists in microelectronics and are among the richest countries in Asia. By the same token, what we now call sweatshop conditions were standard in Europe and the US a century ago. Industrialization may not be very pretty in its early stages, but every country

A billboard promotes a private "EPZ" in Ho Chi Minh City, Vietnam. These special no- or low-tax areas are designed to attract foreign business, and they're associated with the worst type of sweatshop abuse.

that's wealthy today, we're told, has been through this process – and only once people become wealthier will they be able to demand better environmental and labour conditions.

Things aren't quite this simple, of course. For a start, despite the fact that some multinationals might pay relatively high wages, many others have successfully lobbied governments for exemption from minimum wage laws. They also frequently choose to use factories based in the notorious **export processing zones**, or **EPZs**, where labour law is even slacker than elsewhere. In the words of the ICFTU, EPZs "have become a symbol of crude free market globalization, where workers are made to take amphetamines to get them to work harder and faster, where violence and abuse are a daily reality for thousands upon thousands of workers, and where attempts to form unions and bargain collectively for a fair deal are often met with reprisals, sackings and even death threats".

// Globalisation has the potential to bring prosperity to people across the world, but today crude free market globalisation is pushing standards down and leading to massive exploitation. //

Guy Ryder,
General Secretary,
International
Confederation of Free
Trade Unions

Furthermore, while Taiwan and South Korea may have got richer through sweatshop-style manufacturing, they did so at a time when there was less global trade, and hence much less **competition between poor nations**. Today, poor countries struggling to make money through sweatshops have to deal with the fact that other poor countries can try to undercut them on price (and labour conditions), hence slowing development down. Today, it's a race to the bottom, campaigners claim, with real-terms minimum wages in some areas of China (the leader of the race) having *fallen* in the last ten years.

Furthermore, it doesn't make sense to isolate this discussion from a whole range of bigger issues. The poverty of many poor countries is inextricably linked to a whole host of factors: the unsustainable **debt** foisted on them decades ago by the West; colonial and post-colonial **wars**; the rich world's **farm subsidies** that erode poor-country agricultural societies; currency instability helped along by the International Monetary Fund's strong-arm opening of poor-world financial markets. And so on. So when ex-farmers voluntarily work fourteen-hour days producing lampshades for Britain, or green beans for the US, that choice may have been shaped by an unjust global order which has made their previous life impossible.

Finally, even if export factories and farms are comparatively high-paying for those people who choose to work in them, they may bring nothing but misery to others, such as villagers who find that their water is being drained by a nearby plantation, or that their air and rivers are being polluted by factory effluent. In at least one case in Kenya, for example, cash-crop growing has been linked to the starvation of local people.

Demanding better standards

If shunning third-world goods is unconstructive, how about using our power as consumers to demand that companies improve conditions throughout their supply chains? Certainly this seems like a more sensible strategy, though – as ever – not everyone is convinced it's a good idea. Free-marketeers claim that, while it's laudable to desire better standards and wages for third-world workers, their "cheapness" is exactly what allows them to undercut the West and create jobs and wealth – it's their **comparative advantage**, to use the economics jargon.

If Western consumers demand better ethical standards, they risk limiting this advantage, thereby reducing the incentive for companies to invest in, and provide jobs in, developing countries. Hence the fact that, in international trade negotiations with the West, governments of poor countries have often objected to the idea of making trade deals conditional on the enforcement of better labour or environmental standards.

However, the argument that consumer pressure for better standards is likely to harm third-world workers isn't very convincing. For one thing, many of the improvements that could be made – such as clamping down on abusive managers and ending humiliating restrictions on when workers can visit the toilet – don't cost anything economically. Indeed, they may end up saving money, since, as numerous recent studies have shown, workers treated with respect are more productive than those who aren't (no surprise there).

Another thing that costs very little – at least, if the companies have got nothing to hide – is **transparency**. Hardly any big firms that make use of cheap developing-world manufacturing reveal exactly where their products are made, which means that it's difficult for anyone other than investigative journalists to get an independent view of conditions. Usually, the excuse is not wanting to give away valuable business secrets to their competitors. It would be "a little like giving your playbook to the opposing team before a game", according to the Nike website. But it's hard to believe that big businesses operating in the same countries, and sometimes the same factories, cannot find out relatively easily where their competitors' goods are produced.

Even those improvements which will cost money, such as better health and safety, and ensuring that wages are high enough to provide a decent standard of living, are likely to cost little in comparison with the money saved by sourcing from developing countries in the first place. Indeed, labour costs are as much as fifty times lower in poor countries than rich countries so, even when you factor in transport and import costs, there's room for substantial improvement before it becomes economically non-viable for companies to source from the developing world – as many fair trade suppliers are already showing.

Big brands, big business
No logo, pro logo and CSR

In general, the bigger, more visible and more strongly "brand-name" a company is, the more it's disliked by those who describe themselves as ethical consumers. This is due to both a widespread distrust of transnational companies themselves and a distaste for the logos, advertising and chain-store outlets associated with them.

Anti-corporate, anti-advertising sentiment is nothing new, of course, but it's been running at an all-time high since the 1990s, and especially since the publication of **Naomi Klein**'s bestseller *No Logo*, which catapulted modern branding strategies and sweatshop labour firmly into the public consciousness. Klein made the case that big companies are getting bigger, and that their focus is shifting away from real-world activities such as employing staff and manufacturing products (which they increasingly outsource to low-wage contractors in the developing world) and towards the insidious process of branding: using logos and advertising to make people think that their produce "means" something. This trend has inherent social downsides, she argued, but is especially ugly when you consider that the companies constantly appropriate people's icons and aspirations for their advertising and logos, which they force ever further into our public spaces.

Though Klein has never really been an outspoken advocate of ethical consumerism (she tends to be more concerned with political issues such as the deals brokered at the World Trade Organization), her arguments have undoubtedly entered the ethical consumerism debate. The heavily branded companies she criticized – such as Starbucks, McDonald's, Nike and Gap – were never popular among ethically minded consumers, but since *No Logo* they have been at the top of most people's list of companies to avoid.

All this raises an important, though rarely asked, question: are the big brands – indeed, big companies in general – less or more ethical than the rest? How do they compare with manufacturers of **non-name-brand** goods, or less high-profile retailers?

> **//** Quite simply, every company with a powerful brand is attempting to develop a relationship with consumers that resonates so completely with their sense of self that they will aspire, or at least consent, to be serfs under these feudal brandlords. **//**
>
> Naomi Klein, *No Logo*

No group better sums up the anti-brand ethos than Adbusters, a self-proclaimed "global network of artists, activists, writers, pranksters, students, educators and entre- preneurs who want to advance the new social activist movement of the informa- tion age". It's best known for its striking, witty spoof ads, which often adorn the cover of *Adbusters* magazine, its print outlet for ecological, anti-corporate and anti-brand comment. But it has its finger in many other pies. For example, it pro- duces Blackspot trainers (see p.250) and runs PowerShift, an "advocacy adver- tising agency", which helps like-minded organizations to promote their cause visually.

Branding as accountability?

Klein's critics, as exemplified by the "Pro Logo" writers at *The Economist*, say that she has it all wrong. In practice, they claim, the more heavily branded a company is, the more visible it is, and the more accountable to consumers it becomes. One foot wrong from a famous global brand and consumers can take revenge within hours. "Even mighty Coca-Cola has been humbled", they point out: "Told of a contamination incident in Belgium, its then-boss, Doug Ivester, is said to have dismissed it with the comment: 'Where the fuck is Belgium?' A few months later, after a mishandled public-relations exercise that cost Coke sales across Europe, he was fired."

Indeed, the *Economist* writers continue, branding is "an effective weapon for holding even the largest global corporations to account". And this accountability extends to ethical matters, so that when Klein and others attack heavily branded companies for, say, exploiting sweatshops, these companies fear a consumer boycott and are forced to clean up their act. Nike has been forced to "revamp its whole supply chain" due to just such a fear, they point out – but only because its branding (the ubiquitous name and swoosh logo) makes it such an easy target. Had it produced unbranded, no-name products, it wouldn't have been so vulnerable to consumer pressure. In fact, it probably would never have had investigative writers visiting its factories in the first place.

Commentators who take this line admit that there are clearly jarring contradictions between, say, the inclusive, one-world imagery cynically used in a big sportswear company's marketing campaigns and the reality of its factories. But surely, they argue, the important issue is simply how good or bad the working conditions are, not whether they're at odds with a few Western adverts, which everyone knows are a load of marketing claptrap anyway.

Few people would disagree with that last point. But are big, visible brands and retailers *really* more conscientious and good for the world than the non-name-brand equivalents? Well, it's undoubtedly true that as a group – and especially those with high-profile brands that have been targeted by activists – big companies have issued more ethical statements and introduced more **codes of conduct** than less visible companies. Indeed, the field of corporate social responsibility (see box opposite) is now thriving – the UK even has a Minister for Corporate Social Responsibility and a CSR Academy. And it's mainly the big companies that are driving all this.

Take food retail. Nearly all the major supermarkets are signed up to the Ethical Trading Initiative (see p.61), which aims to ensure good labour practice in their developing-world suppliers. You won't find your local corner shop on the list. Or take the clothes sector. Many involved in the social and environmental auditing of developing-world factories treat it as a given that conditions are worse in the small-business-dominated, non-name-brand garment sectors, where margins are tighter, consumer

A protester outside the US supreme court takes a stand against what many see as our "brand new world", on the day of Nike vs Kasky (see box on p.240). But how do the corporate giants compare to smaller, non-name companies?

CSR: ethical big business?

One of the defining business buzzwords of the last decade has been **CSR**, or **corporate social responsibility**. There's no single definition of what this means, but it usually involves a company "aligning its business operations with social values" by drawing up codes of conduct and reporting its social and environmental achievements (and failures) in public, self-penned documents.

This issue splits those in the ethical shopping movement down the middle. While most people agree that a company prepared to acknowledge ethical issues is better than one which is not, some see most CSR as **greenwash**: a cheap smokescreen to satisfy ethically minded consumers, get rid of annoying protesters, and persuade governments that there's no need for the thing that big companies really fear: laws and regulations that *force* them to behave well all the time.

It's certainly true that CSR contains a fundamental limitation, at least in the case of companies owned by shareholders: it can only include things that are likely to increase profits. Doing anything else would violate the basic obligation of company directors to their shareholders: to maximize returns. So while a company's CSR report may talk about wanting to be a "good corporate citizen", this can only go so far. If it can be shown, for example, that reducing carbon emissions will save money, then the change will probably be made – and the company will make a proud public statement about its solid commitment to the environment. But if it looks set to harm profits, then things are very likely to stay as they are.

Can CSR claims be believed anyway? According to many anti-poverty NGOs, the answer is often no. "Corporate practices do not match ethical policies", wrote Oxfam recently about the sportswear industry. At almost the same time, Christian Aid examined the ethical claims of some high-profile companies such as British American Tobacco (on health and safety in developing-world plantations), Coca-Cola (on their promises not to harm local communities by extracting too much groundwater) and Shell (on its social impact on communities in Nigeria and elsewhere). They concluded that in each case the claims were not reflected on the ground and that in general CSR was "a completely inadequate response to the sometimes devastating impact that multinational companies can have in an ever-more globalised world – and that it is actually used to mask that impact".

To try to prove that their codes of conduct are enforced, many of the more progressive companies employ **independent monitors**. But even this can be contentious: while some companies employ expert, non-profit monitors such as Verité (see www.verite.org), others employ companies that may sometimes have a financial interest in not uncovering all the problems (the same kind of conflict of interest that lay behind the Enron scandal).

CSR's defenders argue that all this criticism and scepticism is unhelpful, pointing out that some very positive results have already been achieved and claiming that CSR is sowing the seeds of wider change in a deeper, more effective way than enforceable regulation could ever do on its own.

pressure non-existent and campaigners nowhere to be seen. The head of one auditing body told Rough Guides that, in the ethical stakes, "non-name brands tend to be bottom feeders".

Even the most despised big firms may be better in some ways than their small-scale rivals. McDonald's uses free-range eggs, shuns milk from cows that have been injected with the controversial protein known as bovine growth hormone, and has phased out eco-unfriendly polystyrene in its packaging. Can your local burger joint say the same? And can your local café claim to have as good a coffee sourcing policy as Starbucks (see p.205)?

Of course, the argument continues, the big companies are a very long way from perfect. As already discussed, many of them refuse to publish their list of developing-world suppliers. And, inevitably, some of their ethical policies are overblown PR efforts – in a recent case, Nike settled out of court after exaggerating its ethical standards (see p.240). Still, surely their efforts are better than nothing? Surely a code of conduct and a team of factory auditors is better than the code-free, no-promises approach of the faceless companies that supply bargain stores and street markets?

As one economist from the Bank of England put it, while we might push for global *regulation*, in the meantime we can at least have global *reputation*. And without reverting to small-scale localization, in which you might know the individuals who grew your food and sewed your T-shirt, that reputation is most precious to the bigger, more visible brands and retailers.

One hand gives, the other takes away...

The obvious conclusion to the above is, sure, avoid big brands and shops if you think that advertising is inherently distasteful, that global logos and high-street chains are destroying cultural diversity and homogenizing public space, and that big firms are draining money from local econo-mies. But don't fool yourself that the no-name alternative is any better in terms of workers' rights or environmental awareness – in all probability it's considerably worse.

It's a fair point. As ever, though, it's not quite so simple. For one thing, it's not necessarily true that the big, visible companies are the most ethi-cally enlightened. The world's biggest chain retailer – **Wal-Mart** (which owns ASDA) – is often given as an example of exactly how ethical busi-nesses *shouldn't* behave. For example, its private owners famously don't recognize the fundamental labour right to join a union (see p.220).

The Ethical Trading Initiative

The term "ethical trade" is often used interchangeably with fair trade, but it has a more specific meaning in the context of the **Ethical Trading Initiative** (ETI). Set up in 1998, this is one of the more widely respected corporate social responsibility initiatives, a project that brings NGOs and trade unions together with companies in order to help the latter develop and implement credible codes of conduct relating to **labour and human rights practices** in their supply chains. The ETI membership includes many household-name companies, all of which have committed to implementing a "base code", which specifies that:

- ► Employment is freely chosen
- ► Freedom of association and the right to collective bargaining are respected
- ► Working conditions are safe and hygienic
- ► Child labour shall not be used

- ► Living wages are paid
- ► Working hours are not excessive
- ► No discrimination is practised
- ► Regular employment is provided
- ► No harsh or inhumane treatment is allowed

Significant is the reference to a **living wage**, which the ETI defines as one which "should always be enough to meet basic needs and to provide some discretionary income". This is a commitment that is missing from most corporate codes of conduct, and its presence here is one reason why many labour and anti-poverty groups describe the ETI rules as constituting "a model code". However, that's not to say that the same groups hold up the companies which belong to the ETI as corporate angels. Indeed, the list includes many names that have long been the bane of anti-sweatshop campaigners and trade unions – such as ASDA, owned by union-bashing Wal-Mart. Moreover, though the ETI rules specify that the implementation of the code should be independently monitored, some commentators have questioned how consistently and effectively this happens.

ETI members

ETI members include a number of major companies as well as international trade unions and a plethora of charities and NGOs (including the Fairtrade Foundation, Oxfam and Save The Children). Following are some of the better-known corporate members. For a full list, and for more information about every aspect of the ETI, see: www.ethicaltrade.org

- ► ASDA
- ► The Body Shop
- ► Boots
- ► Chiquita
- ► The Co-operative Group (CWS)
- ► Debenhams
- ► Fyffes

- ► Gap
- ► Levi Strauss & Co
- ► Marks & Spencer
- ► Monsoon
- ► Mothercare
- ► New Look
- ► Next
- ► Safeway

- ► Sainsbury's
- ► Somerfield
- ► The Tea Sourcing Partnership (Taylors, Tetley, Twinings and others)
- ► Tesco
- ► WH Smith

However, even if you're prepared to accept, for the sake of argument, that big, visible companies *are* more likely to be ethically accountable than their smaller, no-name rivals, there remains a case for saying that – very often – their whole way of doing business may still be contributing to lower labour and environmental standards. This view, which has been put forward by numerous pressure groups such as Oxfam, holds that once a brand or retailer has grown big enough, it can exert extraordinary leverage over its suppliers, forcing them to produce faster, more cheaply and more "flexibly" (being able to turn around big orders very quickly, for example).

Once that leverage is available, critics of corporations maintain, a company will invariably exercise it, no matter how many factory auditors it employs or CSR reports it publishes. This allows the brands and shops to pass savings on to consumers and shareholders. But the cost is shouldered by the suppliers, who – in order to meet their ambitious production targets, and stay on good terms with the big buyers – have to cut corners. The likely result for workers is more overtime, less job security, frozen wages, less spending on health and safety in the workplace and poorer environmental standards.

While decent codes of conduct are to be welcomed, says Oxfam, they may be ignored on the ground, because the big brands' "supply-chain purchasing practices are undermining the very labour standards that they claim to support". Even the World Bank has acknowledged this, publishing a report in 2003 that pointed to "tension among price, quality and delivery time on the one hand, and CSR requirements on the other".

On a different level, there's also a fundamental limitation with thinking of corporate size and visibility as a form of accountability: most branded products are made from virtually **untraceable commodity** supply chains over which brands have no ethical control. So even if, for instance, a big clothes company is relatively "ethical" in its factories, its codes are unlikely to cover the farmers growing the cotton they use. Likewise, even the most ethically enlightened electronics brand can't claim to know the provenance of the bauxite or coltan used in its new laptop series. This might all seem a touch pedantic, were it not for the fact that mineral extraction is one of the most dangerous, exploitative and ecologically damaging of all industries (faceless mining conglomerates don't feature much in the mainstream press, but they do crop up in reports on human rights and the environment). Coltan, a black, tar-like mineral used in mobile phone and computer circuit boards, has for years been funding devastating civil war in central Africa.

According to many campaigners, what these "invisible" commodity sectors need is a clear and strict **international legal framework** to enforce decent standards and hold companies that behave badly to account. But big business is not often in favour of this. Indeed, the same high-street brands who claim to be ethical trailblazers are often major players in the corporate lobby groups which spend millions lobbying *against* any across-the-board enforceable regulations. The UN's proposed **Human Rights Norms for Business** are a good recent example: they have met fierce resistance from big-business-dominated trade groups such as the International Chamber of Commerce. Furthermore, as discussed below, in many cases big business bolsters its lobbying case by giving money to politicians. Even where they are making positive developments in their own supply chains, then, big companies may be having a negative effect elsewhere.

So, once again, there are no simple answers for ethically minded consumers. Big brands and retailers do generally have more developed ethical policies than those producing no-name goods, but their codes only go so far, and arguably their aggressive buying practices, lobbying and political donations (not to mention their invasive advertising, fat-cat pay and other corporate trappings) offset the good they do with their moral efforts. Thankfully, however, in a growing number of cases, we can get the best of both worlds by favouring ethical specialists and formal certification schemes, many of which are listed in this book.

Political donations
Voting with your wallet – literally

Though we might get annoyed about what certain politicians get up to, we often fund those very same politicians via the companies we support. This issue affects many countries, including the UK, but it's perhaps most pressing in the US, where campaign contributions are huge and where the politicians influenced by these donations have more international clout than anyone else. So, for example, we might lament George Bush's stance on Iraq, climate change and the International Criminal Court, but most of us continue to buy from the huge list of companies which support him and his party (see box overleaf).

Financial contributors don't determine the outcome of every decision made in Washington, of course, and a causal link between contributions and policy decisions is extremely difficult to prove. But research by organizations such as the US's Center for Responsive Politics certainly suggests a very real link between the voting patterns of elected politicians and the desires of the companies that helped fund their campaigns. Which isn't really very surprising. No one would claim that companies donate to campaign funds for altruistic reasons. (Ideology doesn't seem like a very likely motive either, considering that many companies – such as Microsoft and AOL – have donated large sums to both major parties.)

Some people claim that political donations from companies are healthy – the necessary counterbalance to equivalent donations from trade unions. But even if you agree with that, it doesn't change the fact that as consumers we have a choice: we can either buy goods from companies giving money to politicians we dislike, or we can shop elsewhere. The only problem is that it can be very hard to pin down exactly who's giving what to who, not least because the political funding may not come from

Who elected George W Bush? You did!

Maintained by *Ethical Consumer* magazine and drawing on research from Open Secrets, the Boycott Bush website encourages consumers to shun those companies who have donated the most to George W Bush's election campaigns. The project was launched on Bush's rejection of the Kyoto Treaty, but also objects to his "illegal invasion of Iraq and other regressive steps such as opposing weapons proliferation treaties". Following is their list of major UK brands owned by the top 25 Bush donors with consumer brands, focusing on the 2000, 2002 and 2004 election cycles.

▶ **Computers, Internet and media** AOL, Microsoft, Walt Disney, magazines published by IPC (includes Loaded, NME, Practical Parenting, TV Times, Woman)

▶ **Couriers** UPS, FedEx

▶ **Financial** Citibank, store cards owned by GE Capital Bank (includes those offered by Monsoon, Kwik-Fit, Laura Ashley, New Look, Debenhams and House of Fraser)

▶ **Food and drink** Bird's custard, Budweiser, Bud Ice, Carte Noire, Dairylea, Dime Bar, Doritos, Granose, Horlicks, Kenco, Kraft Foods, Lucozade, Marabou, Maxwell House, Michelob, Milka, Pepsi, Philadelphia, Protoveg and Realeat meat substitutes, Quaker Oats, Ribena, Suchard, Sugar Puffs, Terry's, Toblerone, Walkers

▶ **Medicine and personal hygiene** Amway, Anadin, Aquafresh, Artistry skin care, Beechams cold remedies, Benadryl, Calpol, Contac, Coppertone, Diflucan antifungal, Eumovate eczema treatments, Euthymol toothpaste, Feldene P gel, Listerine, Macleans, NiQuitin, Nutrilite vitamins and supplements, Panadol, Rappell,

the company itself, but from individual directors or (in the US) from so-called Political Action Committees. Luckily, there are a number of websites that will help you navigate the murky world of political giving:

CleanPolitix (UK donations) www.cleanpolitix.com
Open Secrets (US donations) www.opensecrets.org
PoliticalMoneyLine (US donations) www.tray.com

Beyond donations: lobby groups and think tanks

Even when companies aren't donating directly to politicians, they may be having an even greater – and even less transparent – impact on government policy and media content through their contributions to corporate lobby groups and think tanks. We've already seen how even the most mainstream business groups – such as the US Chamber of Commerce – have taken a firm stance against the Kyoto Treaty and the UN's Human Rights Norms for Business. A number of similar examples crop up elsewhere in this book.

Solpadeine painkillers, Sudafed decongestant, TCP throat pastilles, Zovirax coldsore treatment

▶ **Supermarkets** ASDA

▶ **Tobacco** Marlboro, Parliament

▶ **Travel and transport** American Airlines, BP, Esso, Fiat, Ford, Isuzu, Iveco, Jaguar, Land Rover, Mazda, Mobil lubricants, Range Rover, Saab, Subaru, Suzuki, Texaco petrol, Vauxhall, Volvo

Note that, technically speaking, it's not necessarily the companies that make the donations: due to US political contribution laws, it's very often organizations "affiliated" with the company, or their employees. But the effect is the same. Also note that some of the businesses listed above (such as TimeWarner, owners of AOL) have given more money to the Democrats than the Republicans. Finally, be aware that this list looks at the period 2000–04. Since it was compiled, at least one company listed – BP – has promised to stop all political donations.

For the most up-to-date list, methodology and background on the campaign, go straight to the sources:

Boycott Bush www.boycottbush.net
Open Secrets www.opensecrets.com

Just as sinister as these giant groups are the small but highly influential think tanks – many of them funded largely or entirely by corporations – which exist solely to push for big-business-friendly agendas on everything from animal testing to nuclear power. It's beyond the scope of this book to look into this area – not least because accurate information about which companies are giving to which think tanks is very difficult to come by. But if you fancy exploring the issue, check out SourceWatch.

SourceWatch www.sourcewatch.org

☛ *For more on responsible shopping, turn to the chapters on House & Garden Products (p.121), Food & Drink (p.145), Clothes, Cosmetics & Jewellery (p.227) and Money Matters (p.261).*

Part II

The guide

Home energy

When we flick on a light switch or turn up the heating, we rarely stop to think about where our energy comes from and the impacts of its use. But we should. Powered primarily by fossil fuels, domestic heating and electricity account for between a quarter and a third of the UK's greenhouse emissions. (The exact figure depends on whether you include aviation and imported goods in the national figures.) The average UK household creates six tonnes of CO_2 every year.

Climate change is by far the most pressing reason to limit our home energy consumption, but it's not the only one. Fossil fuels have caused countless conflicts over the past two centuries, and refining and burning them generates huge quantities of pollutants such as benzene (which can accumulate in the flesh of animals and humans), volatile organic compounds, polycyclic aromatic hydrocarbons and the oxides of sulphur and nitrogen that cause acid rain. Most of the UK's non-fossil-based power comes from nuclear energy, which raises its own questions, most obviously the safe disposal of radioactive waste (a discussion beyond the scope of this book).

Clearly, then, home energy is a key area for anyone concerned with their impact on the planet. Thankfully, it's also an area where there's much we can do. According to the Energy Saving Trust, the average British household could reduce its CO_2 emissions by a third – and save up to £250 per year – simply by becoming a bit more energy efficient.

Assessing your energy profile

A good first step is to take stock of how your home energy use breaks down. The pie-chart overleaf shows such a breakdown for a typical UK home. As it makes clear, **space and water heating** are by far the biggest consumers of domestic power, accounting for between six and seven times more energy than lighting and appliances.

Of course, the exact figures vary from home to home, so the ideal way to understand your energy use – and potential savings – is to have an expert assess your property. **Home energy audits** can usually be arranged for free via your local Energy Efficiency Advice Centre. Call 0800 512 012 for more details.

Energy use in the UK: total and domestic

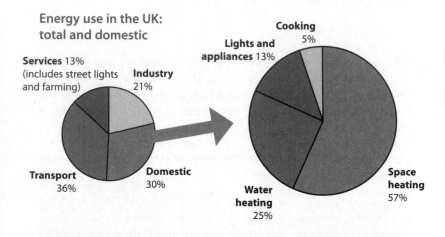

Services 13% (includes street lights and farming)

Industry 21%

Transport 36%

Domestic 30%

Lights and appliances 13%

Cooking 5%

Space heating 57%

Water heating 25%

Grants and offers

Various grants are available to people wanting to make their homes greener and more energy-efficient. If you're aiming to improve your heating and insulation, investigate **Warm Front**, a government scheme offering up to £2700 to certain income groups. Call 0800 316 2814 to see whether you qualify. Also try your gas and electricity suppliers. Under the government's Energy Efficiency Commitment, utility companies are obliged to set a certain percentage of their profits aside to provide their customers with offers on insulation and other energy-saving measures.

For renewable electricity installations, meanwhile, there's the **Low Carbon Buildings Programme**, launched in April 2006 and managed by the Energy Saving Trust. Of the £80 million initial fund, £6.5 million is ring-fenced for householders. However, a successful application depends on your home already having basic levels of energy efficiency in place, including 270mm of loft insulation, cavity wall insulation if possible, low-energy light bulbs, thermostatic radiator valves (TRVs), and a room thermostat and programmer. The application process is fairly simple and you'll normally get a decision within thirty days.

Low Carbon Buildings www.lowcarbonbuildings.org.uk ▷ 0800 915 0990

Electricity
From green tariffs to growing your own

Currently, around three-quarters of the UK's electricity is generated by coal and gas plants, which pump vast quantities of CO_2 and other pollutants into the atmosphere. The government aims to make the national supply more climate-friendly over the coming decades by expanding renewable and nuclear capacity and developing next-generation fossil-fuel plants which are more efficient and able to sequester (bury) the carbon dioxide they produce. But even if you trust the government to meet its targets, and even if you have no ethical problems with nuclear power, it still makes sense to reduce your electricity consumption as much as possible. In the short term, every unit you use leads directly to CO_2 emissions.

Of course, renewable sources already provide some of our electricity – nearly 5% at present, with targets of 10% by 2010 and

The dirty power behind our plug sockets: a bellowing smokestack at a fossil-fuel power station

20% by 2020. Ironically, though, much of our current "renewable" capacity comes from burning the gas formed as our rubbish decomposes in landfill sites. Over the next two decades, wind will become the dominant renewable source, though it remains to be seen how much this development will be held up by opposition to wind-farm planning applications. If you'd like to voice your support for wind power in your area, drop into:

Yes2Wind www.yes2wind.com

But what can consumers do directly to become greener users of electricity? One option is to buy your power from renewable sources – or even buy the equipment to generate your own. People argue about whether the UK could be entirely reliant on green sources, such as wind and solar, but few doubt that the more we generate, the better. Another option is to simply consume less power – something we can do surprisingly easily with a bit of thought, as the following pages reveal.

Green electricity tariffs

There are a wide range of **green electricity tariffs** on offer – both from major power suppliers and from specialist companies which only deal in renewable energy. The basic premise of most of them is that you pay a little bit more and the company supplies you with energy generated from renewable, environmentally friendly sources. Obviously, the actual flow of electrons arriving in your plug sockets won't be any different from before, but the supplier will agree to put green-generated electricity into the national grid to match all (or some, depending on the scheme) of the power you buy.

In practice, however, it's not quite so simple. The complication comes from the fact that UK law requires all electricity providers (except those in Northern Ireland) to buy a proportion of their power from renewable sources. This is known as the **Renewables Obligation** and requires 6% of electricity to be derived from renewable sources in 2006, rising each year to 10% in 2010. This is good news but, annoyingly, the companies can use the green electricity they provide to people who have specifically signed up for it to help them meet their legal obligation. So even when you go out of your way to choose a tariff whereby the supplier agrees to "put renewable energy into the National Grid to match the amount you use", in many cases you'll simply be helping the company achieve the quota of green energy it was going to have to buy anyway. As such, you probably won't be having any direct effect on the amount of green electricity being produced.

Even if your supplier buys more than the legal minimum from renewable sources, it doesn't necessarily make them more green. For each unit of renewable energy that a company buys, it gets a Renewables Obligation Certificate (**ROC**); if it buys more than the legal requirement, it can sell the extra ROCs to other companies, which in turn can use them towards their own legal minimums. So, at present, the only green tariffs that

Switching power companies

Ever since the electricity and gas markets were opened to competition in the early 1990s, we've all had the choice of switching suppliers and tariffs. One reason to do this is to save money: if you've never compared your current providers with others, it's almost certain that you're paying more than necessary. Another reason is to choose one of the ethically minded tariffs listed over the next couple of pages.

If you're thinking of switching but reluctant to change on the grounds of loyalty to your "local" supplier, bear in mind that it's probably not that local at all. Most of the big suppliers are owned by multinationals – for example, Northern Electricity is part of Mid American Energy, London Electricity and South West Electricity are owned by Electricité de France (EDF), and Eastern Electricity and Midlands Electricity are part of Powergen (itself part of German giant E.ON AG).

Various websites make it quick and easy to compare your current electricity and gas tariffs with those of other suppliers, including the various green options. Such sites are all much the same, but use Switch and Give and a donation will be made to a charity of your choice if you do decide to change supplier.

Switch and Give www.switchandgive.com

directly increase renewable power generation are those from companies that buy more than the required percentage of green power and then keep ("retire") some of the extra ROCs. This would all change if more than 6% of the population signed up for a green tariff (since that would be more than the Renewables Obligation), but right now that doesn't look likely.

To complicate things further, with certain tariffs the supplier commits to putting some of the money from your bill into funding new wind farms or renewable energy research. So, even if they *are* selling all their extra ROCs, they may still be doing some good.

Another issue is how ethical the electricity provider is on a broader level. For example, you may wish to avoid suppliers which own inefficient coal power stations ("carbon dinosaurs" in the words of Friends of the Earth). Depending on your point of view, you may also want to shun companies such as EDF – which generates 88% of its energy from nuclear.

So, which tariff?

With such a complex set of factors to consider, it's not easy to rank the various green tariffs. Until 2004, Friends of the Earth maintained a useful online league table, but they stopped due to the difficulties of evaluating the various products and conveying their findings in an intelligible way.

Instead, they are now lobbying energy regulator Ofgem to produce a transparent, green-tariff accreditation scheme. You can add you support to this campaign via the Friends of the Earth website:

Friends of the Earth Climate Campaign www.foe.co.uk/campaigns/climate

There are other sources of advice, but they're not entirely unbiased. For example, the website Which Green (www.whichgreen.com) ranks tariffs according to the amount invested in new renewable energy generation. Ecotricity come in miles ahead of the rest, investing £117 per customer in new wind turbines; but then the same company created the site and chose the methodology. A study by Oxford University's respected Environmental Change Institute (funded by Ecotricity's competitor, Good Energy) proposes that the number of ROCs retired is a better measure of greenness than investment per customer.

Green specialists

Ecotricity

www.ecotricity.co.uk
▷ 0800 032 6100

The only green electricity company actively developing new wind farms. They do not retire any ROCs but in 2005 invested £7 million in new projects. Annual price for typical household: £384.

Good Energy

www.good-energy.co.uk
▷ 0845 4561 640

Supplies nothing but 100% renewable electricity. Does not invest in new projects but buys energy from small generators through its Home Generation scheme. Retires a few percent of ROCs above the legal minimum. Annual price for typical household: £425.

Green Energy UK

www.greenenergy.uk.com ▷ 0845 456 9550

Buys 79% of its energy from renewable sources but doesn't appear to retire any ROCs (at least we couldn't find any evidence that they did, and they didn't return our calls). Intends to invest in new renewable developments in the future. The first 100,000 subscribers also get the offer of becoming shareholders. Annual price for typical household: £441.

Eco Energy (from Northern Ireland Electricity)

www.nieenergy.co.uk ▷ 08457 643 643

The issue of selling on green energy certificates doesn't apply in the case of this tariff, because Northern Ireland has no laws regarding minimum green-electricity purchasing. Annual price for typical household: £364.

More options

Juice (from NPower)

npower juice

www.npower.com

Endorsed by Greenpeace, Juice doesn't cost any more than NPower's standard tariffs. However, no ROCs are retired and NPower is part of RTE, which also owns Thames Water – which tops the Environment Agency's list of the most polluting companies.

RSPB tariff (from Scottish and Southern)

www.scottish-southern.co.uk ▷ 0800 028 8552

Donates £20 to the RSPB when you join. Was previously in the Friends of the Earth's top five choices, but now offers Air Miles as an incentive to sign up, which somewhat defeats the object.

For more information on green electricity tariffs, visit Green Electricity Marketplace. Or to see a breakdown of the energy sources used by each power company, see Electricity Info.

Green Electricity Marketplace www.greenelectricity.org
Electricity Info www.electricityinfo.org

Socially equitable electricity

One completely different option for your power supply is an account with **EquiPower**, a non-profit organization which focuses on social equity rather than the environment. With conventional electricity suppliers, the poorest members of society end up paying the most per unit, for various reasons – they often use expensive pre-pay meters, lack bank accounts enabling them to benefit from direct debit savings, or pay a disproportionate amount via standing charges. EquiPower has one price, regardless of the payment method. Yet, because it's non-profit-making, the company is able to offer competitive rates even without direct debit offers and the like.

One downside is EquiPower's size. As a very small company they are not as easy to get hold of as their bigger competitors and only rate two stars (out of five) for service on the Switch and Give site. For more information and price details, see:

EquiPower www.ebico.co.uk ▷ 0845 456 0170

Generating your own electricity

If you want to put renewable power in your home on a more tangible level, there are a number of options. Most of the renewable energy sources – from wind and solar to hydro and geothermal – can be exploited on a household scale. And since Conservative Party leader David Cameron famously determined to install a wind turbine on his Notting Hill roof, home-generation has been more popular than ever.

In some cases, micro-generation systems make sense not only from an environmental perspective but also from a financial one: you may save money in the long run, and there are grants available to contribute to the price of installation (see box on p.70). You may even be able to feed any extra power back into the national grid and get paid for it. For example, NPower and Good Energy will pay about 5p for each kilowatt hour of electricity generated.

That said, a system that will make you anywhere close to self-sufficient in electricity will require massive up-front investment, and in most cases it's far more efficient to start off by improving your heating (see p.88) and insulation (see p.97). Following is the low-down on each of the main micro-generation options. Also see p.92 for information about combined heat and power set-ups.

Planning issues

The UK government recently proposed making changes to the planning system so that installing micro renewables on existing houses will be classed as a permitted development. In the meantime, it would be advisable to contact your local authority planning department before you start work. Typical issues that need addressing include visual impact, noise and changes to the character of listed buildings or conservation areas. Planning applications cost around £120–200. Micro hydro schemes need an abstraction license from the Environment Agency.

Micro wind turbines

Wind turbines create electricity from the kinetic energy of moving air, most commonly with a three-blade rotor. There are two categories of micro turbines. The first type, designed to be mounted on buildings, range from tiny 100 watt models used to charge 12–24 volt batteries to 2.5 kilowatt turbines that can export any excess electricity to the grid. The second, designed to be mounted on stand-alone masts (3–15m high), range in capacity from 600W to more than 20kW.

Two Swift Turbines on a domestic building in Berwickshire

▶ **How much power?** The power output of a wind turbine depends on the length of the blades, the wind speed and whether there's any air-flow obstruction from other buildings or trees. As a guide, a small 1kW roof-mounted turbine with a 1.75m blade might realistically produce about 650kWh per year at an average wind speed of 4.5 metres per second. That's about 20% of a typical household's needs.

Stand-alone turbines have fewer restrictions on where they can be located so you should aim to find a windy site with minimal obstruction. Wind speed increases with height, and an appropriately sited 6kW turbine with a blade diameter of 5.5m, raised 15m above the ground, should be capable of producing 7500kWh from an average wind speed of 5mps. This is about double the needs of a typical home so you would be able to export the surplus to the grid.

Energy units and prices

Energy consumption is defined in terms of watts and hours. If a 100 watt light bulb is used for ten hours, then the power used is 1000 watt hours. For ease we refer to 1000 watt hours as 1 **kilowatt hour (kWh)** and this is the standard unit that appears on our electricity bills. Gas bills normally specify the number of cubic metres of gas consumed but also convert the figure into kWh.

Unit prices at the time of writing are 2.5p per kWh for gas and 12p per kWh for electricity. An average three-bedroom semi-detached house uses 15,000kWh for space heating, 5000kWh for water heating and 3000kWh for electricity, costing a total of £890 – and resulting in around six tonnes of CO_2 – per year.

▶ **Space requirements** You don't need loads of space, but best results are achieved at 10m or more above surrounding buildings and trees – which is usually impossible with a roof-mounted turbine. In mounting any turbine, avoid sites with excessive turbulence, which will reduce performance and shorten the turbine's working life.

▶ **Costs and grants** You should expect to pay about £3000 per kW, which will include the turbine, mast, inverters and batteries (if required). It's most economical to consume the electricity that you produce. If you wish to sell any surplus to the grid you will need to install an export meter, which costs around £400. Large, stand-alone turbines may also require foundation work, which can cost an additional £3000.

The Low Carbon Buildings Programme offers a grant of £1000 per kW installed, up to a maximum of £5000 or 30% of the total project costs.

▶ **Payback period** You might break even in 15–20 years with a stand-alone turbine. Most smaller units struggle to pay for themselves during their lifetimes, though a steep rise in energy prices could change this.

▶ **Maintenance** The service schedule will be specified by the manufacturer. At the very least an annual inspection should be

Community wind

Somewhere between installing a wind turbine on your roof and signing up for a green tariff is investing in a renewable energy project on your doorstep. In Denmark, 22% of wind farms are owned by local residents and although the UK is a long way behind, there are quite a few examples of wind co-ops and many more in the pipeline. Such schemes typically have a minimum and maximum investment, with first refusal offered to people living in the vicinity of the project. This way, the benefits can be realized by as many people as possible, each member has an equal say, and the local community develops a real sense of ownership over the wind farm.

The **Baywind** community wind farm in Cumbria (www.baywind.co.uk) is the oldest example in the UK. It was set up in 1997 and has 1300 members, 43% of whom live in Cumbria and Lancashire. The co-operative raised nearly £2 million for six turbines on two sites, which produce enough electricity to power 1800 homes. Baywind has frequently provided annual returns of about 7% gross and also promises that the capital sum invested will be returned at the end of the scheme (25 years). An additional benefit is the tax relief that members get in the form of the government's Enterprise Investment Scheme.

For more information about community wind projects, see:

Energy4All www.energy4all.co.uk

performed to check for damage or wear to the blades and other components.

▶ **Worth looking into?** Possibly. It depends on your budget and the average windspeed around your property. You can find windspeed estimates for your postcode online. See:

UK Wind Speed Database www.bwea.com/noabl

For more information on micro wind turbines, see:

British Wind Energy Association www.bwea.com/small

And for some examples of UK-made wind turbine models, visit the following manufacturers' websites:

Windsave www.windsave.com
Proven www.provenenergy.com
Swift www.renewabledevices.com/swift

Solar photovoltaics

Photovoltaics or **PV** systems involve two or more thin layers of semiconducting material (usually silicon) which generate electrical charges when exposed to sunlight. The voltage from a single cell is low, so many cells are connected to form a solar panel. These panels are in turn combined into a solar roof or some other kind of "array". There are currently only around 1500 arrays in the UK, compared to more than 100,000 in Germany.

One problem with PV cells is that they are quite energy-intensive to make and can take up to five years of solid use just to repay their carbon debt (the amount of CO_2 emitted during manufacture). If the system is used in conjunction with batteries, the carbon debt may even be ten years.

▶ **How much power?** A 1kW system might produce 800kWh of electricity per annum, depending on your location in the country (the intensity of solar energy is much greater in Dorset than in Dumfries). That would be sufficient to provide the baseload of your electricity use – about 25% of your total yearly requirements. In most cases, the limitation for bigger systems is roof space.

▶ **Space requirements** A 1kW system requires an area of 10 square metres of south-facing roof.

▶ **Costs and grants** Expect to pay around £5000–£10,000 for a 1kW system. It's most cost-effective to use all the electricity that you produce.

If you wish to export surplus to the grid you will need an export meter costing £400.

The Low Carbon Buildings Programme offers a maximum grant of £3000 per kW installed, up to a maximum of £15,000 or 50% of installation costs.

▶ **Payback period?** An £8000 PV system producing 800kWh per year would yield an annual saving of around £96 relative to electricity bought via a green tariff. The system would be expected to last for 25–30 years but electricity prices would need to increase by a further 70% to see a payback during the panels' lifetime.

▶ **Maintenance** Virtually none is required, though it's a good idea to check annually to see if any debris has fallen on the PV cells. The panels can be cleaned with soapy water and a soft brush.

▶ **Worth looking into?** Only if you have a big budget and an unobstructed south-facing roof in a sunny part of the country. It also helps if you tend to consume electricity in the day (if you work at home, for example), since that's when the sun shines. For more information on solar photovoltaic systems, see:

British Photovoltaic Association www.greenenergy.org.uk/pvuk2

Micro hydro

If you happen to have a river or stream on your property, or you live near to one, you could investigate micro hydro. In such systems, water flowing steeply downhill – over a natural waterfall or man-made weir – is diverted via a pipe called a **penstock**. This directs the water through an enclosed turbine, which rotates to produce electricity. After leaving the turbine, the water is discharged back into the river.

▶ **How much power?** Micro hydro systems can provide a great deal of power, depending on the height that the water falls (the **head**) and the volume of water passing through the turbine each second (the **flow**

rate, measured in cubic metres per second). The flow of the water will vary throughout the year so a 10kW system might be able to achieve its full potential only 40–50% of the time. This would still enable the production of 35,000kWh per year, enough electricity for ten homes.

▶ **Costs and grants** Low-head schemes (with a height of 5–20m) usually cost about £3000–4000 per kW. So a 10kW system would cost around £30,000–40,000.

The Low Carbon Buildings Programme offers grants of £1000 per kW installed, up to a maximum of £5000 or 30% of installation costs.

▶ **Payback period** This depends on the price you get for any power you export to the grid. It might be possible to get as much as 8p per kWh. A 10kW system producing 35,000kWh per year would bring in an annual income of £2800. A £40,000 project would therefore pay back in around twelve years. If you use all the electricity yourself, the payback would be reduced to around eight years (at current energy prices).

▶ **Worth looking into?** Perhaps – particularly if your land has an old water mill on it, as this will significantly reduce infrastructure costs. There are 30,000–40,000 disused water mills in the UK, only a handful of which are currently used for power production. On a smaller scale, hilly areas with spring-fed streams and a head of just 1m can also be suitable. For more information, visit:

British Hydro Power Association www.british-hydro.org

Slimming down your electricity use

Unless you've spent your life savings going energy self-sufficient, it pays – environmentally and financially – to reduce your household electricity consumption. This doesn't have to mean drastic lifestyle changes, as at present a large proportion of our household power is simply wasted, frittered away by the likes of energy-inefficient fridges, overfilled kettles and TVs on standby.

UK householders currently spend £5.3 billion on domestic lighting and appliances. White goods are easily the biggest power eaters but high-tech devices are starting to catch up (see p.86). When buying any electric device, it makes sense to choose the most energy-efficient model available; some appliances use double the energy to get the same job done. Various labelling schemes make it easier than ever to find energy-efficient devices (see p.83).

Fridges and freezers

Household fridges and freezers run non-stop and collectively consume more energy than the total used in running all the offices in the country. If you have an old, inefficient model, seriously consider upgrading. It will pay for itself in a few years and make CO_2 savings from the moment you plug it in.

If you don't want to invest in a new fridge you could still make savings with a **SavaPlug**, available from various websites and shops. It replaces the fridge's normal plug and has a sensor that reduces the amount of electricity used to pump the refrigerant around the fridge. Savings of more than 20% can be achieved, but before buying be sure to check that your model isn't on the incompatible list at:

Savawatt www.savawatt.com

Whatever type of fridge you have, its energy consumption is influenced by the amount of time the door is left open and, strangely, how clean and ice-free it is. So defrost regularly and once in a while check the grille at the back for dust and dirt. This will add to the efficiency and lengthen the fridge's working life.

Washing machines

The average UK household uses their washing machine 274 times each year. Typically, 90% of the resulting energy consumption goes towards heating water, so select the lowest temperature – and the shortest cycle – that will get the job done to a satisfactory standard. A 40 degree wash is sufficient for most non-heavily soiled clothing. If there's an economy setting, use it. For even greater CO_2 savings, always let clothes dry on a line or rack rather than using an energy-hungry dryer.

Dishwashers

As with washing machines, most of the energy consumed by a dishwasher is used to generate heat – both to warm the water and, for drying cycles, to warm the air inside the machine. So always opt for the coolest setting that will get the job done.

As for how dishwashers compare with washing up by hand, this depends on the individual machine (some models use less than fifteen litres of hot water per load), the efficiency of your hot-water heater and, most impor-

Shopping for energy efficiency

A number of energy-efficiency labels now appear on electrical goods. The main ones are:

▶ **EU Energy Label** By law, all retailers – whether shops, mail-order or online – must show the EU Energy Label on or alongside all new fridges, freezers, washers, tumble dryers, dishwashers, lamps, ovens, light bulbs and air conditioners. Each item is ranked from A (efficient) to G (inefficient) in terms of its power consumption under standard running conditions. These days all washing machines available in the UK tend to be graded above D and fridges/freezers above C, so a "middle" rating is actually relatively low.

The label also generally contains other information – such as water usage, and how well the machine actually does what it's supposed to do ("performance"). Washing machines are usually given a three-letter rating, in the form AAB, referring to energy efficiency, wash performance and spin performance, respectively.

The EU label usually includes a measure of energy consumption per cycle or per day, measured in kWh (kilowatt hours). If you're trying to balance cost with efficiency, factor in the future savings you'll make by multiplying this kWh figure by 127 (the average price in pence of one kilowatt hour) to give the cost in pence.

▶ **Energy Efficiency Recommended** Administered by the UK's Energy Saving Trust, the Energy Efficiency Recommended Logo (EER) was developed to point customers to the most energy-efficient products on the market. It can be found on light bulbs and appliances as well as boilers, heating controls, insulation and more. The criteria are strict. For example, to bear the logo at the time of writing, fridges must be A+ or A++ (25%–45% more efficient than standard "A" models) and washing machines must be AAA. You can find endorsed products online or by phone: www.est.org.uk/myhome/efficientproducts ▷ 0800 915 7722

▶ **EU Ecolabel** You may occasionally see products bearing the EU Ecolabel flower, usually alongside the main EU Energy Label. This means the product has passed numerous environmental criteria, relating not just to energy efficiency but also to its expected lifespan, ease of disposability and the like. The scheme also covers everything from paints to tissues to computers, but right now very few labelled products are available in the UK. The Ecolabel criteria have been criticized as too lax by some, such as Ecover, who refuse to display the label. For more info and an online product catalogue, see www.eco-label.com

Low-carbon cooking

▶ **Picking pans** Choosing the right size pan for cooking and keeping a lid on for most of the cooking process can reduce the energy needed to cook food by 90%.

▶ **Only boil what you'll use** Nothing's more wasteful than filling a kettle to the brim to make one or two cups of tea. So get in the habit of using the water gauge.

▶ **Gas vs electric** As with heating, gas cookers are far more environmentally friendly than electric ones. However, try to avoid too much unburnt gas leaking from the hobs before you light them. Methane is 24 times more powerful as a greenhouse gas than CO_2.

tantly, how economical you are when washing up by hand. A much-cited 2004 study from the University of Bonn suggests that dishwashers use less energy overall than the typical person at a sink, but this doesn't include the significant energy costs of producing, delivering and eventually disposing of the machine. Moreover, the study gives figures for hand-washing that can be slashed with just a bit of care, and assumes you run your machine with full loads, skipping extra features such as "pre-rinse".

Lighting

Light bulbs account for around 10–20% of domestic electricity usage – that's more than £1 billion each year in bills between us – yet around 95% of the energy that typical incandescent bulbs use is lost in heat. Energy-efficient **compact fluorescent** bulbs reduce energy waste by more than 75% and they also last around ten times as long.

Decent efficient bulbs cost around £5 each (the cheapest ones tend to produce slightly "artificial" light) but will pay for themselves within a year if used for four hours a day. Each bulb will save you around £100 in power and replacement incandescent bulbs during its lifetime. If you want to spread the cost, replace old bulbs when they stop working, putting the efficient bulbs in the rooms where you use lights the most (not forgetting outdoor security lights).

What about **halogen** lights? These are a subset of incandescents, and tend to be mid-range performers in the efficiency stakes. Better-quality halogen bulbs are around twice as efficient as typical incandescents and half as efficient as compact fluorescents. However, halogen light fittings often take multiple bulbs, raising their overall energy consumption.

Sunpipes

If you live in a house that needs the lights on during the day, even in the middle of summer, then consider having a **Sunpipe** installed. These super-reflective tubes carry natural daylight from your rooftop into dimly lit areas, diffusing the light around the room by a translucent ceiling fixture. Sunpipes can provide 100W of light in the winter and up to 500W on a sunny summer day. For more information, see:

Sunpipe www.sunpipe.co.uk

Regardless of which type of bulbs you use, you can reduce their carbon footprint by turning the lights off when you leave a room. This alone can knock £15–30 off your annual electricity bill.

Don't standby, turn off

An incredible 8% of our domestic electricity is consumed by appliances such as TVs, DVD players, stereos and computers left on standby. Many devices – especially TVs – use almost as much energy in standby mode as when they're in use. Amazingly, the average microwave oven uses more energy powering its digital clock than it does cooking food (costing the owner around £7 per year).

Appliance	Average time in use	Time on standby/ plugged in	kWh used	Percent of electricity used on standby	Cash savings of switching off	CO2 savings of switching off
Normal TV (80 watts playing, 15 watts on standby)	3 hours per day	21 hours per day	203	57	£13.80	50kg
Video	3 hours per day	21 hours per day	125	74	£11.04	40kg
Battery charger (2 watts)	9 hours per week	159 hours per week	18	97	£2.16	7.5kg
Microwave (8 watts)	20 mins per day	23–24 hours per day	70	98	£8.40	29kg

The government's 2006 Energy Review suggests phasing out inefficient standby modes in consumer electronics. In the meantime, getting into the habit of turning devices off properly can take a decent chunk out of your emissions and bills, as the table on the previous page makes clear.

TVs, computers and gadgets

The proliferation of gadgets and over-sized televisions is more than offsetting the gains made in the efficiency of kitchen appliances. Indeed, electrical goods could result in a 20% increase in household electricity consumption by 2020.

Some of the worst offenders are flat-screen **plasma TVs**, which typically use four times as much energy as old-fashioned cathode ray tube models. A cheap plasma TV is typically rated at about 550 watts. Used for four hours each day, the result will be 800kWh a year, which equates to 344kg of CO_2 and nearly £100 in electricity bills.

Digiboxes used for digital TV reception and broadband routers are also very power-hungry. The Energy Saving Trust predicts that by 2010 the power required for these units alone will cost UK households £30 each per year. If you do need to buy a new TV, consider one with IDTV (integrated digital television). These save energy by only using one power socket and one standby circuit.

Computers vary widely in terms of the energy they consume – both when in use and in standby and screen-saver modes. You can reduce the period of inactivity that causes the machine to enter sleep or hibernation mode via the Control Panel (on a PC) or System Preferences (on a Mac). Unless there's a reason not to, turn off computers when they're not in use for extended periods or, even better, dedicate their downtime to the fight against climate change via ClimatePrediction.net. This Web-based project divides complex climate modelling software into tiny pieces manageable by standard PCs (Macs aren't supported at the time of writing). Once installed, your computer will be helping to predict future climate change whenever

it enters screen-saver mode. For more information, or to get started, see:

ClimatePrediction.net
www.climateprediction.net

Portable devices such as **mobile phones** and **MP3 players** tend to consume relatively little electricity in use and on standby, since this helps improve their battery life. However, around 95% of their total energy consumption is accounted for by chargers that are plugged in and working even after the device is fully recharged. So try to get into the habit of unplugging devices when charged and switching their chargers off at the wall.

Get to know your meter

Most people know roughly how much they spend on shopping but have no idea how much energy they use. Monitoring your meter will help you understand how much electricity you consume and where savings can be made. Even better, get a plug-in power meter that allows you to monitor individual appliances over a number of days to see how much energy they use. Start with your fridge or freezer as this is on every hour of every day, so it's easy to extrapolate its yearly consumption from a few days' use. If any of your appliances give figures that equal or exceed the levels in the table below, you might be better served changing to a more energy-efficient model.

Appliance	Electricity use (kWh per year)	Percent of household electricity demand	Cost to run per year	Efficiency savings of a model rated A+	Annual cost savings	CO_2 savings
Lighting	715	27	£86	75%	£64	230kg
Fridge-freezer	650	20	£78	60%	£35	189kg
Dishwasher	410	13	£49	40%	£13	70kg
Washing machine	270	9	£32	30%	£5	27kg

The government are currently testing a range of technologies that could provide real-time information to households about their energy use. These so-called **smart meters** would allow remote reading, removing the need for house calls and allowing householders with solar panels or wind turbines to plug in to the grid. No date has been set for the rolling out of this initiative. In the meantime, energy suppliers will be required to read meters more often and, from 2007, provide graphical details of their customers' energy use compared with previous years.

If you really want to be in touch with your energy usage, consider an **Electrisave** unit. These £80 devices connect to your meter and transmit real-time usage info (in terms of units, CO_2 and cost) to a wireless display. For more information, or to buy online, visit:

Electrisave www.electrisave.co.uk

Heating
Warm your home, not the climate

Heating accounts for around a fifth of the greenhouse emissions of the average UK citizen, so even a small improvement in the way we warm our homes and water can make a big difference. Currently, the most common heating fuel is natural gas. Essentially methane, this gas is the vapour equivalent of coal and oil, formed underground by decomposing matter over millions of years. Gas extrac-

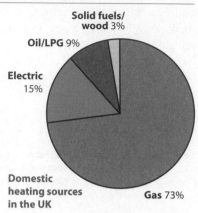

Solid fuels/wood 3%
Oil/LPG 9%
Electric 15%
Domestic heating sources in the UK
Gas 73%

tion, processing and burning is a major source of carbon dioxide but per unit of energy gained gas is less harmful to the environment (in terms of greenhouse gases, particulates and other pollutants) than either coal or oil. These cleaner-burning credentials were one factor in the "dash for gas" phenomenon of the 1980s and 90s, when UK power companies invested in hardly anything but gas power stations. Today, however, North Sea gas production is on the decline and Britain finds itself at the very end of pipelines running from Asia and Eastern Europe. It remains to be seen how prices and reliability of supply will play out in the coming decades.

Regardless of whether you're on the gas network (27% of UK residents aren't), there's probably much you can do to improve the efficiency of your heating system. The first step is to minimize waste; the second is to consider upgrading to a more efficient boiler or even investing in a renewable system powered by wood, sunlight or the ground.

Tweaking your heating

Most households can achieve significant cuts in their CO_2 emissions just by making a few adjustments to the way they use their existing heating set-up. Here are some good ways to get started.

▶ **Turn it down** Reducing your heating and hot-water temperatures by just a small amount can make a disproportionate difference to your

Electric heating: a climate crime

Compared to gas systems, electric heating is profoundly inefficient, producing on average around twice as much CO_2 per unit of heat than does gas. At present, there are 1.64 million UK residences heated by electricity – around 15% of housing stock. Many of these are rural houses that aren't connected to the gas network, but even in cities a significant number of homes – especially rented flats – use electric radiators and storage heaters. It's strange that whilst the government has tightened up energy conservation measures in building regulations they still haven't banned electric storage heaters. As a consequence many well-insulated residences built in the 1990s produce as much CO_2 via heating as poorly insulated houses from the 1890s.

If you own a home on the gas network which uses electric heating, then seriously consider switching over. If you're renting, probably the best you can do is use your heaters as efficiently as possible. With simple electric radiators, this may mean nothing more than setting thermostats at sensible levels and switching the heaters off a while before you go out. With **storage heaters**, which build up heat reserves in the night, when electricity is cheaper, it's a bit more complex. Such heaters usually have two controls: an input and an output. The input regulates the amount of heat that is stored in the heater at night; turn this up during cold weather and down during warm weather. The output dial allows you to control when you release the stored heat. Turn this down a while before going to bed or leaving the house.

energy consumption. You may find you sleep better, too. For rooms, try 16–18°C and throw on a sweater. Each degree you lose will save 114–228kg of CO_2 emissions (and £15–30 on your bills) each year. As for hot water, aim for 50–60°C.

▶ **Keep your tank warm** If you have an uninsulated hot water tank, be sure to equip it with an insulating jacket. For just a few pounds, this could reduce the energy required to heat your water by 25–45%.

▶ **Don't heat empty spaces** Efficient heating controls – especially those that let you specify the temperature of individual rooms, or programme different temperatures for different times of day – can take a significant chunk out of your energy demands. Also look into **thermostatic radiator valves**, which allow you to control each room's temperature automatically.

▶ **Heat rooms not walls** Put foil reflectors behind radiators to reflect heat back into the room. You can make your own, but you'll get better results buying them off the shelf.

▶ **Close the curtains** Draw the curtains at dusk, before the warmth starts to escape.

Gas combi boilers

If you're on the gas network but don't have an efficient **gas condensing combination boiler**, then it's definitely worth considering an upgrade. Combination (aka combi) boilers heat water on demand rather than filling a tank with hot water that may or may not be used. Modern condensing models are also extremely efficient, producing more than 10% extra heat per unit of energy than a typical boiler produced just ten years ago.

Combi boilers aren't cheap, but you could easily save around £1000 (and an equivalent amount of CO_2 emissions) over the space of ten years, depending on your gas demands and future prices. A combi will also let you reclaim the cupboard space occupied by your hot water tank, though on the flipside they don't work in the event of a power cut.

When shopping for a boiler, be sure to look for one bearing the Energy Efficiency Recommended label. You can find a list here:

Energy Saving Trust www.est.org.uk/myhome/efficientproducts/boilers

How to make a combi even more efficient

Depending on where your combi boiler is situated in relation to your tap, it can take up to a minute to actually get any warm water out. In this time you will probably waste 9–12 litres of water. Moreover, once you turn off the tap, warm water remains in the pipe. If you need hot water again soon afterwards, this water will still be warm, but if it's left for an hour then its thermal energy will have dissipated and you'll have to wait another minute for warm water.

There are ways around these problems, allowing you to save energy and water at the same time. One very low-cost measure worth taking when a boiler is being installed is to insulate your hot water pipes. This will keep the water warm for much longer. More elaborate solutions include the following:

▶ **Solar water pre-heat** This option uses a standard solar hot-water system (see opposite) to warm the water before it's fed into the combi boiler. It's quite an expensive set-up to install and you'll need a tank as well as a boiler. Also, note that it will only work with certain boilers, so be sure to check with your boiler manufacturer before ordering.

▶ **Zenex Gas Saver** This is a more compact solution – effectively a boiler "top box" that bolts on to your combi. It extracts otherwise wasted energy from gases exiting the system via the flue, using it to pre-heat the incoming cold water feed. The box costs £575 (plus installation costs) but can pay for itself in three years, since it cuts gas demand by around 11% and saves around 5000 litres of water (around £25 per year on a metered water bill). It will typically reduce your home's CO_2 emissions by almost a tonne per year.

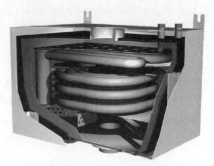

The Gas Saver can currently be used with all Alpha and Veissmann boilers and many others besides. For more information, see:

Zenex Gas Saver www.zenexenergy.com ▷ 0800 328 7533

Alternative heating systems

With rising fossil-fuel prices and an ever-greater sense of urgency surrounding climate change, there's never been a better time to investigate specialist green heating systems. Some only heat your water whilst others provide your entire heating needs. The main options are solar, geothermal, biomass (wood) and combined heat and power.

Solar water heating

Though most people associate solar power with generating electricity, it's also possible to convert sunlight directly into heat. The typical set-up is a roof-mounted **solar collector** panel, which channels the Sun's energy into your hot-water tank. Such systems have been around since the 1970s and there are currently about 80,000 installations in the UK. Generally, the collector is combined with a traditional water heating system; some combi

---

Planning issues for alternative heat

Solar water heating may not be allowed on listed buildings or in conservation areas. With wood fuel systems there are no restrictions in rural areas but as yet there are few products that are eligible for use in smoke-control zones. Environmental Health Officers should be consulted prior to the installation of larger (100kW+) systems. There are no planning restrictions on ground-source heat pumps.

boilers are also compatible. There are various types of solar collector available, with efficiency increasing with price. Beware of junk mail and door-to-door salesmen that promise savings that are too good to be true, and always get several quotes before committing to an installer.

▶ **How much heat?** A typical system will provide all your hot water in the summer and about 50% of your total annual demand.

▶ **Space requirements** A typical three-bedroom house would need three or four square metres of south-facing roof to mount the solar

Micro CHP: the way forward?

Micro **combined heat and power** (CHP) units, which are due to hit the UK market in the next couple of years, are a bit like super-efficient domestic-scale power stations. They replace your standard boiler, burning fuel (usually gas) to generate electricity and channelling the heat produced during this process into water and radiators.

This dual approach reduces energy consumption and carbon emissions by as much as 25%. Furthermore, since the electricity is consumed where it's produced, there are fewer transmission losses, reducing CO_2 emissions even further.

Unlike conventional boilers, most CHP units are designed to run for much of the day, producing a constant low-level heat. A typical model might produce around 2400kWh of electricity each year (worth about £250 per year at current prices) as well as 18,000kWh of heat. Two main brands are currently being tested in the UK: **WhisperGen** by Powergen and **Microgen** by British

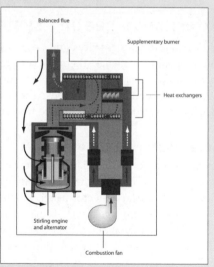

Diagram of a Microgen unit

Gas. Both are expected to be available to residential customers before 2008 and will retail for around £500–1000 more than a normal boiler, with a payback time of just 3–4 years. For more information, see:

WhisperGen whispergen@powergen.co.uk ▷ 0800 068 6515
Microgen www.microgen.com ▷ 01733 393 100

collectors. You'll also need space for a hot-water cylinder, if you don't have one already.

▶ **Cost and grants** Expect to pay around £2500–4000, depending on the type and size of collector. (Installation costs are reduced if combined with other roof work.) The Low Carbon Buildings Programme offers a £400 grant towards the cost.

It is possible to install your own panels, which could reduce the outlay by £1000–2000. However, a DIY installation is not eligible for a grant, and you'll pay full VAT for the panels rather than the reduced 5% level paid by accredited installers.

▶ **Payback period** Savings are best in areas off the gas network. You could expect a payback in 15–25 years when compared to electric water heating. A DIY system could pay for itself in less than ten years.

▶ **Maintenance** Virtually none is required. You may need to replace the antifreeze after about five years. Other than that, just check annually for debris on the collectors, cleaning them when necessary with soapy water.

▶ **Worth looking into?** Perhaps. It makes most sense for those with electric water heaters and especially those with high levels of hot-water demand in summer (such as B&Bs and campsites). For more information, see:

Solar Trade Association www.greenenergy.org.uk/sta

Popular solar collector installation companies include:

Solar Twin www.solartwin.com ▷ 01244 403 407
Powertech www.solar.org.uk ▷ 01202 890 234

Ground-source heat pumps

Heat pumps extract warmth (ultimately solar energy) stored in the ground. A length of plastic pipe is buried in the ground and filled with a mixture of water and antifreeze. This liquid absorbs heat from the ground and an electric compressor raises the temperature to a useful level. The heat is distributed around the home by underfloor heating or radiators. Such systems require some electricity to drive the pump and compressor, but can be made completely renewable when combined with a small wind turbine.

Air-source and water-source heat pumps are also available, though they wouldn't be useful for most UK homes.

▶ **How much heat?** You could produce all your heating with a ground-source pump, but it might be more cost-effective to opt for a smaller system with a fossil-fuel-driven immersion system to kick in during times of peak need.

▶ **Space requirements** The ground loop needs a trench 75–100m long and 1–2m deep for a typical house. Vertical systems are possible but more expensive. The pump itself is a fridge-sized box.

▶ **Costs and grants** A typical 8kW system costs £6000–10,000, not including the distribution system inside the house (an underfloor heating system is ideal although it is possible to use radiators). A total outlay of £10,000–13,000 would be realistic for an average house.

The Low Carbon Buildings Programme offers a grant (regardless of size) of up to £1200 or 30% of total costs.

▶ **Payback period** Savings are best in areas without mains gas. If you replace an electric heating system you could reduce your bills by up to two-thirds, enabling the system to pay for itself in 16–21 years.

▶ **Maintenance** Virtually none is required.

▶ **Worth looking into?** Best for new-build homes where a trench can be excavated during the building works and underfloor heating incorporated in the design. A high level of insulation is necessary to make the most of this technology as poorly insulated properties will require the pump to work harder, consuming valuable electricity.

If you use air conditioning in the summer, you might want to explore reverse-cycle heat pumps that can provide both heating and cooling. Unfortunately the UK grant scheme does not cover these.

For more information, see:

Ground Source Heat Pump Club www.nef.org.uk/gshp/gshp.htm

Small-scale biomass heating

Biomass includes any biological material. In the context of heating, it usually refers to **wood** – in the form of logs, chips and pellets (compressed sawdust) – though **cereal grain** can also be used as a fuel. When wood is burnt, it does produce CO_2 but this is absorbed by new trees planted to replace the mature ones felled. Some additional CO_2 emissions come from harvesting and transporting the wood, but the overall carbon footprint is far smaller than with a fossil-fuel heating system.

Automatic wood heating systems are far more efficient (by 80–90%) than traditional open fires or wood-burning stoves. They also provide a manageable heat source that is controlled by thermostats, and require far less maintenance. They are yet to catch on in a huge way in the UK, but Austria alone already has more than 100,000 installations.

▶ **How much heat?** It depends which technology you go for. A biomass room heater is like having a gas fire or wood stove, providing heating to a single room. Some models can be fitted with a back boiler to provide hot water. Log and pellet boilers are larger and can easily produce enough heat and hot water for a standard home. Wood-chip boilers, meanwhile, produce even more heat and are best suited to large buildings with plenty of space, such as farms.

▶ **Space requirements** Wood has a lower energy content than fossil fuels, so you need more of it to provide the same amount of heating. A room heater fuelled by pellets might only be required for a few hours a day during the winter months. This would add up to an annual heating demand of around 1800kWh, which would require 360kg of pellets. So a year's supply could be accommodated by a typical garage. (The room heater itself will only be around the size of a typical wood-burning stove, though it will require a flue.)

For larger systems providing hot water and central heating, space becomes a more pressing issue. A poorly insulated old house with a total water and heating demand of 25,000kWh would require a tank roughly three cubic metres in size if powered by oil, compared to 10m³ of wood-pellet storage and 38m³ for wood chip. You'll also need space to house the boiler and hopper – generally about double the space required by an oil boiler – and a flue.

▶ **Costs and grants** Standalone room heaters cost around £2000–3000, while log, pellet or grain boilers big enough for a typical house go for £5000–10,000. A 100kW wood-chip boiler for a farmhouse and offices might cost

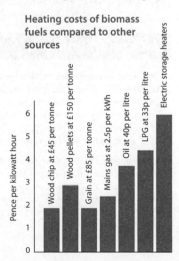

Heating costs of biomass fuels compared to other sources

£30,000. Unlike other renewable technologies you will need to budget for fuel. However, wood chip is very competitive and is currently cheaper than mains gas (see chart on previous page).

The Low Carbon Buildings Programme offers a grant for room heaters and systems with automated wood pellet feed of up to £600 or 20% of the total cost. For wood-fuelled boiler systems (regardless of size) the maximum grant is £1,500 or 30% of the total cost.

▶ **Maintenance** You'll have to empty the ash pan from time to time. This might be weekly for large boilers, or just a few times a year for room heaters. The burner should be cleaned once a year; this can be taken care of as part of a maintenance contract with a fuel supplier or boiler manufacturer.

▶ **Worth looking into?** Yes, especially if you live in a rural area off the gas grid, have ample space to accommodate the boiler and fuel storage and don't mind a hands-on heating system. You could save thousands of pounds – and many tonnes of CO_2 emissions – over the system's lifetime.

▶ **Payback period** A large farmhouse with a heating requirement of 75,000kWh per annum might pay back the cost of conversion from oil or LPG to a wood chip, grain or pellet boiler in just a few years. For a three-bedroom house with an annual demand of 25,000kWh, the best current paybacks are for grain or log boilers. Room heaters won't ever pay for themselves at present fuel prices.

Air conditioning

Once relatively rare in the UK, air conditioning is becoming increasingly popular with British householders. This trend has been driven by the searing heat waves made more common by human-induced climate change. That's somewhat ironic, since AC units themselves are quickly becoming a significant contributor to global warming. One recent report estimated that by 2020 domestic air conditioners in the UK could release almost five million tonnes of CO_2 per year.

A typical home AC unit running at full power uses around 1–2 kilowatts of energy, which makes its carbon footprint roughly equivalent to that of a fan heater. Greener ways to keep interior temperatures down include fans (which are far less energy hungry) and adding pale, reflective blinds to south-facing windows. A more serious option is a ground-source heat pump (see p.94). If you must use electric air conditioning, try to avoid pushing the temperature dial below 25°C.

You can find your nearest woodfuel supplier at:

Log Pile www.logpile.co.uk

Suppliers of wood-based heating systems include:

Rural Energy Trust www.ruralenergy.co.uk ▷ 01664 454 989
Wood Energy www.woodenergyltd.co.uk ▷ 01398 351 349
Econergy www.woodenergy.co.uk ▷ 0870 0545 554
Talbotts www.talbotts.co.uk ▷ 01785 213 366

Insulation
Plugging the leaks

It may not be as glamorous as installing a solar panel on your roof, but improving the insulation of our homes can have just as big an effect. Indeed, in terms of cost-effective ways to reduce greenhouse-gas emissions, making our homes less thermally leaky ranks alongside cutting back on air travel. Decent loft insulation alone can reduce the annual CO_2 footprint of a typical UK home by 1.5 tonnes and reduce heating bills by a fifth. Cavity wall insulation, though more expensive and not suitable for all homes, can have an even bigger effect, while draught-proofing windows and doors can have a significant impact for a tiny investment.

Loft insulation

Current building regulations state that loft insulation in new buildings should be 20cm (8"). If your current insulation is 10cm (4") or less, you should seriously consider topping it up to the 20cm level, and possibly adding even more. If you want a grant to install a renewable-energy technology (see p.70), you'll need at least 27cm (11").

Installing any type of loft insulation is commendable but certain types are greener than others. As a rule, those that use minerals as their raw material use more energy and chemicals in their production – and are less likely to be locally sourced – than those that use natural materials such as wool or flax. The latter – though often more expensive – allow for better circulation of air and help to avoid the retention of toxins in a building, linked by some to "sick building syndrome" (see p.133). Good options include:

Thermafleece

www.secondnatureuk.com ▷ 01768 486 285

Made from the wool of British sheep, Thermafleece is less intensively produced than glass fibre and pays back the carbon dioxide produced during its manufacture seven times faster. It can be installed without gloves or protective clothing, though it's a good idea to wear a mask. If you have a loft measuring 40m² with 4" of glass-fibre insulation, it would cost around £700 to add a further 4" of Thermafleece. At current gas prices, the yearly cost savings would be around £60, so the investment would start saving you money after eleven years.

Warmcel

www.excelfibre.com ▷ 01685 845 200

Warmcel is made from recycled newspaper, with inorganic salts added to provide fire resistance. The material is blown into place with a hose (ideal for difficult-to-access spaces) so there are no off-cuts or different roll thicknesses to worry about. Warmcel is more expensive than glass fibre but cheaper than Thermafleece, costing £8 per square metre to upgrade from 4" to 8". A 40m² loft would therefore cost around £320, paying for itself in just over five years.

Wall insulation

Most houses built after the 1930s have cavity walls – an inner and outer wall with a gap in between. (A typical cavity wall measures 30cm, whilst a solid wall will usually be only around 23cm.) Filling the cavity with insulation can lead to huge energy savings and usually takes only around three hours. The process involves drilling holes in the building's exterior wall and injecting the insulation material, which can be foam, mineral wool or some other option, depending on your budget.

Unfortunately, nearly a third of the UK's 24 million dwellings have solid walls, while a further 1.75 million have cavity walls that are unsuitable for filling. It is possible to insulate solid walls but it's generally more costly and labour intensive. The main decision is whether to go for **internal or external** insulation. The former will reduce your room sizes by around 1cm on each side and will mean complete redecoration; the latter is more expensive and will change the look of your building.

One good option for internal wall insulation is **sempatap**. It can be decorated with any finish (emulsion, wallpaper and even tiles) and enables the wall surface to remain warm, eliminating condensation and

Typical paybacks for insulation products

The exact cost and payback period for each type of insulation and draught-proofing depends on your specific home and heating system, but the following figures show how the various options typically compare.

	Annual savings	Installer cost	DIY cost	Payback period
Cavity wall insulation	£130–160	£260	n/a	1–2 years
Internal wall insulation (for a gas-heated 3-bed semi)	£100–200	£1400 (£40/m^2)	From £800	5–15 years
Loft insulation (from 0 to 270mm)	£180–220	£275	From £230	1–2 years
Loft insulation (from 50 to 270mm)	£50–60	£240	From £200	3–5 years
Draught proofing	£20	From £75	From £50	3–5 years
Floor insulation	£40–50	n/a	From £100	2–3 years
Filling gaps between floor and skirting	£10–20	n/a	From £20	1 year
Hot water tank jacket	£20	n/a	From £10	6 months

black mould growth. By installing sempatap in all rooms, a typical three-bedroom semi-detached house could save around 3800kWh per annum, equating to £95 or 18% of heating costs. However, the up-front cost would be about £1300 (not including redecoration) so it would take at least fourteen years to pay for itself.

Windows

Old single-glazed windows are a major source of heat loss, so it's worth considering **double-glazing**. However, new windows are expensive, and the payback period can be as much as twenty years, so if you have a limited budget it's better to start off with adding loft insulation and replacing inefficient appliances.

If money is no object, the best ethical choice for new windows is wooden frames (with wood from certified sustainable sources). Second best is metal, followed by PVC, which doesn't last as long and can't be recycled.

If you're on a more modest budget, you might explore DIY secondary glazing, which involves adding extra (openable) windows either inside or outside your existing ones.

The very cheapest method of secondary glazing is a special cling-film-like material designed to be applied to standard window frames. You can do a whole house for less than £20, but it's a fiddly, time-consuming job that has to be repeated each year to get the best results.

Selling an energy-efficient home

When deciding whether to invest in energy-efficiency and renewable-energy measures for your home, bear in mind the benefits they might bring if you ever sell the property. A poll carried out by the Energy Saving Trust suggests that 70% of homebuyers see energy efficiency as an important feature. Only 21% consider improving this aspect of their home before putting it on the market, even though 64% of the same people would avoid buying houses with old boilers, single glazing and insufficient insulation.

From summer 2007, everyone selling a house will have to produce a **Home Information Pack**. As part of this process an inspector will produce a Home Condition Report and an Energy Performance Certificate, which will assess the energy efficiency of the home through a simple A–G energy rating, complete with recommendations for improvements.

Waste & recycling

British households produce a staggering 25 million tonnes of refuse every year. That's around half a tonne per person. Add in our share of the country's commercial, industrial and agricultural waste and the figure rises to 4.3 tonnes per head – approximately sixty times a typical person's body weight. Of our domestic waste (which is increasing at 2% per year), less than a quarter is currently recycled. Recent EU laws and various UK government targets will force our recycling figures up steeply over the coming years, but in the meantime there's much we can do on an individual level to reduce the amount of rubbish that we generate.

In doing so, we can help reduce greenhouse-gas emissions – which result from the production of packaging and bin bags, the decomposition of food waste and the collection and processing of our refuse – and cut down on the amount of stuff sent to landfill sites (see box overleaf). In trying to achieve this, the old green mantra of the three Rs – **reduce**, **reuse**, **recycle** – holds strong. This chapter takes a look at each approach in turn.

What we throw out

Following is a breakdown of the contents of the typical UK household's bin.

▶ Garden waste 20%

▶ Paper and board 18%

▶ Food waste 17%

▶ General household sweepings 9%

▶ Glass 7%

▶ Scrap metal/white goods 5%

▶ Wood 5%

▶ Dense plastic 4%

▶ Plastic film 4%

▶ Textiles 3%

▶ Metal packaging 3%

▶ Soil 3%

▶ Nappies 2%

Landfill and incineration

The waste that we don't recycle is either buried or burned. **Landfill** still accounts for more than two-thirds of our domestic waste disposal. It's a simple approach: put the rubbish in a hole in the ground and cover it with a clay "cap". The main environmental problems, aside from the visual impact and the famously bad smells, are the byproducts. These include leachate – water contaminated with heavy metals and various other harmful chemicals – and landfill gas, a mixture of methane, CO_2, vinyl chloride and hydrogen sulphide.

Each tonne of biodegradable waste produces between 300 and 500 cubic metres of landfill gas. Of its ingredients, **methane**, being a greenhouse gas more than twenty times as potent as CO_2, is perhaps the most pressing problem. Many of the bigger landfill sites extract the methane and use it for power generation but where this is uneconomical, it seeps into the atmosphere. All told, decomposing waste accounts for around a fifth of UK methane emissions.

The proportion of our rubbish heading to landfill is going down. Things started to change in 1996 with the introduction of a landfill tax (paid by local government using council tax revenues) of £7 per tonne of refuse. This helped push up recycling rates significantly, and they've climbed even more steeply after recent increases in the tax (which now stands at £18 per tonne and will rise by at least £3 per tonne each year until it reaches £35). Further regulations have come into force following the EU Landfill Directive of 1999, which aims to reduce the amount of biodegradable municipal waste going to landfill by 65% by 2020 (relative to 1995 levels).

You can find out about landfill sites in your area by logging on to the Environment Agency's "What's in my Backyard?" website. If you want to experience one for yourself, the Carymoor Environmental Centre in Castle Cary, Somerset, offers tours of an operational site including the tipping face, composting and recycling operations, leachate treatment and methane electricity generation.

Environment Agency www.environment-agency.gov.uk/maps/info/landfill
Carymoor www.carymoor.org.uk ▷ 01963 350 143

As for **incineration**, the UK currently burns about 9% of its waste (compared to 53% in Denmark and 46% in Sweden). In most cases, the idea is to combine waste disposal with energy recovery methods such as combined heat and power (which generates electricity and hot water from the burning refuse). Hospital waste is one of the main sources for incineration and many Healthcare Trusts now use energy from the incinerators to reduce their heating costs.

Many environmental groups disapprove of incineration. One reason is that they see it as a disincentive to recycling (once a site is built, a steady stream of waste is required). Another is that the incinerators are associated with emissions of poisonous **dioxins** and carcinogenic ash, as well as plain old CO_2. There are now stringent laws in place to combat poisonous outputs, and the technology does exist to significantly reduce them. But even proposed incineration schemes employing state of the art features still often fall foul of local planning regulations. Still, with ambitious targets hanging over them, several local authorities – from Leeds to London – are considering proposals for new incinerators.

Stage 1: **Reduce**
Less in = less out

Recycling and reusing are all well and good, but the very best approach to reducing waste is to generate less in the first place. There are, of course, myriad ways to do this, most of which require little more than a bit of thought. Following are a few good ways to get started.

Food and food packaging

An astonishing 20% of the food that we buy is fed to the bin, either as leftovers or because it's no longer fresh. This waste costs an average household £424 a year and results in considerable emissions of methane. The solutions are simple, though they may require a bit of getting used to: planning more carefully when shopping and cooking; using the freezer to prolong the life of things that are likely to go stale; and making use of leftovers rather than letting them sit in the fridge decaying. Finally, try to compost whatever waste food you do create (see p.143).

Of course, it's not just the food itself that fills up our bins: it's the packaging that it comes in. No one knows exactly how much food packaging we get through each year, but it clearly accounts for a significant proportion of our domestic waste. Perhaps the best strategy here – aside from favouring minimally packaged products – is to follow the advice of the German government and make a point of leaving excess packaging in the supermarket after you've been through the checkout.

Paper

We each use about 200kg of paper per year, the production of which requires three or four trees and thousands of litres of water. Besides cutting back on food packaging, we can reduce our paper use in various ways:

▶ **Go digital** Where possible, download leaflets, brochures and other written material from the Internet, rather than picking up or requesting a hard copy. Also try reading the news online instead of buying newspapers; even the slimmed-down *Guardian* uses more than five square metres of paper per copy (and much more on Saturday). You could also consider helping to cut down on the one billion Christmas cards that British people send each year by opting for a virtual alternative from Friends of the Earth:

FoE Cards www.foe.co.uk/cards

Junking the junk mail

If you're fed up with picking junk mail off the doormat and putting it straight into the recycling bin, register with the Mail Preference Service to have your name removed from the lists of direct mail companies.

Mail Preference Service www.mpsonline.org.uk ▷ 0845 703 4599

To also stop junk mail sent to "The Occupier", write to:

Door to Door Opt Outs Royal Mail, Kingsmead House, Oxpens Road, Oxford OX1 1RX

▶ **Buy recycled** As we'll see later on, despite the occasional magazine or newspaper article that states that recycling is a waste of time, recycled paper is much more environmentally friendly than virgin paper. For a full range of recycled paper products, see:

Recycled Paper Supplies www.rps.gn.apc.org

▶ **Printing** If possible, set up your printer – at home and work – so that printing on both sides is the default option. Before printing, check the Preview option to ensure that the document will come out as planned.

Carrier bags

In the UK, we use an average of 17.5 billion carrier bags per year – that's almost one per person per day. Most of these end up in landfill sites, where, in the case of standard plastic versions, they break down over the space of an estimated 500 years. Many supermarkets now offer biodegradable plastic bags, which can be broken down by micro-organisms. Unfortunately, they still use fossil fuels as their raw materials and they produce CO_2 and methane as they break down. At the time of writing, the government has rejected calls for a plastic bag tax (such as the one introduced in Ireland in 2002), but that shouldn't stop us taking reusable bags with us to the shops whenever possible. Aside from anything else, they're more comfortable to carry and less likely to break than the plastic versions. For some French-style green chic, commission a custom willow basket from a local producer (you can track one down via www.basketassoc.org).

Nappies & sanitary products

Babies account for a small percentage of family bodymass, but when kitted out with **disposable nappies** they can easily generate half the contents of a household's bins. A typical baby gets through around 5000 disposables during its nappy days; across the UK, this adds up to eight million per day and three billion each year. Most of these end up in landfill sites where, according to many environmental groups, the plastic will take hundreds of years to break down, the super-absorbent granules will soak up groundwater needed for the decomposition of other waste, and the excrement and urine may pose a health hazard. Even if these worries are overcautious, as some commentators claim, nappies are energy- and resource-intensive to produce and therefore also expensive to buy. Parents spend an average of £700 per baby on disposables, according to Market Intelligence.

The green advice has always been to opt for washable **cloth nappies** (which are also now promoted by local councils keen to cut down on landfill costs). However, a recent in-depth study from the Environment Agency has left many people wondering whether cloth nappies are worth the hassle. The report concluded that although a baby's worth of disposable nappies uses more oil than washables (93kg vs. 28kg of crude), it leads to less CO_2 emissions (437kg vs. 507kg) and less water usage (34,000 litres vs. 86,000 litres). Cloth nappies from a washing service had the highest CO_2 outputs (705kg), with middle-range figures for oil and water.

These figures have been disputed, however. The Women's Environmental Network, long-standing proponents of washable nappies, point out that the study made various assumptions that wouldn't apply to many green-minded people. They claim that, if you have an energy-efficient washing machine, use a 60 degree wash cycle, limit yourself to 24 nappies, and don't tumble dry or iron them, then the washable option ends up producing a quarter less CO_2 than disposables.

Cloth nappies are very widely available, though you may prefer to look into fair trade and organic options from specialists such as those listed from p.244. The UK Nappy Helpline (01983 401 959) can provide more information about all types of nappy services and products.

Sanitary towels and tampons raise similar issues to nappies. An alternative popular with many environmentally conscious women is a product called Mooncup. Made from soft silicone rubber, it's a small cup that is worn internally and collects fluid without leakage or odour. It needs emptying less frequently than towels or tampons need replacing. Mooncups cost £18 but last for years and will start saving you money in around six months.

Mooncup www.mooncup.co.uk ▷ 01273 673 845

Water

Mention green living and the first thing that comes to some people's minds is minimizing water wastage – a brick in the toilet cistern, perhaps, or turning off the tap while brushing teeth. But how much does saving water really matter?

Most eco-minded articles on the subject fudge the issue somewhat by focusing on the terrible inequality in access to water between rich and poor countries. It's true that this inequality is extreme: UK citizens use around 55,000 litres of water every year, while in other parts of the world more than a billion people lack access to clean water and 21 million people die each year from diarrhoeal diseases caused in part by poor sanitation. It's also true that the outlook is dire: the proportion of people living in water-stressed areas is expected to grow from one-third to two-thirds over the next 25 years. Appalling though these facts are, no one is suggesting that we ship our spare water abroad, so it's hard to see how any of this is relevant to our own water use.

A more pressing reason for saving water is that we might one day not have enough within the UK. Recent hosepipe bans in the South East have shown how a combination of dry winters, warm summers and leaky infrastructure can leave us with only just enough to go around. Add in a growing population in certain regions, ever-more water-hungry appliances and increasing numbers of people living on their own, and it's true that there could be water stresses in the future. Water companies are already being forced to extract more from underground reservoirs, which are not being replenished, and there are plans to build a desalination plant on the Thames at Beckton (Borough of Newham).

Another reason to cut back on unnecessary water consumption is that every drop we consume has been treated; and every drop we put down the plughole or toilet is later treated again. All of this treatment requires energy, and therefore results in greenhouse-gas emissions. Indeed, the water industry uses around 6000 gigawatt hours of energy to provide water and treat sewage each year, producing 2.7 million tonnes of CO_2 – around 0.5% of total UK emissions. (If the desalination plant is built, this would shoot up by around 10%.) To put these figures in perspective, a family of four uses approximately 200,000 litres of water per year, which requires 94kWh to supply and 83kWh to treat, resulting in 78kg of CO_2. That's equivalent to an average car travelling 1100 miles.

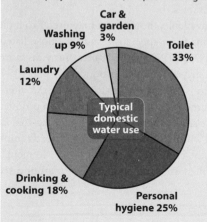

Washing up 9%
Car & garden 3%
Toilet 33%
Laundry 12%
Typical domestic water use
Drinking & cooking 18%
Personal hygiene 25%

With all this in mind, the Centre for Alternative Technology suggests that we should aim to reduce our daily water use to about 80 litres per person. Following are some tips for doing just that. If your water is metered, you'll save money, too.

▶ **Toilet flushing** Cisterns that predate 1993 tend to use around 9.5 litres of water, whilst later models typically use around 7.5 litres. Aside from flushing less frequently (as per the old saying "If it's yellow let it mellow, if it's brown flush it down"), the easiest way to make savings is to put a displacement device in the cistern. A water-filled plastic bottle will do the trick, as will a built-for-the-job Hippo Watersaver (www.hippo-the-watersaver.co.uk). If you are fitting a new toilet choose an eco-flush which allows you to choose a full or half setting (such as those available from www.greenbuildingstore.co.uk). Finally, think about what you flush: if you don't like seeing tampons and condoms floating in rivers and the sea then don't put them down the loo. It only takes a blockage at the sewage works for such items to back up into our waterways and end up in rivers and on beaches.

▶ **Taps** You can reduce the flow of taps with Tapmagic inserts, which provide a spray when the tap is turned slightly but full flow when turned more fully. They're less than £5 each and are easy to fit yourself. See www.tapmagic.co.uk

▶ **Baths and showers** A five-minute shower typically uses around 25 litres of water, compared to 80 litres for a bath and 120 litres for a power shower. For maximum green points, if you do use a bath, consider recycling the water for your garden. This is possible with a Drought Buster syphon pump, available from www.droughtbuster.co.uk.

▶ **Watering the garden** Watering the garden with a hose can consume more than 1000 litres per hour, so it makes sense to use alternative sources as much as possible. The first thing to do is get a water butt fitted to the down pipe from your roof and start collecting rainwater. Plants actually grow better in natural water sources so this makes sense from every perspective. Combine a water butt with a solar-powered irrigation system (see www.solarflow-garden.co.uk) and the garden will even water itself. However you water the garden, you can minimise evaporation by doing it in the evening and watering the base of plants rather than the leaves.

Tapmagic inserts can cut water use for a particular sink by as much as 50%

▶ **Recycling and harvesting water** Grey water is water that has been used in baths, washing machines and sinks. With a bit of careful plumbing, it can be stored in a tank and recycled for toilet flushing. Even more serious is a rainwater harvesting system. You'll still need a mains supply for your drinking water but will save around 50% on consumption. Such systems cost around £2000–3000 for a typical home and pay for themselves in around 10–15 years (this will fall if water bills rise as expected by 10% a year for the next five years). There are currently fewer than 500 water harvesting systems in UK homes, but across Europe around 100,000 are being installed each year. To find out more, see www.ukrha.org and www.rainharvesting.co.uk.

▶ **Getting serious** If you really want to cut your incoming and outgoing water levels, you could consider a reed-bed sewage treatment set-up or even do away with a conventional toilet altogether and use a composting model (see p.119).

Stage 2: Reuse
Don't throw it – donate it

Much of what we throw away is in perfect working order but no longer useful to us. In the UK, we're quite good at giving away unwanted books and clothes to charity shops and jumble sales, but many other usable items are simply junked, including some which could easily be donated to good causes. Following is a list of items which charities will gratefully take off your hands.

For items not listed, try Freecycle – a website used by millions of people around the world to give things away to people in their local area. Sign up for your nearest group (it's free) and you can offer anything, with the exception of living creatures, to the other members. If someone wants something that you've offered – and in big cities, especially, the replies come surprisingly thick and fast – then it's up to them to come and collect it. The only problem is that, once you've signed up, reading the offerings of the other Freecyclers can be rather addictive.

Freecycle www.freecycle.org

Bikes

The Re~Cycle project gathers secondhand bicycles and ships them to various African countries. Partner groups teach local people how to repair and maintain them.

Re~Cycle www.re-cycle.org

Computers

You can donate old computers to charities through ComputerAid and Computers For Charities, who will send them to developing countries. However, they only accept machines less than around five years old. You can also offer computers, components and peripherals to other individuals in the UK via Donate A PC.

Computer Aid International

ComputerAid www.computeraid.org ▷ 01323 840 641
Computers For Charities
www.computersforcharities.co.uk ▷ 020 7281 0091
Donate A PC www.donateapc.org.uk

Curtains

If you have some high-quality curtains that you no longer want (nothing old accepted), the Curtain Exchange will try to sell them, and donate them to charity if nobody bites.

Curtain Exchange www.thecurtainexchange.net/secondhand.htm

Furniture

There are many charitable organizations across the UK who take unwanted furniture and pass it on at affordable prices to those who most need it. The Furniture Re-use Network (FRN) is the co-ordinating body for such groups. Because of rules on electrical goods and fireproofing it is always worth telephoning a charity before delivering.

Furniture Re-use Network www.frn.org.uk ▷ 0117 954 3571

Hearing aids

Help the Aged clean and distribute working, unwanted hearing aids throughout India. Simply post them to:

HearingAid Appeal Help the Aged, FREEPOST LON13616, London, EC1B 1PS

Paint

Many local-authority recycling centres accept old paint. In order to stop it drying out, cover with cling film, put the lid back on firmly and store upside down. If the label has been lost write the colour with a marker pen on the can. Alternatively donate it to Community Repaint so it can be used to decorate a community building.

Community Repaint www.communityrepaint.org.uk

Spectacles

More than 200 million people in the developing world would benefit from a pair of spectacles, so consider donating old pairs. Some local authorities accept spectacles as part of their doorstep recycling schemes. Alternatively, give them away via:

Help the Aged World in Sight Appeal www.helptheaged.org.uk ▷ FREEPOST LON 13109, London, N1 9BR ▷ Drop off service at any Dolland and Aitchison opticians
Vision Aid Overseas Second Sight Project www.secondsightproject.com ▷ Drop off at any Kodak Lens Vision Centre.

Stamps and coins

Many charities can make money out of old stamps and coins. It is useful to separate your stamps into UK and foreign categories as a kilo of UK stamps will make about £1.50 while a kilo of foreign stamps might make £12.50. The following all accept stamps and coins.

Guide Dogs for the Blind Association www.gdba.org.uk ▷ 0118 983 5555
Oxfam www.oxfam.org.uk ▷ 0870 333 2700
Royal Society for the Protection of Birds www.rspb.org.uk ▷ 01767 680 551

Tools

Tools are badly needed in many developing countries, so if you have spare hammers, spanners or pretty well anything else, give them away via one of the following charities:

Tools With A Mission www.twam.co.uk ▷ 01473 210220
Tools For Self Reliance www.tfsr.org ▷ 02380 869 697

Toys

Toys can be donated to The National Association of Toy & Leisure Libraries, who offer them on free loan to parents around the country.

National Association of Toy & Leisure Libraries www.natll.org.uk ▷ 020 7255 4605

Stage 3: Recycle
Why it's worth it and how to do more

Recycling of household waste in the UK has doubled in the last four years, but the UK still trails far behind some of its neighbours. We currently manage an average of 18% (more in the south, less in the north), even though most experts agree that 60% is perfectly feasible and 80% may even be achievable. The main obstacle – aside from people failing to use the services that already exist – is the expense of collections (£9 per household per year) relative to the current low value of recycled materials. Aluminium cans are worth £700 per tonne but you need 60,000 cans to make a tonne. Recycled plastic bottles can sell for £200 per tonne but steel (£60 per tonne) and glass and paper (£20 per tonne) are not exactly money spinners. The government has set up WRAP (the Waste and

Recycling saints and sinners

The top recyclers in the UK are the residents of St Edmundsbury in Suffolk, who recycle or compost more than 50% of their household waste. In Europe, the greenest region is Flanders in Belgium, which manages a remarkable 71%.

On a national level, the Netherlands tops the EU table, recycling 64% of total municipal waste, followed by Austria (60%) and Germany (57%). The UK, with 18%, is a poor performer, though way ahead of Greece (9%) and Portugal (4%).

Globally, New Zealand is perhaps the most progressive country when it comes to waste and recycling and is aiming to minimise "and eventually eliminate" waste from domestic, construction and demolition sources. For more information, see:

Zero Waste www.zerowaste.co.nz

Resources Action Programme) to develop markets for recovered materials, but there's still some way to go.

This low value has led some commentators to suggest that recycling is a waste of time, but such people often ignore two facts. First, recycling almost always saves energy and greenhouse emissions compared to using virgin materials (not to mention cutting down on landfill and the environmental impacts of resource extraction). Second, the value of a product is the result of all kinds of factors, including tax structures. If the EU cracked down hard on greenhouse emissions, for instance, then the value of recycled materials would shoot up.

That said, it's hard to gauge the full environmental footprint of recycled materials since there's no official record of where they end up. In 2004, the *Guardian* reported that "More than a third of the waste paper and plastic collected by British local authorities, supermarkets and businesses for recycling is being sent 8000 miles to China without any knowledge of the environmental or social costs". To be fair, however, most of this shipping makes use of containers that would otherwise be empty and it's inevitable that materials – raw or recycled – will be in greatest demand in countries with active manufacturing industries.

Most recycling in the UK is still done at bottle banks and civic amenity sites, but the number of doorstep collections has expanded widely, and should cover everyone in the country by 2010. If you don't have doorstep recycling, or you want to recycle something too big for your box, locate your nearest recycling bank by calling 01743 343 403 or visiting:

Recycle Now www.recyclenow.com

What can be recycled?

Different local authorities accept different items in their recycling schemes, but in some cases there are other ways to recycle.

Aluminium foil

Unless it's really dirty, it makes sense to recycle aluminium foil, as creating aluminium from bauxite ore requires around twenty times more energy than creating it from recycled products. However, some "foil" – such as that used in tea bags and crisp packaging – looks like aluminium but generally isn't. You can tell with the scrunch test: if it springs back it isn't aluminium and should go in the bin.

Batteries

Batteries are environmentally problematic, since they contain heavy metals such as cadmium and nickel. They are easily recycled and yet 98% of used batteries from UK households end up in the bin. If your doorstep collection scheme accepts batteries, then use it; otherwise, store them in a box and use your local recycling point once in a while.

Also consider replacing old batteries with rechargeable ones. Modern recharging units are effective and inexpensive. For maximum green points, pick up a solar-powered recharger from the Centre for Alternative Technology (www.cat.org.uk).

Cans

Steel is used for most food tins, while aluminium is used for around three-quarters of drinks cans. Both metals can be recycled indefinitely, leading to substantial energy and landfill savings (we currently landfill fourteen million dustbins' worth of recyclable aluminium cans each year). So, try to recycle all your tins and cans – including petfood cans, which many people throw in the bin to avoid washing out. If you don't have doorstep recycling, and you're short of space, a wall-mounted can crusher might help. They're available for £14 from www.recyclenow.com

If you're really keen, consider setting up a can recycling point at work and donating the cans collected to good causes through Novelis Recycling's Cash for Cans initiative:

Cash for Cans www.thinkcans.com

Cooking oil

Used cooking oil can be turned into biodiesel vehicle fuel (see p.230), but in most cases it's impractical for fuel processing companies to collect small quantities, such as you might use at home. One option is to set up a local collection depot (schools are a good bet, not least because they generate waste cooking oil themselves) where people can drop off their used oil and a local biodiesel producer can pick it up. You can find local producers via:

Allied Biodiesel Industries www.biofuels.fsnet.co.uk

Electrical equipment

The average UK citizen generates 3.3 tonnes of waste electrical and electronic equipment (WEEE) in their lifetime – products such as fridges, computers and TVs. For white goods, most retailers will take away your old machine for recycling or safe disposal when you buy a new machine. For smaller items, such as PCs, try your local recycling centre (and the donation services listed on p.108) before resorting to the bin. Businesses with computers, monitors, printers, circuit boards and cables to recycle should contact:

WEEE Care www.weeecare.com ▷ 01757 708 180

If you'd like to see what 3.3 tonnes of electrical waste looks like, check out the WEEE Man project at:

WEEE Man www.weeeman.org

Engine oil

Used engine oil is highly polluting if not disposed of properly. It's easily recyclable, but you'll need to find your nearest oil bank. That's easily done with this service from the Environment Agency:

Oil Banks UK www.oilbankline.org.uk ▷ 08708 506 506

Glass

Glass is made from sand, soda ash, limestone and additives for colour and durability. There are no shortages of these materials but recycling saves energy and emissions, as well as reducing the environmental scars of mining. Recycling just two bottles saves enough energy to make five cups of tea, while recycling a tonne saves 315kg of CO_2 emissions.

In 2005, Brits recycled 50% of used container glass (more than a million tonnes). That's a respectable figure but we're well behind the Swiss and Finns, who managed 90%. One issue in the UK is that we import a lot of wine in green bottles and export a lot of whisky in clear bottles. Hence we end up with a lot of recycled glass that isn't much use to our domestic drinks industry (as such, green bottles made in the UK use 85% recycled material, but the clear ones use much less). Excess green glass can, however, be turned into other useful materials – from sand for golf-course bunkers to "glassphalt" for road resurfacing (fourteen million bottles were used to surface the M6 motorway). For more information about the products made from recycled glass see:

WRAP Glass Recycled Products Guides www.recycleglass.co.uk

The business sector has an appalling record on glass recycling. Each year, 600,000 tonnes of bottles and glasses from pubs and clubs ends up in landfill – mainly because green, brown and clear glass gets mixed and it is not economical to sort this prior to recycling.

Mobile phones

There are an estimated ninety million unwanted mobile phones languishing in British homes. These can be donated to charity – for example, to Oxfam's Bring Bring scheme, which has already raised more than £300,000 and stopped 22,500kg of electronic waste from being landfilled. Either drop them off at a local Oxfam store or put them in a jiffy bag and send to:

Oxfam Bring Bring Scheme Freepost LON16281, London, WC1N 3BR

hand over your handset to Oxfam here

Oxfam can now give your old mobile a new lease of life – a life full of meaning and purpose. They can turn unwanted handsets, and their accessories, into tools, seeds, school books, blackboards – in fact anything that will help Oxfam to support poor communities around the world.

So go on, do the right thing – bring in your old mobile phone and put it in the special collection box.

bRing bRing
your old mobile to Oxfam

Oxfam

Recycling symbols

 The so-called **mobius loop** simply specifies that an item can be recycled. That doesn't mean that it can or will be recycled in your local area.

 The mobius loop with a percentage symbol in the centre tells you what proportion of an object has been made with recycled materials.

 In certain European countries, the **greendot** symbol is used to show that the producer of a piece of packaging has contributed to the cost of its disposal or recycling. Within the UK it means nothing at all – so don't think items bearing the greendot can or will be recycled.

Plastics

Most plastic packaging displays a small symbol specifying the type of plastic used. The following shows the scientific names and common uses for each of them. Numbers 1,2 and 4 are the most widely recycled in the UK, but check with your local council to find out which they will and won't accept.

 PETE
Polyethylene terephthalate: fizzy drink bottles and oven-ready meal trays

 HDPE
High-density polyethylene: milk and washing-up liquid bottles

 V
Polyvinyl chloride: food trays, cling film, soft drink and shampoo bottles

 LDPE
Low density polyethylene: carrier bags and bin liners

 PP
Polypropylene: margarine tubs, microwaveable meal trays

 PS
Polystyrene: yoghurt pots, foam, meat and fish trays, hamburger boxes, egg cartons, vending cups, plastic cutlery, protective packaging

 OTHER
Melamine: plastic plates and cups

If you are a charity and would like to get involved with mobile phone recycling contact:

Answer the Call www.answerthecall.co.uk ▷ 01603 882 800

Paper

This one's a no-brainer. Each tonne of recycled paper can save 17 trees, 1700 litres of oil, three cubic metres of landfill space and 32,000 litres of water. Indeed, making new paper from old paper, compared to making it from virgin fibres, uses 64% less energy and 58% less water.

In addition to new paper, recycled paper can be turned into everything from cat litter and paints to loft insulation (see p.98).

Plastics

Eight percent of the world's current oil production is used to produce plastics, and the resulting products occupy around a quarter of the typical landfill site. Recycling plastic can save 66% of the energy consumed in manufacture, reduce water use by 90% and cut emissions of sulphur dioxide, nitrogen oxides and CO_2 by more than 50% each. Recycled plastic is very versatile and can be turned into products ranging from window frames and filling for sleeping bags to clothes (25 two-litre drinks bottles makes one fleece jacket).

Despite all this, comparatively little plastic is recycled at present. That's due partly to technical difficulties involved in processing large-molecule materials and partly to problems related to separating the various different types of plastic (see box on previous page). Most local authorities currently accept plastic bottles only – often via bottle banks only – while some supermarkets offer plastic bag recycling. Even in these areas we score poorly, however. The average UK household gets through more than one plastic bottle per day and recycles only one in ten. Recycling rates for plastic bags are even worse.

When recycling plastic bottles, it makes sense to crush them to reduce the space they take up – and hence the diesel used in their collection. Plastic bottle crushers can be bought from Plascan (www.plascancrusher. com). Don't be tempted to put yoghurt pots and margarine tubs in a plastic bottle bank: they're usually made of polystyrene or blends and generally cannot be recycled (look for the numbered symbol on the side). It just creates hassle and contaminates the load. If you want your council to do more, write to your MP (see p.5).

Printer cartridges

Over two million non-biodegradable printer cartridges are sent to UK landfill sites every year. Many of these can be reused or recycled. You can refill inkjet cartridges and save 60% off the price of new ones via services such as:

Cartridge World www.cartridgeworld.co.uk ▷ 0800 183 3800

Laser printer toner cartridges can be donated to various charities who can make money from recycling them. These include:

Action Aid www.actionaidrecycling.org.uk
Rain Forest Concern www.rainforestconcern.org

Tetra Pak cartons

Most milk and fruit juice that doesn't come in plastic bottles comes in Tetra Pak cartons. These are made of 75% paper, 20% polythene and 5% aluminium film. The fibre within them is quite valuable and can be recycled into new paper products that require strength. However, you'll probably find that your local authority doesn't accept them for recycling.

If you're determined to recycle as much as possible, check the following website to see if there's a carton recycling point near you. If there isn't, the same site offers downloadable address labels to post the cartons to the nearest one. But it's probably easier (and certainly cheaper) to simply avoid buying Tetra Paks where possible.

Drinks Cartons Recycling www.drinkscartons.com/docs/recycling_uk.htm

Tyres

In the UK, 28 million tyres are discarded each year but from 2006 the EU Landfill Directive no longer permits their disposal in landfill sites. As they have an energy content of 32 gigajoules per tonne there is significant economic potential for tyre incineration. But it makes no sense to burn a tyre until it's no longer functional. Virtually all tyres can be retreaded several times. Each retread prevents the manufacture of one new tyre, saving twenty litres of oil for a car tyre and 68 litres for a truck tyre. Find out more about retreads from:

Retread Manufacturers Association www.retreaders.org.uk ▷ 01270 561 014

Composting

Over 50% of our domestic refuse is organic in nature, such as garden and kitchen matter, paper and cardboard. Many local authorities are now setting up doorstep collection schemes for this waste or have specially designated skips at the local tip. This is a breakthrough and will divert much material away from landfill. However, if you already have your own compost heap, keep up the good work – this is still the most ecologically friendly way to treat your kitchen scraps. As long as the heap can "breathe" it will not produce methane. You can't use everything but with a bit of patience you'll end up with a lovely crumbly compost that will help your garden thrive.

How to make your own compost

There are many schools of thought on composting, but the crucial thing is to get good results without creating bad smells or attracting vermin (especially important if you only have a small garden and there are children about). The best bet is to buy a sealable compost bin, which many local authorities will sell you at a highly subsidized rate. These are mostly made from thick plastic and will take virtually any organic matter. If you build your own compost bin on bare soil and leave it open at the top, you should avoid all foodstuffs except fruit, vegetables and things like tea leaves and coffee grounds (meat, dairy and grain-based products are a magnet for rodents).

Whichever option you go for, ensure you have a good mix of carbon-rich **browns** – for example dried flowers, woody stems and cardboard – and nitrogen-rich **greens**, such as fresh grass cuttings and kitchen waste. Best results are achieved by cutting large items into smaller pieces to accelerate the process. Build the heap in layers (rather than just piling it up) and introduce air on a regular basis by occasional turning or by adding a layer of cardboard and paper every now and then. You want a moist heap rather than a wet or dry one; so if it's too wet add more dry material and if too dry add water, or – if you can stomach it – urine, which is a great accelerator as it's very rich in nitrogen. Other good accelerators are young nettles and comfrey leaves. Your heap will take between six months and two years to turn into sweet-smelling dark crumbly compost.

For the intrepid a **wormery** is another option. These come in all shapes and sizes (so can be good for small spaces) but they demand rather more care and attention than a normal compost heap. For more information, or to buy online, visit:

Wiggly Wigglers www.wigglywigglers.co.uk

If your garden has plenty of deciduous trees, it's well worth gathering the fallen leaves in autumn and storing them either in a separate heap or – if there aren't that many – in a black bin liner. By the following year this will have produced a nice crumbly mould which can be used as a mulch or to enhance the texture of your soil (evergreen leaves take much longer).

If you're feeling really adventurous, you might consider recycling your own human waste via a composting toilet. There are now a surprisingly large number on the market. For information and further links, go to:

Composting Toilet World
www.compostingtoilet.org

For more information on composting in general, visit:

Composting Association www.compost.org.uk
Recycle Now www.recyclenow.com/home_composting

A can-o-worms wormery from Wiggly Wigglers

Find out more

For more information about waste, recycling and related issues, drop in to the following websites:

Recycle Now www.recyclenow.com
Recycle More www.recycle-more.co.uk
Waste Online www.wasteonline.org.uk

For advice on minimizing waste and reducing environmental impact from a business perspective, try:

Envirowise www.envirowise.gov.uk ▷ 0800 585 794

Or to *buy* recycled products, from toilet tissue to plant pots, find your nearest suppliers via:

Recycled Products Guide www.recycledproducts.org.uk

House & garden products

Perhaps the two most pressing ethical issues raised by our homes are energy use and waste, which are discussed in the previous two chapters. But the products we buy for our homes and gardens are also worth considering – from furniture and bedlinen to detergents, paints and compost.

Cleaning & laundry products
A green clean?

Partly because of the ubiquity of "green" alternatives, most people already have a suspicion that there may be something slightly dodgy about conventional surface cleaners, washing-up liquids, washing powders, polishes and the like. The main issues are what's in them and who makes them – including whether or not the company in question carries out tests on animals.

The chemical question

Different categories of cleaning and laundry products are based on different types of chemicals. Many of these chemicals are uncontroversial, but others, according to environmental and consumer groups, pose risks both to human health and to the environment.

The detergents that form the basis of products such as washing-up liquids are chemicals known as **surfactants** ("surface active agents"), which function by dissolving partly in water and partly in organic substances such as food and grime. Some surfactants – especially those derived from petrochemicals – are toxic and relatively slow to biodegrade, especially compared to the plant-derived alternatives used by the eco specialists. However, surfactants rarely feature on the list of the most potentially risky chemicals: at the levels used, they're not widely believed to be a serious health hazard to humans, and with water quality in UK rivers improving all the time, not everyone is convinced they do that significant damage to aquatic life.

More worrying, according to campaigners such as Greenpeace, are the additive substances used, some of which were recently classified as "chemicals of high concern" by the EU. Some of these substances, such as the **phthalates** found in certain multi-surface cleaners, are thought to pose a threat to our hormone systems, while others are known to be carcinogenic (cancer causing) in animals. Furthermore, some of the chemicals in question, such as the **artificial musks** widely used as fragrances in laundry powders and other cleaning products, are **bioaccumulative**, meaning they can build up in the body tissue of humans and other organisms, and be passed on through the food chain or by birth.

"Babies are born with toxic chemicals already contaminating their bodies", according to Greenpeace, while wildlife groups have raised concerns that bioaccumulative chemicals are even starting to turn up in the livers of arctic animals such as polar bears, presumably having been passed from plug holes and factories via water treatment systems to plankton, and then up the food chain via crustaceans, fishes and seals, increasing in concentration at each level. They may also pass back to other humans via the consumption of fish.

But how serious are these environmental and health risks? In most cases, we're not exactly sure. In part this is because causal links between specific chemicals and specific effects are almost impossible to prove. Whether you're talking about cancer in humans, or endocrine disruption in arctic birds, there's no simple way to isolate the effect of any single chemical.

However, it's also because not a great deal of research has been done. According to *Chemicals in Products*, a recent government report from the Royal Commission on Environmental Pollution, "Society might reasonably expect that adequate assessments have been carried out on chemicals that are on the market, and that appropriate risk management strategies

are in place for potentially harmful substances. This is not the case..."
Hence the government has only recently set out to discover the effects on
people and the environment of many of the chemicals already widely used
– an initiative called **REACH**. This idea is very popular with anti-chemi-
cal campaigners, but not popular with animal rights groups, since it is due
to involve a huge number of animal experiments.

It's worth keeping all this in perspective. Even if the health risks of these
chemicals are proved, they are almost certainly many orders of magnitude
lower than the risks posed by, say, smoking – or the likelihood of having a
car accident while driving. And the environmental impacts of our cleaning products are minute compared with the output of similar chemicals
from the oil, gas and coal industries that power our plug sockets, cookers
and cars, or the plastics industries that produce everything from our plant
pots to our computer monitors.

As such, cleaning products aren't the "key area" that they're sometimes
described as being. But with greener alternatives to most of the potentially
risky cleaners available, there is certainly a decent case for favouring companies that have promised not to use the most worrying chemicals. This
basically means favouring the green specialists, who usually also shun
animal-based products as well as non-toxic but otherwise problematic
chemicals such as phosphates (which can encourage excessively fast plant
growth and clog up water systems).

Household toxins: beyond cleaning products

The debate about whether or not the chemicals found in our homes pose genuine
risks to people and planet tends to focus almost exclusively on household cleaning products, paints (see p.132), and cosmetics and toiletries (see p.251). However,
many of the same chemicals, and numerous others besides, are found in all kinds
of household items – from carpets and computers (which may contain substances
such as brominated flame retardants) to PVC shower curtains (which may contain
phthalates).

Again, there's no pressing evidence to say that, in the quantities we're exposed to,
the chemicals are really that risky. But many people take the view that ethically
minded shoppers should avoid any company using bioaccumulative, dangerous
and poorly understood chemicals – even if just to reduce the environmental risks of
producing them. If you feel the same, or you simply want to minimize your exposure
to the "chemicals of high concern", visit the Greenpeace Toxic Home website for a list
of "green" and "red" products:

Toxic Home www.greenpeace.org.uk/Products/Toxics

Animal testing

New ingredients for washing and cleaning products are widely tested on animals, both in the UK and elsewhere. Often this is for such useful ingredients as "optical brighteners" – chemicals added to big-brand detergents to make our whites appear more luminously white than white can be. However, unless there is a recognized alternative test, the law requires *all* relevant chemicals to be tested on animals, including those ingredients produced specifically with the aim of reducing environmental impact and toxicity. This sometimes creates a tension between eco-focused manufacturers, who are constantly looking for greener ingredients, and animal welfare groups, who think that no new ingredients should be used if they necessitate animal testing.

What to buy

The vast majority of cleaning and laundry product sales are accounted for by a handful of large companies. Here are the biggest players, and some of their most popular brands:

Colgate-Palmolive Ajax
Procter & Gamble Ariel • Bold • Daz • Fairy • Flash
Reckitt Benckiser Dettox • Finish • Harpic • Haze • Mr Sheen • Vanish
SC Johnson Pledge • Toilet Duck • Mr Muscle
Unilever Comfort • Domestos • Cif • Persil • Surf

Perhaps unsurprisingly, none of these multinationals gets a clean bill of health on the grounds of chemicals, animal testing or various other measures. So how do the alternatives compare?

The best-known and most widely available "green" cleaning range is **Ecover**, which now includes scores of products, from floor cleaner to fabric softener (for the full list, see www.ecover.com). Ecover claim that "environmentally friendly detergents do not exist", but that theirs are about as close as you can get, being almost entirely plant-based and excluding all the high-concern chemicals discussed above. In 2002, the company even released their own detergent's chemical formula, so that other producers could "improve their impact on the environment". Ecover is widely available in both supermarkets and health-food shops, and often comes top in user tests of green household products.

But Ecover does have its critics. For years, the company was even on boycott lists, due to the fact that it was part-owned by **Group 4**, the private security firm criticized for violence against anti-road protesters and for its involvement in the controversial Campsfield immigration detention centre. That link is no longer direct – the two companies just share a significant individual investor – but there's still a tension between Ecover and the animal-rights lobby. The company claims to be actively "against" animal experiments, and they won't use an ingredient animal-tested in the last five years. However, this kind of "rolling cut-off date" policy – as opposed to picking a fixed cut-off year and sticking to it – leaves open the option of Ecover using ingredients being tested on animals now or in the future. Granted, they don't necessarily make use of this option, but their quest for greenness means they don't want to rule out a future eco-friendly ingredient just because the law means it has to be tested on animals. The same is true of **ACDO** – another popular eco-cleaner company.

If animal-testing is something you feel strongly about, you may prefer to buy products bearing the **Humane Household Products Standard** (HHPS) jumping rabbit logo. Like the

Do green cleaners actually work?

They may be kind to baby polar bears, but are "ethical" cleaning products as mean as they are green? It depends on the individual company and product, of course, but these days the eco options are generally pretty good. Ecover washing-up liquids and surface cleaners, for example, work almost indistinguishably as well as the big brands, despite the washing-up liquid being forty times less toxic to aquatic life than the market leader (if Ecover's PR material is to be believed).

As for laundry, you probably *will* notice a difference in performance between the green detergents and the big brands for clothes that have oily or greasy soiling. But for day-to-day freshening up they work absolutely fine. So perhaps consider mixing and matching.

In truth, however, you can almost get by with no washing powder at all, since sweat and much other dirt is water-soluble and removed perfectly well by the warm water and rotating action of a washing machine. Hence the success of products with names such as **eco-balls**, **eco-discs** or **aquaballs** (www.aquaball.com) that claim to remove the need for detergent by "ionizing" or "magnetizing" the water. Many people swear by them, but few have tried comparing the result to using nothing at all.

longer-established Humane Cosmetics Standard, the HHPS scheme is managed by the British Union for the Abolition of Vivisection and its logo can only be displayed on products made by companies that shun all ingredients tested on animals after a *fixed* cut-off date, and which are audited to prove it.

Since the HHPS scheme is quite new, only a few companies are certified at the time of writing. These include the **Co-op** – for its own-brand cleaners and detergents – and the following two specialists. These three companies all shun the "chemicals of high concern" in their products. For a full list of certified companies, see www.buav.org.

Astonish (by the Oil Refining Company)

www.astonishcleaners.com ▷ 0113 236 0036

The Astonish range includes basics such as washing-up liquid as well as cleaning products for everything from tiles and glass to upholstery and cars. Available online, via mail order, or from retailers such as Sainsbury's, Morrisons and John Lewis.

Clear Spring (by Faith Products)

www.faithinnature.co.uk ▷ 0161 764 2555

Dishwasher products, washing-up liquids, window cleaner, liquid detergent and polishes. Available in health stores, via mail order and online.

Other green cleaners, such as **Ecover**, **Bio-D** and **ACDO**, are available on the high street and from green-living websites, such as:

Ecozone www.ecozone.co.uk
Green Shop www.greenshop.co.uk
Natural Collection www.naturalcollection.com

Back to basics

Trading in your Ajax for baking soda will be uncomfortably close to green extremism for most punters, but this kind of good old-fashioned, eco-friendly alternative works surprisingly well. As does **lemon juice** as a bleach substitute and **white-wine vinegar solution** as a descaler and glass cleaner (though it does smell a bit). The more adventurous among the eco-minded community even swear by **tomato ketchup** (organic, of course) as a pot scrubber.

Furniture & DIY
Home improvements

Furniture, timber & other wooden things

Wood is a natural, renewable, recyclable, biodegradable and non-toxic material. It's more energy-efficient to produce than metal and most other materials and, in theory, if trees are planted in greater numbers than they're cut down, the timber industry can even help reduce global warming by soaking up CO_2. But, unfortunately, some of the wood we buy – whether it's used for beds, floorboards or candlesticks – comes with serious environmental and social costs. Britain still imports large amounts of wood from irreplaceable ancient forests – which continue to be chopped down at the astonishing rate of a football-pitch-sized area every two seconds. And most of the rest comes from quick-growth plantation forests that are also associated with certain environmental problems.

Sumatra in your sitting room?

Next time you admire the rich, dark grain of a mahogany sleigh bed or eye up a teak table, bear in mind that the Western demand for tropical woods such as these has been a consistent driving force of the clearance of the world's **rainforests**. Though this isn't the headline issue it once was, it is still just as massive a problem, with millions of acres being cleared every year. In fact, recent surveying by the National Institute for Space Research found that forest clearance in the Amazon was actually speeding up. Urbanization and the creation of farmland for cattle feed and palm oil are probably the biggest factors, but logging remains a key contributor.

But deforestation is not only an environmental issue: it's also a human-rights one. Many forest-based people have contracted diseases from loggers or been forced off the lands where they have always lived, albeit without any formally recognized rights. From Asia to Latin America, forest-based indigenous people have even been murdered when they've refused to leave. And the wider population can also be affected if the logging – as in Liberia in recent years – is funding a military conflict. You don't have to take the green groups' word for it either: a recent European Commission statement reported that "In some forest-rich countries, the corruption fuelled by profits from illegal logging has grown to such an extent that it is undermining the rule of law, principles of democratic governance and respect for human rights."

The UK imports around four-fifths of its wood and when it comes to rainforest varieties such as mahogany and teak, a great deal of it has been illegally sourced – that is, cut down or exported in a way that breaks the laws of the country it came from. There are no definitive figures, but Friends of the Earth estimates that around 60% of the UK's tropical wood has been illegally sourced, with much of the rest being legal but not from sustainably managed forests. The timber industry disputes such claims, yet cases keep popping up which suggest that wood specialists with ethical policies and big budgets are failing to keep their noses clean (as the Royal Family found out in 2002 when the Queen's Gallery was refurbished with wood from endangered forests in Cameroon).

Illegally sourced wood from the West is much less common, though from the US to Scandinavia campaigners are still having to battle to save the tiny remaining areas of ancient forest. Such forests are under threat of being cleared not only for their hardwoods, but also so that their land can be used for fast-growing softwoods such as pine, from which most of our flatpack furniture and paper is made. Replacing old forests with

Corbis

Sumatran tigers, such as this cub, are the last of the Indonesian tiger subspecies. They are now critically endangered, partly due to habitat loss caused by logging and partly due to hunting. Only a few hundred remain alive in the wild, and many conservationists expect them to become extinct within ten years.

Of cues, caskets and clarinets

Furniture and timber are the products most widely associated with eco-friendly (and eco-unfriendly) wood. But the same issues apply to tree-based products of all shapes, sizes and functions. For instance, Andrew Wasley recently reported in *Red Pepper* magazine that the UK imports nearly 300,000 budget **snooker cues** made "from the timber of the ramin tree – a rare species listed under the Convention on International Trade in Endangered Species (CITES) – chopped down and exported illegally from Indonesia's dwindling tropical forests".

Of the 200 trees estimated to be used in **musical instruments**, meanwhile, more than 70 are included in the World Conservation Union 2000 Red List of globally threatened trees, according to Fauna & Flora International's SoundWood programme (www.soundwood.org). Some of these so-called "tone woods" are critically endangered, including species of ebony used in several string and wind instruments (but not any longer on pianos, Stevie Wonder songs notwithstanding).

Even as we leave the world we may not be treading lightly upon its forests, since some **coffins** are veneered or made out of tropical hardwood such as mahogany. Also widely used are chipboard and plywood, both of which commonly contain illegally sourced wood.

It's difficult to imagine the FSC logo becoming a common sight in music shops, sports stores and funeral homes, but pressure from ethically minded consumers – even if it's only asking questions – will at least encourage importers and manufacturers to consider the issues. As for ethical alternatives, you're unlikely to come across green cues or clarinets. But with the first generation of eco-warriors getting on a bit, there's a growing number of alternative coffins on the market. These avoid not only hardwood, but also MDF sides made with formaldehyde-containing glues, and plastic handles and linings, which all give off pollution when cremated (a UK/EU report estimates that crematoriums are responsible for 12% of UK dioxin emissions). This will be taking things a bit too far in most people's eyes, but if you're really keen to ethically shop till you drop you could look into the recycled cardboard, bamboo or wicker options from companies such as:

Eco Coffins www.eco-coffin.co.uk ▷ 01162 333 566
Greenfield Coffins www.greenfieldcoffins.com ▷ 01376 327 074
Peace Funerals www.peacefunerals.co.uk ▷ 0800 093 0505

new is certainly better than slashing and burning for pastureland, but the process of uprooting the old trees gives off more CO_2, according to *The Ecologist*, than will be absorbed by the new trees in their first ten years. Furthermore, some heavy herbicides (such as napalm) are sometimes used to get the new trees to grow, and the biodiversity of the new forests is limited by the fact that they consist of only one or two tree types. So "one tree planted for every one cut down" isn't necessarily as good as it sounds.

Good wood

Whether you're buying a salad bowl, a bed or a set of shelves, the best way to be sure that your wood has come from sustainably managed forests is to choose products bearing the logo of the **Forest Stewardship Council (FSC)**. There are various sustainable wood labelling schemes out there. But many of them – such as the American Sustainable Forestry Initiative – are highly noncommittal efforts of the timber industry, and the FSC remains the only one that should be taken seriously.

An international, independent, non-profit-making organization, the FSC was founded in 1993 after extensive consultation between "timber users, traders and representatives of environmental and human-rights organizations". It only accredits wood when it can vouch for the entire supply chain – or **chain of custody** – from forest to sawmill to processor. The scheme isn't without its critics: in late 2002 the Rainforest Foundation (www.rainforestfoundationuk.org) released a report entitled *Trading in Credibility*, accusing the FSC of being "seriously flawed" and "knowingly misleading the public" in terms of the gap between its image and the reality of its operations. But even if these accusations are true – and they're not widely supported – it's still by far the best scheme currently around and the only one recognized by the major environmental groups.

FSC-approved wooden objects – ranging from beds and breadbins to firewood and floorboards – aren't too difficult to come by. For a list of products and suppliers go to:

FSC Product List www.fsc-uk.org/product-search ▷ 01686 413 916

Reclaimed wood

FSC-certified wood is a good choice, but environmentalists claim the very greenest option is to favour **reclaimed (recycled) timber** whenever possible. After all, for all its recyclable credentials, wood accounts for a significant proportion of our waste: Friends of the Earth estimate that 3000 tonnes of perfectly good wood are thrown away or burnt each day just from buildings being demolished in the UK. And yet reclaimed wood is often better quality than new stuff, as it contains less water, is less likely to contract and was usually harvested before the advent of quick-growth forests, which are better at growing fast than delivering really fine woods.

The **Reclaimed Building Supply** will help you find local suppliers of reclaimed timber and other products. Also check out the amazing **Salvo** website – which has classifieds for everything from reclaimed floorboards to staircases and cinema seats – and the relevant page of the **WasteBook** site.

Reclaimed Building Supply www.reclaimbuildingsupply.com ▷ 01883 346 432
Salvo www.salvo.co.uk
The WasteBook www.wastebook.org/furnrec.htm

Or for in-depth information about reclaimed timber, try:

Timber Recycling Centre www.recycle-it.org

Or if buying new, uncertified wood...

If buying FSC-certified or reclaimed wood isn't an option, at the very least avoid tropical hardwood such as **mahogany**, **teak**, **redwood**, **rosewood** and **ebony** wherever possible. Such products won't *necessarily* have been

Bamboo

Bamboo is something of a wonder crop. The central building material of East Asia since time immemorial, it has also served as everything from a foodstuff to jewellery. And today it is hailed by some as the future green alternative to hardwood. It's very strong yet doesn't contract as much as wood, and with modern processing it can even be used for flooring. It grows incredibly fast – some species can manage two feet in their first day – making it sustainable to grow in large quantities, unlike many hardwoods.

Significantly, the way that bamboo grows means that when the plant is harvested it isn't killed: it simply grows back up from where you cut it, so the roots remain in place and the soil isn't damaged or washed away. Furthermore, bamboo doesn't require lots of pesticides, can grow nearly anywhere and is even thought to be capable of sucking pollutants *out* of the water cycle. So, while there's no reason to believe that bamboo furniture and other products have been ethically sourced or made in decent working conditions, the material itself would clearly be a contender for the world's most sustainable hardwood. Were it not for the fact, of course, that it's actually a type of grass.

logged from virgin rainforests, but it's not unlikely. Also try to avoid suppliers that can't tell you about the origins of their woods.

For more information about the specific woods and the issues they raise, see the Friends of the Earth website, or order their book, *The Good Wood Guide*.

Friends of the Earth www.foe.co.uk ▷ 020 7490 1555

Furniture & DIY superstores

The furniture market is increasingly dominated by **IKEA** (www.ikea.co.uk). A true giant, this chain has almost 250 superstores in more than 30 countries, and its founder, Ingvar Kamprad, is one of the five richest people in the world. This, along with its global-domination-style expansion policies, has earned IKEA the usual criticism from anti-corporate groups but, for a business of its size, the company has also received quite a lot of praise. Friends of the Earth have lauded its phasing out of hazardous chemicals, and WWF its commitment to eco-friendly wood sourcing. On the latter issue, IKEA has a long-term plan to only sell wood from certified forests (FSC is currently the only certifier it recognizes). But for now, it only buys some FSC wood and, annoyingly, the label is not displayed on products, since the managers "want the IKEA brand itself to stand as a guarantee of genuine concern for the environment and social responsibility". Still, the company claims to ensure that even its non-FSC-approved woods don't come from intact natural forests, and its code of conduct also covers human and worker rights in supplier factories. Research from 2003 by SOMO (www.somo.nl) suggests that breaches of this code are not uncommon. But compared with other companies of its size, IKEA doesn't fare too badly.

The big household/DIY centres such as **B&Q** (www.diy.com) and **Homebase** (www.homebase.co.uk) also both sell FSC-certified furniture. B&Q, especially, is one of the most progressive big firms in the UK. It has an excellent timber sourcing policy as well as codes of conduct on everything from employment practices to the selling of environmentally problematic peat (see p.143). It has even worked with fair trade groups in India.

Paints & other DIY products

Many people dutifully buy their eco washing-up liquid but don't consider environmental issues when shopping for DIY products such as **paint**, brush cleaner, stripper, wood stains, glues and varnishes. This is a touch ironic, since many of these products, which are mostly derived from non-degradable petrochemicals, are on a different level of eco-unfriendliness from washing-up liquids and laundry detergents.

One issue is that many paints, varnishes and solvents – in both their manufacture and application – release **volatile organic compounds**

(VOCs) into the air, leading to the creation of polluting ground-level ozone, among other things. The EU is currently in the process of tightening up the laws about VOCs, and most big paint manufacturers now specify the VOC level on their tins. This development has been widely welcomed, but it doesn't deal with the heavy metals, solvents and other controversial chemicals used in many paints and other DIY products. From dyes to plasticizers, many of these ingredients are fat-soluble and therefore prone to accumulating in our bodies (and those of animals, being passed up the food chain from low-level aquatic life to fish, birds and mammals). Not all of these are known to be harmful, but some are toxic or carcinogenic.

As with all household chemicals, the **health risks** to humans of occasional exposure to DIY products are unproven – and likely to be extremely small. But longer-term use does seem to be harmful. In 1989, for example, the International Agency for Research on Cancer concluded that "occupational exposure as a painter is carcinogenic". Furthermore, paints and varnishes can continue to emit fumes once they're on the door frame or table, and this is thought to be a contributor to sick building syndrome (SBS) – headaches and other health effects which seem to be brought on by a specific building. Though this all sounds a bit New Agey, SBS is an all-too-real malaise, formally recognized by the World Health Organization since 1982.

As for the effect on the wider environment, the amount of VOCs, bioaccumulative toxins and other chemicals released into the atmosphere at the time of application is relatively small with most DIY products. That is, as long as you don't pour any down the sink (instead, give unwanted half-full paint tins to charity; see p.109). But, according to environmental groups, the manufacture of a litre of paint can create ten or more litres of toxic waste – which, considering that the UK gets through a few hundred million litres of paint each year, adds up to a pretty staggering total.

As ever, though, it's worth keeping all this in perspective: most of us account for the release of far greater quantities of problematic chemicals through our cars than we do through our DIY.

Greener DIY products

Due to a gradually increasing awareness of all these issues, an ever-growing range of greener DIY products is available, including a wide selection of paints and some varnishes, strippers, waxes, stains and other related products. The main producers are:

Auro Organic www.auroorganic.co.uk ▷ 01799 543 077
ECOS www.ecospaints.com ▷ 01539 732 866
Ecotec Paints www.natural-building.co.uk ▷ 01491 638 911
Livos www.livos.demon.co.uk ▷ 01952 883 288
Nutshell Natural Paints www.nutshellpaints.com ▷ 08700 331 140
OSMO www.osmouk.com ▷ 01296 481 220

Alternative paints tend to impose a slightly smaller ecological burden on the world. They also give you a chance to avoid the major paint firms, who are mainly owned by chemical companies (such as **ICI**, which owns **Dulux**) that have been widely criticized by green groups. However, "eco" paints themselves vary widely, from those which include synthetic chemicals but no solvents – such as **ECOS** – to more comprehensively "natural" products such as **Auro Organic**. In general, the greener the product, the more expensive it is and the smaller the colour choice (especially for bright colours).

You can get prices, order colour charts and buy online from most of the above suppliers, but for advice you might be better contacting a specialist store, such as:

Construction Resources (London) www.ecoconstruct.com ▷ 020 7450 2211
Eco Merchant (Kent) www.ecomerchant.co.uk ▷ 01795 530 130
Green Building Store (West Yorks) www.greenbuildingstore.co.uk ▷ 01484 854 898
The Green Shop (Gloucestershire) www.greenshop.co.uk ▷ 01452 770 629
NBT (Buckinghamshire) www.natural-building.co.uk ▷ 01491 638 911

Green construction

If you're planning a serious green building project, three of the top firms in eco-friendly building design are:

BBM Sustainable Design, East Sussex
www.bbm-architects.co.uk ▷ 01273 480 533

Gaia Architects, Scotland
www.gaiagroup.org ▷ 0131 557 9191

Bill Dunster Architects, Surrey
www.zedfactory.com ▷ 020 8484 1380

For more info, as well as inspiration, tips, links and books, visit:

Environmental Building News www.buildinggreen.com
The Centre for Alternative Technology www.cat.org.uk
Association for Environment-Conscious Building www.aecb.net

If you'd rather stick to your home-town DIY centre, then consider favouring B&Q, which, as already mentioned (see p.132), is highly progressive for its size.

For some products, though, there's no particularly green equivalent. For example, the Association for Environment-Conscious Building recommends avoiding wood preservative altogether. If it must be used, they claim, **boron** is the best option (it's available from Auro and Livos, both listed above).

Soft furnishings & homeware
Ethical decor

Rugs & carpets

Most of the rugs and carpets we buy are machine-made in the West. The ethical problem most frequently raised in relation to these is the fact that many carpets contain and emit volatile organic compounds, benzene-based flame retardants and other "chemicals of high concern", despite the fact that less potentially harmful alternatives are available. On these grounds, Greenpeace recommends avoiding carpets by **Axminster** and **Stoddard**, and favouring those by **Cavalier** and **Ulster**.

Another issue is resource consumption. The production and transport of carpets (a staggering 70% of which come from one town in Georgia) consumes a great deal of energy and water. According to an early-1990s report by the University of Utrecht, wool carpets are better in this respect than those made of nylon.

More contentious than mass-produced carpets are the high-quality rugs that we traditionally associate with the Middle East, but which are just as commonly made in the Indian Subcontinent. These are usually **hand-knotted** and, with as many as 250,000 knots per square metre, each rug is the result of months of painstaking work.

Carpet making is a venerable tradition that employs millions of poor workers from South Asia to North Africa. However, the sector has become increasingly tarnished by allegations of widespread child labour – including "forced" or "bonded" child labour, with kids being used to pay off debts in conditions roughly equivalent to imprisonment or slavery.

Child workers (sometimes said to be favoured for their small fingers) are found throughout much of the rug-producing world, but there are no accurate figures of exactly how many there are in each country, and how many of them are in forced-labour positions (as opposed to supporting their families, perhaps even in between schooling hours). It seems, though, that the problem is particularly acute in **South Asia**, which saw a boom in carpet production from the 1970s after a crackdown on child labour in Iran. Figures vary widely but it is thought that as many as one million children may be working in the carpet industry in India, Pakistan and Nepal alone.

Rugmark and fair trade carpets

As is always the case with child labour, the question of how to solve the problems of the South Asian carpet industry is a thorny one. It goes without saying that a complete solution is going to require the political will of the governments in each country. But what can consumers do?

One option is only to buy rugs bearing the **Rugmark** label, which identifies carpets made without the use of child labour. Set up in 1994 by a collection of human rights organizations, exporting companies, UNICEF and other bodies, the scheme also guarantees that a proportion of the price of each rug goes towards providing an education for former child weavers that its inspectors have discovered. Rugmark currently only covers India, Pakistan and Nepal, but there are plans to extend it to other countries, such as Afghanistan, Turkey and Morocco, if and when funding permits it.

To put the label on their carpets a company has to agree to anti-child-labour policies and allow random inspection of their premises, both by Rugmark inspectors and by other non-profit child-welfare organizations. To protect against counterfeit, each carpet is individually numbered, allowing it to be traced back to the specific loom on which it was made. Rugmark accredits around 15% of registered Indian looms and its inspectors have "rescued" more than 2500 children, nearly all of whom have received education at affiliated schools.

Some Rugmark lines can be found in most of the major carpet retailers in the UK, but **B&Q** and **Co-op Homemaker** have committed to stocking Rugmark exclusively. For a full list of retailers, see:

Rugmark www.rugmark.org

Like all such schemes, Rugmark isn't without critics. As evidenced by Mark Tully's recent book, *India In Slow Motion*, some in the carpet industry claim that the labelling organization has exaggerated the extent of bonded child labour and, by publicizing the issue, has reduced the demand for all South Asian rugs, including the majority that are made by adults living in extreme poverty. Such critics also point out that no labelling system can genuinely ensure a carpet is "child-labour free".

On the other hand, Rugmark has been criticized for not going far enough, since it focuses on illegal child labour rather than the wider social issues that create it. To be fair, Rugmark does work alongside ethical trade organizations, and their inspectors try to keep an eye on wages and health and safety. But it's true that it doesn't claim to be labelling fair trade rugs, as such. For a more comprehensive ethical approach, check out the following:

Mala Carpets

www.malacarpets.co.uk ▷ 01904 786 880 ▷ 64–68 Low Petergate, York

Mala Carpets sell high-quality Indian carpets produced by Mala Handicrafts, a project aiming to create a pragmatic solution to child labour. Mala seek out working children in Indian villages and give them "a three-year non-formal education course, designed adopting Gandhian principles", without restricting their use of non-school time "to relieve their poverty" (ie working). The rugs, which cost £100–3000, come with a lifetime guarantee and you can rest assured that "60- to 100-count wool" is used "where higher definition is needed", and that "the warps will mostly be strong cotton with two wefts". Shop online, at the York store or through the Third World Craft Centre, Wimborne (01202 849 898), or Adam Flude Rugs, Chichester (01243 786 333).

One Village

www.onevillage.co.uk ▷ 0845 4584 7070 ▷ On the A44 in Woodstock, nr Oxford

If you're after something less expensive, check out the rugs and other floor coverings from "alternative trading organisation" One Village. Instead of expensive hand-knotted carpets, they offer a range that includes soft, unbleached cotton rugs from the Ganges region and tough coir mats from a village co-operative society in Kerala.

Other homeware – from bedding to bowls

We increasingly buy our homeware, such as linen, cushions, kitchenware and ornaments, from giant companies such as IKEA. But there are now quite a few ethical specialists in this field. As with clothes (see p.244), these companies fall into two categories: the **fair traders**, who buy direct from marginalized small-scale producer groups in the developing world; and the **greens**, who attempt to be non-exploitative but focus primarily on organic fabrics and other eco-friendly materials.

The following all sell online and/or via mail order, but you could also check out your nearest fair trade shop (see box). And if you have a penchant for fairly traded homeware, ornaments and the like, consider subscribing to *New Consumer* magazine (see p.320).

Fair trade

Ganesha

www.ganesha.co.uk ▷ 020 7928 3444 ▷ 3 Gabriel's Wharf, 56 Upper Ground, London

A member of BAFTS (see box opposite), Ganesha have a range of nicely designed homeware. Transform your sofa with a cotton handloom throw (£35 from a weavers' co-operative in West Bengal) and a couple of "retro chintz printed" silk cushion covers (£20 from an IFAT member in South India). They also stock drapes, placemats, beautiful bamboo bowls and more.

One Village

www.onevillage.co.uk ▷ 0845 4584 7070 ▷ On the A44 in Woodstock, nr Oxford

One Village (another BAFTS shop) offers a massive selection of good-value "functional interior products". Once you get used to the website's intimidatingly big and confusing pages, you'll find everything from hand-thrown *ökopots* (glazed terracotta tableware) and salad bowls made of mango wood (not FSC-certified but apparently from sustainably managed orchards) to Filipino bamboo lampshades and Christmas decorations.

Traidcraft

www.traidcraftshop.co.uk ▷ 01914 910 591

The UK's leading fair trade organization offers a reasonable household selection that ranges from Bolivian tumblers to Thai candles. Prices are very reasonable, with sets of hand-block-printed Indian bedding starting at £50.

Fair trade shops

The UK has a number of shops, websites and cata-
logues that sell wide ranges of fair trade items, of the
certified and uncertified varieties (see p.24). Most of
these stores are members of the British Association
for Fair Trade Shops (BAFTS), which requires its members to meet a number of ethical criteria.

A few BAFTS shops sell only clothes or rugs, but
most of the rest sell a roughly consistent range of
gifts, **cards**, **foods**, **jewellery**, **clothes**, **hand-made
papers**, **ornaments**, **quilts**, **toys** and **musical instruments**. Many of these items tend towards slightly hippyish styles, and goods include
all the clichés of ethical shopping such as rainbow textiles and even the dreaded
rain-stick. But some fair trade shops, such as London's Ganesha, are *plus chic*.

BAFTS criteria for fair trade shops

▶ Buying a majority of goods from
importers who comply with the FINE
criteria (see p.25) and are listed in the
BAFTS Importers' Directory

▶ Showing good reason for selling
other goods, and explaining this on
the membership application form

▶ Buying from importers and selling
to the public at fair prices, reflecting
the value of the products

▶ Promoting and encouraging
product quality either through the
importers or directly to the producers

▶ Paying invoices in credit time

▶ Showing concern for social and
environmental aspects of products,
including child labour, tropical
hardwood use and animal testing

▶ Ensuring equal opportunities for all
shop staff, whether voluntary or paid,
and actively opposing discrimination

▶ Showing openness to customers,
by having information available on
suppliers, BAFTS, aims and working
practices

▶ Having an educational/
campaigning aspect to the work in
the shop

There are more than 100 BAFTS shops across the UK. To locate your nearest, or for
more information, see:

BAFTS www.bafts.org.uk

As well as fair trade shops, you may also come across the
occasional fair trade event. For example, London has for
years had a Fair Trade Fair each December, with scores of
stalls offering fairly traded Christmas gifts. The screening of suppliers is mainly based on trust, but you're
likely to get a more ethical Christmas sack than you
would on the high street. For more information, see:

Fair Trade Fair www.fairtradefair.org

Eco & organic

Eco Boudoir

www.eco-boudoir.com

Run by designer Jenny White, Eco Boudoir is a purveyor of thoroughly desirable, high-class homeware using "sustainable textile materials" such as organic silks, recycled cotton and fur, and chrome-free leather and sheepskin. Aiming to provide "luxury with a conscience", their collection ranges from gorgeous silk blankets and cushions (£150 and up) to more risqué items such as eye masks and bed ties.

Ecotopia

www.ecotopia.co.uk ▷ 0845 094 2181

Ecotopia aims to be a one-stop shop for goods that "assist people in leading a more natural and lower impact lifestyle". The site is dominated by cleaning, health and beauty and energy-saving products, but there's some homeware on offer, such as a magazine holder and chairs made from recycled plastic and vases of recycled glass.

Greenfibres

www.greenfibres.com ▷ 01803 868 001 ▷ 99 High St, Totnes, Devon

Bedroom and bathroom linen, as well as duvets and mattresses, in organic and eco-friendly textiles. The range is impressive but prices aren't low. Organic bed sheets, for example, come in cotton classic, cotton poplin, cotton/organic or cotton flannel, ranging from £25 to £45. Organic mattresses are for serious green shoppers only, starting at around £500.

Natural Collection

www.naturalcollection.com ▷ 0870 331 3335

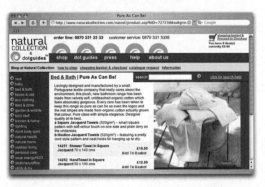

Selling online or via a catalogue, Natural Collection offer a wide range of eco-friendly goods (or, in their less prosaic words, "eclectic, unusual, useful and interesting products carefully chosen to inspire ideas towards a sustainable future"). The household selection includes everything from organic bedding and towels to FSC-approved wooden furnishings and a log maker (£30) which will turn yesterday's newspaper into a brick-shaped "pulp log" capable of burning for an hour.

Cut flowers

The overwhelming majority of our cut flowers are imported. Some come from Holland, but we also import massive quantities from further afield, in particular from Kenya, Israel and Colombia. This raises a whole mix of environmental and social concerns. On the environmental side, there's the fact that flowers (due to their short shelf life) are usually **air-freighted** into the UK, with the global-warming impact that implies. Furthermore, the demand for cosmetically perfect blooms means that huge quantities of **pesticides** are used in their production. This is not only an environmental issue but also a labour one, since these chemicals can be dangerous to workers when not carefully regulated. According to the US-based International Labor Rights Fund (www.laborrights.org), flower workers in Colombia and Ecuador are exposed to up to a hundred different agrochemicals (some of them extremely toxic, and banned elsewhere in the world), and one in five suffer from work-related health problems – from nausea to congenital malformations in their offspring.

In Kenya, meanwhile, the industry has provided much-needed jobs and most of the suppliers are governed by codes of conduct (such as those demanded by the UK supermarkets which are members of the **Ethical Trading Initiative** – see p.61). However, according to the Kenya Human Rights Commission, many of the workers earn less than one dollar per day, have poor health and safety conditions, little collective bargaining power and no job security. The industry is also accused of seriously burdening local water sources. As for Israel, that's another can of worms, of course, since the country's activities in the Occupied Territories put it near the top of most lists of oppressive regimes.

A few specialist food shops and box schemes now offer UK-grown – even organic – flowers. These have environmental advantages, but, as ever, boycotting those from the poor world is likely to cause more harm than good for those people who rely on the sector for work. In the future, we may start to see a decent range of flowers bearing the **Fairtrade Mark**. The first – roses from Kenya – were introduced by Tesco in time for Valentine's Day 2004.

Another ethical labelling scheme in the pipeline is **FFP** (Fair Flowers & Plants). This Dutch-based, EU-funded project aims to unify the various existing ethical initiatives within the flower industry to create an accreditation scheme roughly similar to Fairtrade, with each link of the supply chain audited to ensure decent labour and environmental standards. The scheme is well under way, but there's plenty still to do, so don't expect to see the label on flowers and plants before late 2007 or even 2008. For the latest news, see:

fair flowers fair plants

FFP www.fairflowersfairplants.com

In the meantime, the best thing consumers can do is to raise questions of labour and environmental issues with retailers. This can only help accelerate improvements within the industry.

Gardening products
Even greener fingers

With so much agricultural land being given over to mono-crop industrial farming, some commentators hope that gardeners could be the saviours of British **biodiversity**. But certain garden products can have the opposite effect, causing harm to the environment either through their toxic contents or through their extraction from the earth.

Pesticides and alternatives

As the abundant health warnings on the packets attest, many garden **herbicides** and **insecticides** contain some nasty substances. Some of these not only hit the target species, but also poison birds and other wildlife, and pollute local water systems. As with many household chemicals, they're also likely to be the result of a polluting manufacturing process.

Just as with farming, however, weed and pest killers can be largely avoided with a bit of effort. For weeds, this generally means pulling or digging them out by hand, but if an area has been invaded by pernicious weeds (such as bindweed or ground elder), the best bet is to dig over the ground and then cover it with old carpet or plastic in order to deny the plants light. If the weeds haven't taken over completely, a less drastic measure is to cover the dug ground with a layer of newspaper and then a light-excluding mulch such as wood chippings.

Pests – in particular slugs and snails – can be the bane of the gardener's life. Fortunately the natural solution is often the best. Birds (like thrushes) will crack open and eat snails, slugs are part of the hedgehog's diet, while ladybirds and lacewings keep aphids in check. You can encourage birds and hedgehogs either by the way you plant (birds will nest in thick hedges) or by having strategically placed nesting boxes. If you must use slug pellets, make sure they are a variety that is harmless to all other creatures.

Companion planting – the growing of specific plant species in close proximity – provides another option. This has a number of benefits, such as repelling pests, attracting certain insects (such as aphids) away from one plant and on to another, and forming a protective barrier. For more information on chemical-free gardening, see the website of the HDRA (Henry Doubleday Research Association), or, for supplies, go straight to their catalogue/online store (see p.144).

HDRA www.hdra.org.uk

Compost: the peat problem

Of the various garden products collected at cost to the environment, the worst is **peat**, which is the basis of much of the compost on sale in garden centres and elsewhere. The problem is that harvesting peat means draining and digging up irreplaceable **peatland bogs**, which are home to a wide range of increasingly rare plant and animal species (and which also serve a valuable role in stabilizing ground-water levels). According to a 2003 report from two environmental groups – the WWF and Traffic (see www.traffic.org) – around 2000 hectares of peatland bogs are dug up in Ireland each year, mainly to supply British gardeners.

The advice of most green groups is to only buy compost specifically labelled as peat-free. Such composts make use of sustainable alternatives such as **coir peat**, a biodegradable byproduct of the coconut industry. Peat-free compost isn't difficult to find in the big home-improvement chains but it can be trickier in supermarkets, independent garden centres and at branches of Wyevale, which came bottom of the list in a recent survey, conducted for London's Deputy Mayor, of how successfully peat is being phased out (B&Q came top). It's worth noting that a peat-free growing medium does not hold moisture as well as a peat-based one, so in summer you should water less heavily but more often.

Alternatively, **make your own compost**. This not only gets around the water issue but also helps minimize the amount of food you throw away. For more on composting see p.118.

Flower pots

Most plant pots are made from polypropylene or polystyrene. Few garden centres will take them back for reuse (there's a risk of spreading pests and diseases) and they can't easily be recycled. So if purchasing pots separately from plants, consider opting for ones made of vegetable byproducts, such as those by Earth Buddy. Such pots last well but can eventually be broken up and composted. Some enlightened garden centres also sell bedding plants in coir pots which can be planted straight into the ground – the roots simply break through and the pot gradually disintegrates.

Earth Buddy www.earthbuddy.co.uk

For ornamental plants, terracotta pots are built to last and look good. If broken, they can be used as drainage in pots or recycled for use as hardcore. It's worth trying to buy locally made ones, since those bought at a big garden centre are likely to have been shipped from the Far East.

More garden tips

▶ To minimize the use of a hose (and maximize your supply plant-friendly rainwater) fit up your garden with **rain butts**. As well as taking the water from the roof guttering of your house, these can be set up against garden sheds or outhouses. For more on home and garden water use, see p.106.

▶ Wooden garden furniture is usually made of hardwood, so be sure to look out for the FSC logo (see p.130) when buying.

▶ Avoid "water-worn", "Irish" or "weathered" limestone. Limestone pavements (outcrops of rocks that have been weathered into a paving-stone pattern) support rare plants and wildlife, but most of those in the UK have been carved up and made into rockeries and water features.

▶ Favour garden centres and nurseries which either cultivate their own plants and flowers or are sure where their stocks came from. As Traffic and the WWF recently reported, legal records suggest that the illegal collection of bulbs from British woodlands is a growing problem. This issue relates primarily to bluebells and snowdrops.

▶ For low-carbon outdoor lighting, check out the sun-powered options. A selection of solar lights, ranging in price from £10 to £99, are available from Green Fingers (www.greenfingers.com ▷ 0845 345 0728).

▶ For lounging around in your eco-friendly garden, you could invest in a South Indian canvas hammock from One Village (see p.138). Apparently it's "the Rolls-Royce of hammocks", no less, and "the best you can buy, for extreme comfort and delight".

Where to shop

For eco-friendly garden supplies, try one of the following sites. As its name implies, the Organic Catalogue is also available in paper form.

Green Gardener www.greengardener.co.uk
Organic Catalogue www.organiccatalog.com ▷ 01932 253 6660
Wiggly Wigglers www.wigglywigglers.co.uk

Food & drink

7

No consumer area is so politically charged as food, which is at the centre of debates ranging from farmer exploitation, animal welfare and international trade rules to public health, biotechnology and environmental degradation. Some of these issues are discussed in general terms in chapter three, but here we look in more depth at the ethical implications of the food and drink we buy. The chapter covers some general topics – intensive farming, organics, food miles, genetic modification and the environmental burden of meat production – before focusing on specific foods and drinks (from p.175) and the pros and cons of different places to shop (see p.216).

"Cheap" food vs. organics
Is organic food and drink more ethical?

Agriculture in the UK has undergone a remarkable transition in the last sixty years. In the aftermath of World War II, the UK's drive to produce as much as possible as quickly as possible saw massive **state subsidies** awarded to the biggest, most industrialized farms. Small producers that relied heavily on manpower and produced a range of crops and animal products were gradually eclipsed by larger businesses that focused on just one or two crops or meats and relied primarily on technology, economies of scale and large quantities of **agrochemicals** (such as fertilizers and pesticides).

One impact of this process of industrialization has been a massive decrease in the number of farm workers. Indeed, there are now nearly half a million **fewer agricultural jobs** in the UK than there were a few decades ago – and although the amount of food we import has played a part in this, the main factor has been the increased efficiency allowed by technology and chemicals. Depending on who you ask, this reduction of the farm workforce is either a disaster (as family traditions have been destroyed and thousands of workers have lost their jobs) or a good thing (since fewer people are subjected to back-breaking work in rainy fields).

Another impact of subsidized industrial agriculture has been **a fall in the price of the food in our shops**. The average UK household is now estimated to spend less than one-tenth of its total budget on food. This compares with around one-third just fifty years ago, and that's despite the fact that we're eating more expensive and exotic ingredients than ever before. Of course, much of this drop in how much of our money we spend on food is down to increasing wages and the fact that food prices are kept artificially low by our tax-funded subsidies. But even taking these factors into account, food has become significantly less expensive as farming has got more industrial.

Most people would agree that cheaper food is a good thing (despite the worsening problem of obesity in the UK). However, according to many commentators, we're not getting something for nothing. The hidden costs of industrial farming – to **human health**, the **environment** and long-term **food security** – are big and getting bigger.

In the words of the staff writers at *Nature* (a peer-reviewed science journal, not a bastion of eco-warriors), "Mainstream agronomists now acknowledge ... that intensive farming reduces biodiversity, encourages irreversible soil erosion and generates run-off that is awash with harmful chemicals – including nitrates from fertilizers that can devastate aquatic ecosystems." And that's before you consider the impact on **animal welfare**, and the massive wastefulness that accompanies intensive meat farming (more on this later).

Some saw these problems coming right from the beginning. As agricultural industrialization took off, a small bunch of philosophically minded farmers, worried primarily about the potentially damaging effect on soil, planted the seeds of the **organic movement**, which, after decades on the fringe, has seen an amazing boom recently, with annual sales in excess of £1 billion and rising every year.

Soil

Soil may not seem like the most interesting thing in the world, but it's actually pretty amazing stuff and it's at the centre of debates about organic and industrial farming. Indeed, despite its dull appearance, earth is absolutely packed full of life. The UN's Global Biodiversity Assessment suggested that a single gram of soil "could contain 10,000 million individual cells comprising 4000–5000 bacterial types, of which less than 10% have been isolated and are known to science", and that's before you consider snails, earthworms, termites, mites and other invertebrates. But soil not only *contains* life, of course, it also gives it: without fertile earth, there'd be no plants, no animals and no humans.

The world is covered by an extremely thin and delicate skin of this fertile dirt. (If the world was the size of a football, the layer of soil would be many thousands of times thinner than a piece of paper wrapped around the ball.) And yet humans have been rather cavalier in their treatment of this precious resource, battering it with intensive, chemical-heavy agriculture, urbanization and deforestation. According to a report by the UK's Royal Commission on Environmental Pollution, around 10% of the world's total soil has been lost through human-induced causes. Even more amazingly, in just the last forty years, nearly a third of the world's arable crop land has been abandoned due to soil erosion. Considering that it takes around 500 years to form just a few centimetres of soil in agricultural conditions, we're clearly losing our life-giving earth far more quickly than it can be replaced, in the process endangering the future world's ability to feed itself.

It was precisely these worries that led to the establishment of the organic movement. Hence the fact that its longest-standing organization is known as the Soil Association.

Source: All figures quoted in Biodiversity for Food and Agriculture, *a report by the Sustainable Development Department of the United Nations Food & Agriculture Organization*

Organic questions and answers

What is organic food?

Since the EC passed legislation on it in 1993, the term "organic" has been governed by strict legal **definitions and regulations** across the European Union. Any product labelled as organic – wherever it was produced – must have been grown or raised according to a set of minimum EU standards and possibly extra standards imposed by the individual country and certification body (see box overleaf).

As most people are aware, at the core of the organic movement is a policy that shuns synthetic **fertilizers, pesticides, herbicides, fungicides** and other man-made "inputs". Instead of these, organic farmers rely on a mixture of special growing techniques and "natural" alternatives. In place of chemical fertilizers, for example, soil fertility is maintained through the use of **animal manure** and **crop rotation**.

Crop rotation is a farming technique in which the same field is used for growing different crops in successive months or years, the idea being to ensure that the nutrients some crops take from the earth (most notably nitrogen) are put back by others. It can also reduce the need for pesticides and herbicides, though other techniques are usually also necessary. These range from manual weeding to the introduction of predatory insects to a crop (to eat the pests) or the use of "natural" pesticides such as Bt, derived from a bacterium.

Organic rules also ban **additives** such as artificial sweeteners, colourings, preservatives and flavour enhancers as well as hydrogenated fats and genetically modified ingredients. But this doesn't tell us the whole story. The organic "idea" is an entire agricultural philosophy, taking in **animal welfare** and **social justice** as well as environmental and health concerns (see box).

In the case of prepared foods, to bear an organic label they must contain at least **95% organic ingredients**; the rest, where applicable, may be non-organic, but only from a list of approved ingredients.

Who enforces the rules?

Anyone who produces, imports, packages or processes organic food has to register with an official **certification body**, which will inspect them at least once a year. In the UK, there are currently ten certification bodies, all of which impose minimum standards defined by the UK government, and some of which add extra rules of their own. The best known of the ten, the

The organic charter

Though the exact details of organic rules vary around the world, a definitive set of principles was recently agreed by the **International Federation of Organic Agricultural Movements** (www.ifoam.org). Here, then, are the four principles, followed by a bit of further explanation about each, drawing on the official IFOAM commentaries.

▶ **The principle of health** Organic Agriculture should sustain and enhance the health of soil, plant, animal, human and planet as one and indivisible

▶ **The principle of ecology** Organic Agriculture should be based on living ecological systems and cycles, work with them, emulate them and help sustain them

▶ **The principle of fairness** Organic Agriculture should build on relationships that ensure fairness with regard to the common environment and life opportunities

▶ **The principle of care** Organic Agriculture should be managed in a precautionary and responsible manner to protect the health and well-being of current and future generations and the environment

The first principle "points out that the health of individuals and communities cannot be separated from the health of ecosystems" and conveys that "the role of organic agriculture, whether in farming, processing, distribution or consumption, is to sustain and enhance the health of ecosystems and organisms from the smallest in the soil to human beings".

The second principle "states that production is to be based on ecological processes and recycling … and should fit the cycles and ecological balances in nature". It also reflects the organic movement's desire to reduce inputs and energy consumption "in order to maintain and improve environmental quality and conserve resources" and "to protect and benefit the common environment including landscapes, climate, habitats, biodiversity, air and water".

The third principle deals with the lesser-known aspects of organic farming: social justice ("those involved in organic agriculture should conduct human relationships in a manner that ensures fairness at all levels and to all parties – farmers, workers, processors, distributors, traders and consumers") and the humane treatment of animals (which "should be provided with the conditions and opportunities of life that accord with their physiology, natural behaviour and well-being"). The idea of fairness also applies to preserving resources for future generations.

The final principle reflects the ideas that "organic agriculture should prevent significant risks by adopting appropriate technologies and rejecting unpredictable ones, such as genetic engineering", and that increased efficiency and productivity should never come at the cost of risks to health and well-being. It also gives the official organic line on science, which is viewed as "necessary to ensure that organic agriculture is healthy, safe and ecologically sound. However, scientific knowledge alone is not sufficient. Practical experience, accumulated wisdom and traditional and indigenous knowledge offer valid solutions, tested by time."

Soil Association, is often described as having the most comprehensive rules.

Every organic product sold specifies the certifying body. Even if you don't see the name and logo, you'll see a code written in the form "Organic Certification UK3". For a list of the bodies and their numbers, see:

DEFRA www.defra.gov.uk/farm/organic

Is organic food definitely better for the environment?

There's no single, definitive answer to this question, because environmental impact can be measured in so many different ways, and because the relevant research is a long way from comprehensive. However, according to most non-partisan commentators – including a recent summary of the scientific evidence by the staff writers at *Nature* – organic farms are certainly more environmentally friendly in many ways.

Compared with conventional farms, for example, they tend to encourage greater **biodiversity**, such as insects, birds and other wildlife (because of the absence of pesticides and the fertility of the soil). They also tend to use less **energy** and create less global-warming CO_2 per kilo of produce (in part because man-made fertilizers are so energy-intensive to manufacture) and they generate less **waste** (such as fertilizer packaging). In some areas, such as phosphorous run-off into streams and the all-important question of retaining soil quality, a lack of many long-term comparative studies makes the benefits difficult to prove beyond doubt, but, according to *Nature*, "many studies" suggest that organic production lives up to its promises.

The United Nations Food and Agriculture Organization (FAO) seems even more convinced, claiming in 2003 that "If organic agriculture is given the consideration it merits, it has the potential to transform agriculture as the main tool for nature conservation. Reconciling biodiversity conservation and food production depends upon a societal commitment to supporting organic agriculture." They also noted that organic farming "encourages both spatial and temporal biodiversity … conserves soil and water resources and builds soil organic matter and biological processes".

That's not to say that organic is *necessarily* the most eco-friendly farming system in the world – for now or for the future. A growing number of

How cheap is cheap food?

Supporters of organic and other "alternative" agricultural systems claim that, while organic food is undeniably more expensive, this is partly because the price we pay for conventionally farmed goods at the supermarket check-out doesn't reflect their true cost. In the words of Jules Pretty, a professor at the University of Essex, food "only appears cheap in the shop because we are not encouraged to think of the hidden costs … we actually pay three times for our food – once at the till in the shop, a second time through taxes [for subsidies] … and a third time to clean up the environmental and health side effects". Here are some of the "external" costs – beyond the barcode price on the packet – that we, or others, pay for elsewhere.

▶ **The financial cost** The industrial agriculture machine needs financial oiling at many points. In the UK, this happens most demonstrably via billions of pounds' worth of direct subsidies, the majority of which go to the biggest, most intensive farms (though, to be fair, some also go to organic farms). However, the taxpayer also bails out industrial farming in less direct ways, such as cleaning up the massive environmental damage it causes. According to Jules Pretty's calculations, the *measurable* extra costs – such as dealing with the damage done to the environment and to human health – amount to around £2 billion a year (£35 per person) and that's without the massive costs of crises like BSE and foot and mouth. Sadly, consumers who buy organic, opting out of the industrial farming system, still have to pay for all these extras.

▶ **The human cost** People debate the health risks posed by agrochemical residues on and in our foods (see p.196). However, less widely discussed is the more measurable impact on farm and plantation workers who apply the stuff. Figures from the World Health Organization (www.who.int) and the World Resources Institute (www.wri.org) suggest that there are between 3.5 and 5 million acute pesticide poisonings annually, tens of thousands of which result in death. And the impact is particularly bad in the developing world, from where a significant proportion of our produce now comes: according to one study published in the *World Health Statistics Quarterly*, 99% of pesticide fatalities occur in poor countries, despite the fact that they only account for a minority of the world's pesticide use. The drive to make food ever cheaper has also arguably exacerbated the problem of child labour. An estimated 70% of the world's child labourers work in agriculture, especially on plantations growing coffee, tea and sugar (as well as tobacco and cotton).

▶ **The cost to animal welfare** When it comes to animal products, intensive farming is generally very bad news for livestock. And though things are slowly improving – veal crates and the worst battery farm cages are on their way out, for example – the conditions that many farm animals are subjected to are still atrocious. As described later in this chapter, they are often treated as mere commodities, living their short existences in chronically over-crowded sheds, never seeing natural light until being packed into a truck on slaughter day.

To this list we could also add the potential cost to human health of routine antibiotic use for livestock (see p.174) and the environmental cost of intensive meat farms (see p.168).

scientists advocate a middle ground that builds on organic concepts but doesn't rule out all synthetic inputs or GM processes – some of which, they claim, are less harmful (both to the environment and to health) than the "natural" alternatives. Still, this middle ground isn't something that's being adopted and it's not something that we're offered in the shops: for now, the choice is basically between the produce of "conventional" or organic farms, and the latter are indeed better environmentally.

Still, even if organic *farms* are a good thing for the environment, that doesn't necessarily mean the same can be said of organic *food*. At least, not according to two arguments often made by critics of the organic movement. The first is that a huge amount of organic produce is **flown or shipped** into the UK from the other side of the world. This contributes unnecessarily to climate change, via the CO_2 emissions of the planes and boats that transport it. It's a fair point – Europe and North America account for practically all organic food sales, yet around half of total organic food production takes place in Asia, Australia and Latin America. But it's also perhaps irrelevant: a criticism of food imports as a whole, not organic farming. If we grew more organic food at home, there'd be less need to import it.

The second argument is that organic farms tend to produce **less food per acre** than their more industrial counterparts. Therefore, if everyone went organic we'd either not have enough food, or we'd have to reclaim more land to use for farming by cutting down vast areas of forest, which of course would be an environmental catastrophe...

Could organic farming feed the world?

No one knows exactly how much food an exclusively organic world could grow, but by most estimates it would be substantially less than the amount currently produced. Even such keen organic exponents as Lord Melchett (former director of Greenpeace UK and himself an organic farmer) admit that it's an unknown quantity.

However, any question of feeding the world has to ask how much food the human population actually needs. After all, much of what we currently produce ends up squandered in the rearing of **cheap meat**. Indeed, as discussed later in this chapter, the world's rainforests *are* already being chopped down to make way for more farmland. But this isn't to grow organic carrots; the crop of choice is intensively farmed soya (much of it GM), the vast majority of which is used in the inefficient and environmentally burdensome process of feeding up cattle.

On these grounds, some in the organic movement claim that if we gave up our desire for cheap, intensively farmed meat (which we would have to, since huge monocrop soya farms aren't exactly suited to old-fashioned crop rotation), an exclusively organic world could easily feed itself.

Others aren't convinced we'd even need to change our diet very much. Several food economists have pointed out that many small farmers in poor countries have actually *increased* their yields by adopting organic practices. As Nadia Scialabba wrote in a report for the FAO, "In developing countries ... properly managed organic agriculture systems can increase agricultural productivity and restore the natural resource base."

Furthermore, it's clear that solving world hunger is as much to do with increasing **political will** and reducing waste as it is with producing more. Even according to the cautious figures of the US Department of Agriculture (www.usda.gov), one-fifth of America's food ends up in the bin – enough to feed the people who starve each year around the world twice over.

Still, even if a completely organic world could feed itself now, it may struggle in the future. After all, the global population is predicted to rise to around ten billion by 2050 according to the UN. The main sticking point is the fact that organic rules currently ban the use of man-made fertilizers, which have been central to boosting world food productivity in the last few decades, and which – though they can cause serious environmental problems when applied irresponsibly – are not necessarily all that bad when used carefully.

Hence it is sometimes said that green-minded consumers should certainly support organic farming, but should accept that, in the long run, the rules may need to be made slightly more "flexible", to allow, for example, carefully regulated additions of synthetic fertilizer.

Why is organic food so expensive?

There's no way of avoiding it: organic food is more expensive. And, largely because of the higher labour costs, it looks likely that this will never change. However, it's pretty clear that the "real" difference in price isn't quite as great as it currently appears, for two main reasons. First, conventional non-organic farming comes with a number of external costs that our taxes pay for, ranging from subsidies given to farmers to the clearing up of their environmental mess (see box on p.151) – not that organic shoppers are excluded from paying these costs, of course. Second, organic foods are usually treated as premium products by supermarkets, which means they charge a larger mark-up on them.

Whether organic food is worth the money is for each of us to decide. But bear in mind that you can always **be selective**. Just because you have no intention, or lack the cash, to go 100% organic, it needn't stop you from just buying, say, organic animal products – which score a hat-trick in terms of animal welfare, antibiotics and pollution issues (all of which are discussed later on in this chapter). Also, bear in mind that organic produce can very often be found at sub-supermarket prices via box-schemes, greengrocers and farmers' markets (see p.222).

Is it better for the farmers?

Organic farming can certainly offer some advantages to farm owners and workers. For example, it removes the considerable **health risks** associated with over-exposure to agrochemicals – a huge issue on developing-world plantations in particular (see pp.198–199). It also means that small farmers are less likely to find themselves getting caught up in a spiral of **debt** driven by the cost of chemical inputs. This is a common problem since, as soil quality goes down and chemical-resistant pests develop, farmers can find they need to spend more on inputs each year. As the UN has reported, "the conventional food production model ties farmers into conditions of dependence on large corporations to buy agricultural inputs (seeds, fertilizers, pesticides) and to sell their produce".

That said, it's certainly not the case that life is rosy for all farmers and workers growing organic produce. Though the organic codes on worker welfare are much better than nothing, the organic food we import from the third world still generally comes from farms where the employees see little reward for the fruits of their labour. And in the UK, too, while some farmers have profited from converting to organic, many others have struggled to make a decent income from their produce. Some blame the supermarkets for taking too big a slice of the organic pie, others the direct and indirect subsidies that make conventional farming appear cheaper than it really is.

Whatever the truth, there's an ever-increasing amount of organic **Fairtrade** produce available – and these products certainly offer farmers a better deal. And the Soil Association has recently launched its own Ethical Trade label (see p.201).

Not quite organic

Set up in 1991, **LEAF** (Linking Environment and Farming) is a UK farm certification scheme that aims to encourage an integrated and environmentally responsible approach to agriculture.

The rules are less strict than those of organics, but this, in theory at least, means that the scheme can appeal to the majority of growers who, for financial or other reasons, haven't decided to go properly organic. So pesticides are allowed, for example, but must be used responsibly. Though it's been around for more than a decade, the leaf "marque", as they call it, is one label that you're still unlikely to come across in most food outlets. Waitrose is currently the only major retailer involved.

The **Wholesome Food Association** (WFA), meanwhile, has similar rules to organic certifications – including no synthetic inputs – but the system is based on trust rather than inspections and paperwork. The idea is that farmers interested in ecologically sound production and local sales can participate without the cost of official organic certification.

For more information see:

LEAF www.leafmarque.com
WFA www.wholesomefood.org

Is organic food healthier?

Organic foods are widely marketed as safer and healthier, but the benefits are not universally accepted. The claims fall into two separate categories, the first of which relates to the potentially harmful effects of **pesticide residues** in our food. Unsurprisingly, organic foods carry incomparably fewer of these residues, and few people deny that this is a good thing. However, many toxicologists aren't convinced that the levels of pesticide residues in conventional food – even those that exceed the official safety limits – are a serious cause for concern (for more on this topic, see p.196).

The second issue is whether organic foods are more **nutritious**. There have been studies showing organic food to contain higher levels of vitamin C, essential minerals, cancer-preventing phytonutrients and other beneficial things. But the differences tend to be slight, and there's a possibility that organic food may bring risks, too, such as – according to at least one study – a higher proportion of certain bugs in chicken meat.

Where to buy organic food and drink

Though the supermarkets now stock a pretty wide range of organic foods, there remains a strained relationship between organic farmers and the retail giants in whose stores the majority of their produce is sold. One point of contention is the issue of profit margins: like all farmers, organic producers feel that supermarkets' near-monopoly powers give them the ability to demand unreasonably low prices while making massive profits.

But beyond this, supermarkets also have various habits that many feel are the very antithesis of the organic philosophy: flying in produce from abroad, even when UK stock is available; packing organic fruit and veg in completely unnecessary plastic packaging; and contributing to the corporatization of the organic movement itself by favouring large organic suppliers rather than independent local farms.

For these reasons – and various others (see p.216) – you might prefer to buy your organic food via local box schemes, farmers' markets and farm shops. To find them, turn to p.222. Or, for organic views and news, visit:

Plan Organic www.planorganic.com
Links Organic www.linksorganic.com
About Organics www.aboutorganics.co.uk
DEFRA www.defra.gov.uk/farm/organic

Food transport

Meals and miles

Europe has been importing food and drink from far and wide for millennia – tea from China, spices from India, coffee from Ethiopia. But the globalization of modern food markets is on a completely different scale. These days we fly in fruit from the global South when it's **out of season** in the North, and we ship in goods that we could grow in the UK, but which can be **sourced more cheaply** from elsewhere.

Though only a small proportion of the food produced in the world is traded internationally – probably around 90% is consumed in the country where it is grown – the distance travelled by the food we put on our plates in the UK is thought to have roughly doubled in the last two decades. Today, the contents of an average shopping basket of goods – including

Let's play swap!

Regardless of the debated costs and benefits of our increasingly globalized food industry, international trade in food is unquestionably more wasteful and environmentally damaging than it needs to be. For such is the weird and wonderful world of global commodity markets that countries often end up exchanging exactly the same products. Local specialities changing hands, you might think. But no: even such generic products as milk are exchanged. In *Stopping the Great Food Swap – Relocalising Europe's Food Supply*, Green Party MEP Caroline Lucas documents this phenomenon, drawing on data from the UN's FAO Food Balance Sheets. Here are just a few of her examples:

▶ In 1998 the UK imported 60,000 tonnes of poultry meat from the Netherlands and exported more than 30,000 tonnes to the same country.

▶ In the same year the UK exported 109,533 live pigs while importing 203,174.

▶ In 1997 we imported 126 million litres of liquid milk (powdered is another story) and exported 270 million litres.

To read the report online, visit:

The Great Food Swap www.carolinelucasmep.org.uk

organic foods – can be the result of tens of thousands of miles' journeying, by road, sea and increasingly air (see box overleaf).

For food grown in the UK, too, the distance from "farm to fork" is bigger than ever, not least because supermarket systems rely on everything being delivered to the shop via massive distribution centres. Since these are few and far between (Sainsbury's only has a dozen or so, for example), long truck journeys are inevitable. One much-cited study traced vegetables on sale in a supermarket in Evesham: they were grown just up the road, but had arrived via a huge round trip taking in Hereford, Dyfed and Manchester. Some defenders of the supermarket-style system – such as Tony Blair's "rural tsar", Lord Haskins – claim that this may actually be better than millions of half-full smaller vans making shorter journeys. But it's a contentious argument.

The most obvious problem with extra "food miles" is their environmental impact, especially in terms of **global warming**. According to a 2006 government report, UK food transport now accounts for 18 million tonnes of CO_2 – and also costs the country £9 billion in congestion, accidents and other externalities. Petrol used to transport food in vans or lorries at least has a tax payable on it, but aviation fuel – used, for example,

Long-distance dining

In a study called *Eating Oil*, the campaign group Sustain measured the miles travelled by our foods and the energy that the transportation consumes. One of their case studies looked at a basket of imported foods you might pick up in any UK supermarket:

From abroad to the UK

▶ **5kg of chicken from Thailand** 10,691 miles by ship

▶ **1kg of runner beans from Zambia** 4912 miles by plane

▶ **2kg of carrots from Spain** 1000 miles by lorry

▶ **0.5kg of mangetout from Zimbabwe** 5130 miles by plane

▶ **5kg of potatoes from Italy** 1521 miles by lorry

From the UK to the distribution centre

▶ **1kg of sprouts produced in Britain** 125 miles by lorry

▶ **All the imports to the distribution centre** 625 miles by lorry

From the distribution centre to the store

▶ **British sprouts, plus all the imports (total weight 13.5kg)** 360 miles by lorry

Add it all up and, collectively, these goods would have travelled almost **25,000 miles**, using up 52 megajoules of energy in doing so – equivalent to boiling the kettle for around 700 cups of tea. By contrast, an equivalent basket of seasonal produce from a farmers' market went only 376 miles, using up just one megajoule (around 13 cups of tea).

Organic foods aren't likely to be any more local. The UK imports the overwhelming majority of its organic produce, partly because we don't produce enough, and

to fly in out-of-season strawberries from South Africa to the UK– isn't taxed at all (see p.302).

It may not always be the case that local food is more eco-friendly. As economist Philippe Legrain argues, "growing Kiwi fruit in heated greenhouses in England gobbles up more energy than transporting them from New Zealand". This may be true, as long as they are shipped rather than flown. But the point only relates to "exotic" produce that is hard to grow in the UK – not the majority of food imports.

Environmental damage isn't the only criticism that local-food advocates make of our increasingly long-distance dining. In the case of shipping live

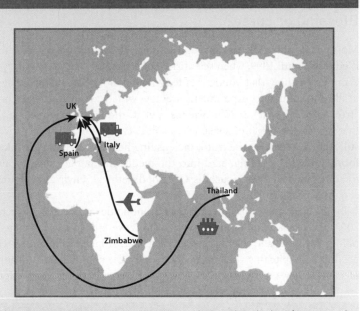

partly because imports are cheaper. Sustain worked out that a basket of 26 imported organic products could have travelled nearly 150,000 miles, releasing as much CO_2 as "an average four bedroom household does through cooking meals over eight months".

For more information see:

Sustain www.sustainweb.org

animals, longer-than-necessary distances raise the likelihood not only of animal welfare abuses but also of the **spreading of diseases** such as foot and mouth. And these can end up costing astronomical sums of money: the total bill for the UK's foot and mouth crisis of 2001–02, including lost tourism revenue, is estimated to be around £10 billion.

On the other hand, as already discussed, the trade in food has been a key source of income for many developing countries, so that needs to be factored in when deciding whether to favour local or foreign foods. See p.46 for more on this topic.

GM food
Blessing or curse?

Most people in the UK had never given much thought to genetically modified foods until 1999, when scientist **Árpád Pusztai** caused an outcry by claiming to show that young rats fed GM potatoes were showing signs of ill health. Pusztai's experiments are now widely accepted to have been "irrevocably flawed", as *New Scientist* put it, though some greens claim that he was the target of a shameless smear campaign and that his work still stands. Whatever the truth, the ensuing health scare about **frankenfoods** provided a springboard into the media and public consciousness for other related issues, such as GM food's ethical, environmental and economic implications.

By the time the government staged a public debate on the subject in 2003, the overwhelming majority of Britons were dead against biotechnology for food, and the big supermarkets had stopped selling most GM products. Despite this, the first UK licence for the commercial cultivation of a GM crop was given out just a few months later. In the event, the licen-

GM food: what, when, where?

Genetic modification is a kind of **biotechnology** in which the DNA of an organism, most commonly a crop, is altered. This can be done either by changing an existing part of the DNA or by adding a new gene from elsewhere – usually from a bacteria, a virus or another plant – allowing scientists to "cross" two organisms that couldn't cross in nature. GM has been a theoretical possibility ever since the discovery of DNA in 1953, but it was in the early 1980s that the techniques were actually developed, and in the 1990s that GM foods became a commercial reality.

Though the potential applications are very wide-ranging, the only commercially available GM food crops at the time of writing are **soya**, **maize**, **cotton** and **canola** (with wheat probably on the way soon). The majority of current modified plants are engineered to be **herbicide tolerant** – capable of dealing with special herbicides that would kill normal crops. The rest have been made **insect resistant**, with their cells modified to produce an insecticide known as Bt toxin. Some GM crops are both herbicide tolerant and insect resistant.

A public outcry has temporarily halted GM planting in Britain, but there's been no such hold up in much of the rest of the world. At the time of writing there are around six million farmers growing GM crops on roughly 75 million hectares (approximately twice the land space of the UK). **Monsanto** soya products account for the majority of these, with most of the planted area being in the US and Argentina, followed by Canada and China.

see – Bayer CropScience – decided to abandon the UK as a potential market, which means that no GM crops are likely to be grown in Britain for some years to come. But modified ingredients and animal feed continue to be imported to, and sold in, the UK, and the arguments have broadened from questions over the safety and ethics of "tampering with nature" to claims that, by shunning GM crops, Western shoppers are inadvertently harming both the environment and people in the third world.

The following pages outline the cases for and against "biotech" food, before looking at how to avoid GM in the shops.

Health concerns

There is nothing concrete to suggest that the current generation of GM food is more harmful or less healthy than any other foods, and the American population, as the biotech industry is always keen to remind us, has been eating it for years with no measurable side effects. However, critics such as Michael Meacher – the Environment Minister sacked by Tony Blair after expressing scepticism about GM – claim that this isn't enough proof of their safety, pointing out that there have been no proper "human feeding trials", in the US or elsewhere, to rigorously screen the health of GM consumers.

Furthermore, not all scientists are convinced that the current laws, which require biotech firms to show that their crops are "substantially equivalent" to their non-GM counterparts, are enough to rule out potential increases in the levels of plant toxins or reductions in the levels of nutrients. And the tests that *have* been done have been largely carried out by the GM companies themselves, and have been, according to Meacher, "scientifically vacuous".

Overall, the scientific consensus seems to be that the risk of serious damage to human health is low. But if a danger were found at some point down the road – by which time the GM crop in question would probably have widely cross-pollinated with its conventional cousins – it could be almost impossible to solve.

Environmental impact

Environmental groups have led the campaign against GM, but biotech advocates say they're shooting themselves in the foot, since GM technology could offer considerable environmental benefits. Their claims are numerous. Insect-resistant plants – with "natural" pest resistance built in – can mean **less pesticide** being pumped into fields, hence improving soil

Anti-GM food protesters ripping up biotech crops in Banbury, Oxfordshire
Photo: Adrian Arbib

fertility and reducing both pollution and poisoning of farmers. Herbicide-resistant crops, meanwhile, allow for special "designer" weedkillers that are safe to use and quick to break down in the soil, and which make it easier for farmers to adopt **non-tillage** (plough-free) techniques, which reduce soil erosion and degradation.

GM could also make possible higher-yield crops, or ones able to grow in soil that's been left saline by irrigation (pumping water onto crops often results in salty groundwater rising up and damaging the soil). Both these technologies could help the world meet its ever-increasing demands for food without having to cut down forests to claim new farmland. And the applications aren't limited to food: biotechnology is already being used to research ecologically sound replacements for products such as bleach and formaldehyde.

The green movement is largely unconvinced by these claims. After all, in the case of herbicide-resistant crops, there's as much evidence to suggest they end up **increasing weedkiller use and harming wildlife** as there is to suggest the opposite. In parts of Argentina, for example, the development of weeds resistant to the designer herbicides has led to huge amounts of other herbicides being used, harming local people's health and crops. There's also the concern that different herbicide-resistant GM crops will cross-pollinate with each other, resulting in **super-weeds** resistant to multiple herbicides. Even the British government's **farm-scale evaluations** of four GM varieties suggested that three could be harmful to wildlife. And that was comparing them to their equivalents from conventional intensive farms; a more meaningful study would compare GM crops to organically grown produce, environmentalists claim.

As for increasing the world's food supply, that's also a red herring, the greens argue. Most GM crops are simply supplying feed for the intensive livestock industry, the land for which is now one of the most important drivers of the disastrous clearance of Amazon rainforest (see p.171). Hence we should be looking to consume less meat and redistribute more, not simply increase production.

There is one area where some GM critics concede that biotechnology may have proved environmentally beneficial. Pest-resistant crops – such as **cotton plants** engineered to produce Bt toxin, the pesticide based on a naturally occurring bacterium, and used by many organic farmers – are widely recognized to have helped reduce pesticide use in China and elsewhere (see p.229). But the question remains as to whether we should release any GM crops into the wild without absolute certainty that they won't cause environmental or health problems. After all, **contamination** (or "cross-pollination", depending on who you're talking to) is inevitable, as farmers in the US and Canada have already found. And even if this doesn't prove dangerous, it limits consumer choice and risks the livelihoods of **organic farmers**, since no GM-tainted crop can be sold as organic.

Some GM advocates, such as molecular biologist Conrad Lichtenstein, claim that organic farmers should simply embrace biotechnology: "GM technology … is by definition a very organic technology", he once wrote. "There is no contradiction between organic and GM." Most organic farmers and consumers beg to differ.

Corporate control of the food chain

No part of the GM debate is as heated as the claims about the potential benefits for the world's poor. The biotech industry and the US government talk of **high-yield crops** able to resist harsh winters or droughts, which could reduce hunger and increase food security in regions afflicted with problematic climates and soils. And special nutritionally improved staples have already been designed to help farmers and their children get the vitamins and nutrients they are currently lacking.

True, these have so far failed to live up to their creators' promises. So-called **golden rice**, for example, aimed at combating the vitamin A deficiency which blinds and kills thousands of children in poor countries every week, needs to be consumed in vast quantities to have the desired effect. Still, it's "much better than nothing", GM scientist Michael Wilson told Rough Guides, and we should remember that this is only "first-generation technology". At some stage, life-saving and environmentally beneficial GM crops are inevitably going to become reality and, by shunning biotechnology as consumers, we risk being the "GM Jeremiahs" – in the words of the *Guardian* columnist Nick Cohen – who slow this essential process down.

It's a contentious case, made all the more so by the fact that many leaders of poor countries, as well as most anti-poverty groups, have spoken out against GM. In 1998, for example, a group of African delegates to the UN issued a joint statement saying that they "strongly object that the image of the poor and hungry from our countries is being used by giant multinational corporations to push a technology that is neither safe, environmentally friendly nor economically beneficial to us". ActionAid, meanwhile, considers GM crops to be currently "largely irrelevant for the poorest farming communities – only 1% of GM research is aimed at crops used by poor people – and they may pose a threat to their livelihoods".

Even when pro-poor GM crops do evolve, some argue they are failing to deal with the underlying problems. In *So Shall We Reap*, for example, Colin Tudge writes that vitamin A rice is the "heroic, Western high-tech solution to the disaster that Western commercial high-tech has itself created", pointing out that vitamin A deficiency doesn't exist "so long as people have horticulture", which has always been part of "traditional farming". The problem isn't low-tech rice, he claims, but a global agricultural ideology based on "obsessive mono-culture" and global trade.

But the main concern of ActionAid is that "four multinationals dominate GM technology – giving them unprecedented control over their GM seeds and the chemicals that go with them". The companies in question are Monsanto, Syngenta, Bayer CropScience and Dupont. Like many other GM sceptics, ActionAid worry that these companies' virtual monopoly on **seed distribution**, combined with a lack of education in some countries about the legal implications of using GM seeds (for example, the requirement to buy new seeds each year), allows them to effectively force their products on farmers, who will then find themselves taking on avoidable debt.

Moreover, the big companies are registering ever more **patents**, giving them the sole rights to perform certain types of genetic manipulation on certain plants. So even if public-sector organizations stumble across potentially positive GM crop developments, they are likely to find them all wrapped up in legal red tape.

The biotech companies tell us not to worry – that they are out to apply their technologies for the good of the world. Yet they tend to behave in a way that suggests consumers would be right to be sceptical of such claims. For example, the firms spend millions on **political donations and lobbying**. According to a Center for Responsive Politics report from 2003, biotech firms have made "close to $26 million in individual, PAC and soft money contributions since 1989". And, along with the Biotechnology Industry Organization (their main trade group), they "also spent nearly $143 million to lobby Congress, the White House and the Food and Drug Administration between 1998 and 2002". And that's only the start of it, according to campaigners. For full critical resumés of these companies, check out www.corporatewatch.org.uk.

In the short term at least, some farmers are clearly already benefiting from GM technologies – or thousands of them wouldn't be voluntarily choosing biotech crops in Argentina, China, India and elsewhere. And, in the longer term, there is no reason why GM shouldn't be part of a solution for a better world. Certainly the UN Food and Agriculture Organization thinks so: "biotechnology is capable of benefiting small, resource-poor farmers" was one conclusion of a recent *State of Food and Agriculture* report.

But whether the world *needs* GM crops, whether they're part of the solution or the problem, and whether it's the industry or consumers who are holding up any potential positive benefits, is highly questionable. After all, if crops truly beneficial to the world's poor are proved to be effective and safe, and offered at reasonable prices and terms, it will surely take more than a few European fears about modified cornflakes to stop them being taken up around the world.

GM foods: what's in the shops?

At the time of writing, no GM crops are commercially grown in the UK. And since Bayer CropScience decided to stop pursuing its goal of commercializing its **Chardon LL** modified maize (the only GM crop given government approval), it looks unlikely that there will be any British GM cultivation in the immediate future. In mid-2006, an application was made for a trial of blight-resistant GM potato, but it remains to be seen whether the project will win approval. Either way, genetically modified crops are still imported from abroad, both as **ingredients** and as **animal feed**.

After a tightening of EU law in April 2004, all food derived from a GM organism must be **labelled** as such. And this includes all products that contain individual ingredients with a GM content of 0.9% or higher. So if a brand of biscuit, say, contained a small quantity of soya oil, which itself was 1.5% GM, a label would be required. If the soya oil, for "accidental or technically unavoidable" reasons, was 0.5% GM, no label would be needed. In practice, though, this is all academic, since the major UK supermarkets, and many of the major food processors, have imposed their own stricter standards, and don't sell anything that would come close to requiring a label. The **Co-op**, for example, won't sell any foods containing ingredients consisting of more than 0.1% GM-derived produce.

The major exception to the EU's strict GM labelling rules relates to **animal products**. Despite the fact that most biotech crops are grown as animal feed, there's no requirement to label meat, fish, eggs or dairy products that came from farm animals fed GM crops. There isn't any evidence to suggest that GM DNA can be passed from animal feed into meat or milk, but anti-GM campaigners such as Greenpeace point out that this hole in the labelling laws makes it **impossible for consumers to boycott** biotech foods completely. That said, Marks & Spencer have stopped selling products from animals which have been fed GM crops. As for the rest, Friends of the Earth rate Sainsbury's, the Co-op and Waitrose as having "room for improvement" and Tesco, Morrisons, ASDA, Iceland, Somerfield and Budgens as being "bottom of the pile".

Similarly, no labels are required on food produced with the aid of, but not actually containing, GM-derived substances. For example, the **chymosin enzyme** – "rennet" – used to separate the curds and whey in cheese production is usually produced with modified yeast or bacteria (the main exception being traditional cheeses made with rennet from calves' stomachs). Finally, certain GM-derived foods produced before April 2004 may still be on sale and not labelled. But this only includes products – such as vegetable oil from GM rapeseed – that have been processed to the point of being chemically indistinguishable from the non-GM equivalents.

There are rules also for cafés and restaurants. Owners aren't obliged to specify GM ingredients on the menu but the staff must – in theory at least – be able to inform you, if asked, of any dishes that would require a label if sold in a shop.

Going GM-free

As explained above, most people in the UK aren't currently buying or consuming GM foods in any serious quantities. But if you'd rather be consuming none at all, including products from animals fed on GM crops, you may want to check out Greenpeace's near-comprehensive online shopping guide, which gives thumbs up or down to hundreds of products, including supermarket own-brands:

Greenpeace GM Shopping Guide www.greenpeace.org.uk/Products/GM

Alternatively, buy organic, since the organic rules ban all use of GM technologies. Even this may not completely remove all traces of modification from your diet, since accidental contamination of organic food by GM crops has already been spotted. According to a study published by Mark Partridge and Denis J Murphy in the *British Food Journal*, out of 25 "organic/health foods containing soya beans ... ten tested positively for the presence of GM material"; eight of these were labelled organic. Still, it's about as close as you can get to completely sidestepping GM.

GM links

To read more about GM from various different perspectives, see:

Biotechnology Information Resource www.nal.usda.gov/bic
European Federation of Biotechnology www.efbpublic.org
Food Standards Agency www.foodstandards.gov.uk
Friends of the Earth www.foe.co.uk
Genewatch www.genewatch.org
Union of Concerned Scientists www.ucsusa.org

Eating animals
Waste, pollution and the ethics of meat

The consumption of animal products raises a number of ethical issues. The most obvious is the long-standing question of whether it's right or wrong to eat animals in the first place, as discussed in the box on vegetarianism below. Others include the hidden environmental and social costs of meat production, the dangers of routinely administered antibiotics and concerns over animal welfare.

The ethics of vegetarianism and veganism

"Ethical", humanely reared meat is all well and good, but is it really justifiable to kill any animals simply so we can have the pleasure of eating them? This must be one of the longest-running of all ethical consumerism debates: exclusively non-animal diets have been relatively common in Asia since the development of ancient religions such as Jainism, and Europe first grappled with the concept just as long ago. Pythagoras, Plato, Socrates and Ovid all expressed doubts about meat.

However, Western vegetarianism as we know it today didn't really take off until the beginning of the nineteenth century, when the tireless campaigning of the appropriately named **William Cowherd**, a reverend from Salford, started the ball rolling. The term itself was coined in 1847 by the UK's newly formed **Vegetarian Society**, which made a point of deriving it from *vegetus*, Latin for lively, rather than vegetable (though this seems a bit academic considering that both words come from the same Latin root). Numbers have grown ever since, and today surveys suggest that 4–6% of the UK population describe themselves as vegetarian, with many more consciously limiting their meat intake.

Besides individual views about killing animals unnecessarily, numerous more objective ethical arguments can be made for vegetarianism. The two most convincing are that most meat and farmed fish is **wasteful** to produce, and that **animal welfare** standards are often very low (both subjects are explored elsewhere in this chapter). Organic and other non-intensive meat and fish is available, of course, but it's more expensive, harder to find in restaurants and still typically more wasteful than non-animal foods.

Some other arguments, however, such as the idea that we're herbivore by evolutionary design, are flawed. People disagree about the exact diets of our ancestors, but it's actually pretty clear that early humans, like the chimps they evolved from, ate at least some meat when it was available. As for claims of better **health**, vegetarians do tend to live longer and suffer fewer serious problems, but it's difficult to work out how much of this is due to a meat-free diet, and how much of it is down to other attributes that, according to the stats, happen to be common to most vegetarians,

Environmental and social issues

Beyond animal welfare concerns and the standard moral questions that surround killing animals for food, there are some serious ecological problems with our consumption of animal products – especially those which come from intensive farms.

Many of the problems stem from the fact that most animal products are **inefficient to produce**. Take beef, for instance. There's no single definitive figure, but producing a single kilo of intensively farmed beef typically takes in the region of 10 kilos of grain for feed. Beef is among the worst

such as a middle-class background and general health consciousness. Still, whatever the reasons, most vegetarian diets tend to be comparatively healthy.

But what about **eggs and dairy products**? The rearing of egg-laying chickens (p.182) and dairy cows (p.185) is associated with animal-welfare problems at least as great as those of the meat trade. Egg-laying chickens are killed after only weeks of life, ending up as meat in pet food, while dairy products rely on a constant stream of calves being born, most of which are slaughtered for meat (if they weren't, we'd end up with an ever-growing bovine population). So "lacto" vegetarians still kill animals, you might argue, and intensively farmed milk and eggs are not necessarily morally superior to, for example, organic, free-range chicken.

These contradictions lie behind the growing number of **vegans**, who abstain from all animal products, including dairy, eggs and even honey. Veganism grew out of the vegetarian movement in the first half of the twentieth century, and it generally sees itself as the logical conclusion of that movement (as is implied by the term "vegan": the beginning and the end of the word vegetarian). It is a much bigger commitment than vegetarianism, ruling out many foods and guaranteeing a considerable degree of inconvenience when eating out or travelling. But it's ultimately a more coherent ideology, at least from the animal-welfare and ecological perspectives.

Still, even veganism isn't enough for some, who ask why we should draw the line at plants. **Fruitarians** only eat foods – such as fruits, berries, olives and tomatoes – that can be eaten without deliberately harming any organism, and also save energy by eliminating the need for cooking, refrigeration or even washing up. This is one branch of ethical consumerism that it's hard to see ever really taking off.

For more information, visit:

Vegetarian Society www.vegsoc.org
Vegan Society www.vegansociety.com
The Fruitarian Site www.fruitarian.com
Beyond Vegetarianism www.beyondveg.com

culprits, but similar problems apply to most meats, farmed fish and, to a slightly lesser extent, dairy and eggs. Obviously all these foods have relatively high energy and protein levels, so a kilo of feed is not directly comparable to a kilo of meat. But even taking this into account, the simple fact remains: we get less food out of most farm animals than we put in.

Animal produce *can* be made far more efficiently on **mixed, closed-system farms** of the type often favoured by small-scale and organic growers. Chickens, for instance, can be fed on scraps that might otherwise go to waste. Equally, some animals graze on land that would be no good for

Making meat

The exact quantity of feed required to make each kilogram of meat or fish varies according to breed and farming method – and there are also great differences between the figures favoured by campaigners, on the one hand, and the meat industry, on the other. The following "middle-of-the-road" estimates come from the non-partisan Council for Agricultural Science and Technology.

Kilos of feed required to produce 1 kilo of food

Farmed fish	1.5–2.0	
Poultry meat	2.1–3.0	
Pork	4.0–5.5	
Beef	10	

The amount of water required to produce certain meats is also often very high (though naturally the significance of this fact varies from country to country). According to a study by D Pimentel, published in *Bioscience*:

Litres of water required to produce 1 kilo of food

Potatoes	500	
Wheat	900	
Maize	1400	
Rice	1910	
Soya beans	2000	
Chicken	3500	
Beef	100,000	... and 180 more

crops, with a diet largely consisting of grasses, perhaps supplemented with crop byproducts. For these reasons, the most efficient food production systems of all *do* actually include some animal products. But in reality, the majority of farmed animals consume feed that could be more effectively used elsewhere.

This is no minor issue. Global meat consumption has rocketed by around 500% since 1950 – the world today contains around twice as many chickens as humans, plus 1 billion pigs, roughly 1.3 billion cows and 1.8 billion sheep and goats – and there is no sign of this slowing down. According to agricultural commentator Colin Tudge, if the current growth rate of animal-product consumption continues, by 2050, livestock will consume as much food as the entire human population did in 1970.

This rising demand for animal feed has a number of implications, one of which is a growing demand for farmland to grow feed crops such as soya. This is already driving the destruction of **rainforest** in the Amazon and elsewhere, causing a whole raft of environmental problems.

A second implication, in the slightly longer term, is a possible threat to the **food security** of the world's poorest people. Unless rainforest clearance and/or a revolution in farm technology manages to keep up both with rising meat consumption and with rising global population, we may soon get to the point where there won't be enough crops to feed all the people and all the farm animals. At this point, demand will outstrip supply and the price of crops will rise. The price of meat will go up more than basic foods, of course, since meat farmers will have to pay more for feed. But such is global wealth inequality that those who consume animal products may be able to absorb this rise in price far more easily than those in poor countries, who already struggle to buy enough basic crops to feed themselves and their families. No one knows exactly how this scenario will play out, but it's certainly a cause for concern.

Other impacts

Even where rainforests aren't at risk, the intensive production of animal products creates a range of environmental burdens. For one thing, the production of feed crops and the farming of animals uses up an astonishing amount of water. It can take 100,000 litres of water to make a single kilo of beef (see box). This isn't usually a big problem in the UK and many other rainy countries. But considering that fresh water stocks are already close to being exhausted in much of the developing world, it's a potentially massive issue when the meat is produced there.

Secondly, the world's livestock produce more than 10 billion tonnes of **mineral-rich effluent** each year. While manure adds to soil fertility in mixed, closed-system farms, it can be a major polluter in intensive farms, finding its way into rivers and groundwater, and raising nitrogen and phosphorous levels higher than aquatic species can survive. Its ammonia content can also contribute to acid rain.

Last but not least there's **global warming**. Astonishingly, farm animals are thought to account for around 10% of the world's greenhouse-gas emissions. Part of this contribution is due to the fact that meat production uses a lot of oil – to power farm machines, make fertilizer for feed crops, transport feed and animals, and so on. All told, meat requires around 10–30 times as much energy input per kilogram as corn or soya. But it's also because cows and other livestock annually burp and fart a staggering 80 million tonnes of **methane**, a greenhouse gas that's over twenty times more potent than CO_2.

The solution?

Various groups claim they have the solution to meat's environmental problems. **Vegetarians** advocate simply cutting out meat from our diet; **localizers** (see p.46) argue that we should move away from a global free market in food, encouraging countries to focus on self-sufficiency through ecologically friendly "mixed" farms; **GM exponents** (see p.160) look to biotechnology as a means of increasing crop productivity and therefore increasing supply to match demand; and some food economists have even suggested the implementation of a global food-chain tax, to add to the cost of meat.

As for what individual ethical consumers can do, the basic facts are simple enough: if you really want to reduce your environmental footprint – in terms of climate change, pollution, water use and deforestation – try to consume fewer animal products, and especially those from intensive farms.

Animal welfare

Even if intensive meat production wasn't environmentally and economi-cally problematic, there are serious issues with the conditions that many animals are subjected to. Specific welfare concerns and recommended ethical options are dealt with in the following sections on red meat, poultry and eggs, dairy and fish. But first here's a quick look at two

Like a lamb to slaughter: animal transport

Farm animals are often transported long distances by lorry within the UK, on their way either to slaughter – as most local abattoirs have been shut down since the 1970s – or to be fattened up elsewhere. Whatever the reason, transport can cause enormous distress to the animals. According to campaign groups such as Compassion in World Farming, animals are often packed into metal containers, struggling for air and in some cases suffering injury or death on the way.

Most UK supermarkets impose a **maximum journey time** for the animals used for their own-label meat, but in general they still allow around eight hours for cows, pigs and sheep and eight to twelve hours for poultry – far more than the EU vets and welfare experts suggest is acceptable. Moreover, according to some critics, supermarkets sometimes move live animals just to add a label to their products: "Scotch beef" and "Welsh lamb", George Monbiot has written, "come from animals pastured in Scotland or Wales for just two weeks. They are trucked all over the United Kingdom so that the stores can change their designation and thus raise the price of their meat."

Importing and exporting live animals is also big business, with millions of animals each year making huge journeys by road (England to Italy takes around 45 hours) or sea (Australia to the Middle East takes weeks). From the UK, exports are down since the foot and mouth crisis and since a 1997 law imposed a maximum eight-hour journey time for the worst vehicles. But campaigners claim that unacceptable conditions are still endured by animals for prolonged periods.

The obvious way forward for concerned consumers is to favour locally produced meat wherever possible.

schemes that claim to guarantee better levels of welfare, one specifically – from the RSPCA – and one as part of a wider set of assurances from the National Farmers' Union (NFU). Ironically, neither is as strict as the **Soil Association's organic standard** (see p.150), which remains the best guarantee of decent treatment of farm animals.

To see how the various supermarkets compare in terms of their animal welfare standards, see p.221.

British Farm Standard

Launched just after the turn of the new millennium in response to growing public distrust of the agricultural sector, the **NFU's Little Red Tractor** scheme labels meat, dairy, veg and cereals that come from farms conforming to British Farm Standards – a set of "exacting" standards relating to the environment, food safety and animal welfare.

BRITISH FARM STANDARD

The scheme sets out some very basic minimum animal welfare standards – such as outdoor animals having access to shelter – but, according to campaign groups such as Compassion in World Farming, the rules still allow such animal-unfriendly practices as narrow farrowing pig crates, battery cages for laying hens, restrictive feeding practices, combinations of breeds and diets that can lead to animal health problems, debeaking of chickens, and tail docking and teeth clipping of pigs. Friends of the Earth have also complained that it doesn't rule out GM or cover the responsible use of pesticides. Find out more on both sides of the argument at:

NFU www.littleredtractor.org.uk
CIWF www.redtractortruth.com

The antibiotics issue

Along with their diet, many animals in intensive farms – especially pigs and poultry, but also cattle and fish – routinely receive drugs. These are mostly **antibiotics**, both to stimulate growth and to prevent the diseases that thrive in overcrowded conditions. Animal welfare campaigners object to this because growth promoters are thought to cause health problems and because they push animals beyond their natural limits. But equally troubling is the potential threat to human health via the growth of **antibiotic resistance**. As "super-bugs" in hospitals have shown, resistance to our most useful drugs is on the up. For instance, a significant proportion of cases of the biggest source of food poisoning in the UK, campylobacter, are now untreatable by antibiotics. Though not all scientists agree, many microbiologists think we're sitting on a time bomb.

Over-prescription in humans is certainly part of the problem – perhaps even the biggest part – but intensive farming is now widely accepted as a potential breeding ground for resistant bugs, which, once developed, may be passed on to humans via meat, milk or even possibly crops grown from animal fertilizer. The chicken industry quietly went back on its much-publicized phasing out of antibiotic growth promoters, but such additives were finally made illegal across the EU at the start of 2006. Still, growth promoters only account for a small proportion of the hundreds of tonnes of veterinary antibiotics used each year, and there are no plans to phase out the rest, which are routinely administered on a prevention-is-easier-than-cure basis.

Drugging animals also raises the question of carcinogenic or otherwise harmful **drug residues** in our meat or milk. Strict regulations setting out periods of "withdrawal" for animals given drugs theoretically avoid this, but various studies have shown residues in excess of the legal maximums, suggesting farmers don't always observe the rules.

If you want to avoid routinely administered antibiotics, buy organic or shop at Marks & Spencer, which claims to enforce a strict policy governing the use of antibiotics by their suppliers.

RSPCA Freedom Food

Established in 1994, the Freedom Food scheme labels eggs, dairy, chicken, pork and some prepared foods. The idea is to label products from animals that – from farm through to abattoir – haven't been denied any of the basic "five freedoms": freedom from **fear and distress**, freedom from **hunger and thirst**, freedom from **discomfort**, freedom from **pain, injury and disease**, freedom to express **normal behaviour**.

As interpreted by the scheme, these freedoms don't preclude many unpleasant practices – hens might still be debeaked and kept in high-density sheds, for example – and this, combined with the fact that farmers pay to join, has led to criticism from some quarters. While Animal Liberation Australia's claims that the RSPCA is "in bed with the egg industry … in the business of harming animals" are a little over the top, it's true that the scheme is laxer than you might imagine, considering who runs it. That said, the RSPCA clearly set the standards at a level which they thought would get the label into the mainstream, rather than limiting it to the "premium" sector. And the rules are certainly far better than nothing.

For more information, or a full list of products available at each supermarket, visit the RSPCA's website. Or for stricter animal welfare standards, go organic.

RSPCA www.rspca.org.uk

Red meat
Pigs, cows & sheep

In addition to the general issues just discussed, each type of meat raises its own specific animal-welfare concerns, with those relating to pork products being perhaps the most pressing.

Pork products

Pigs are highly intelligent social animals – usually compared to dogs in the animal IQ stakes – but they're often reared with little respect for their well-being. Pig farming techniques have become increasingly industrial over the past few decades. Farms are growing to epic sizes (in the US, there are now individual farms with more than a million swine) and the sow has been transformed into a meat-making machine. Relatively recently, female pigs would give birth to around five piglets a year, but 25 is not uncommon today. This is thanks to a mixture of **intensive breeding** practices and the technique of removing piglets from their mothers very early, to maximize the number of possible pregnancies per year.

The UK is better in terms of pig welfare than most of the EU, where many pigs still spend their whole lives in **sow stalls** – barren cages, often so small that the pig can't even turn around – or chained to the floor with a **tether**. Routine "docking" of tails and clipping of teeth is also standard in much of Europe, to avoid the pigs biting each other – something they generally do only in cramped conditions with nothing to keep them entertained. Most of these techniques are due to be made illegal across the EU, but not until 2013.

In the UK, things have been improved by various bits of legislation but the situation is still far from rosy. Most pigs are kept in cramped, dimly lit indoor conditions. According to Compassion in World Farming, fewer than half of them are even provided with straw, leaving them on bare concrete and slatted floors, which can cause health problems as well as preventing normal behaviour. And **farrowing crates** – small stalls into which sows are put for a week or two either side of giving birth – are still the norm. The industry claims these are needed to protect piglets from being crushed by their mother, but organic farmers have shown that with good husbandry this isn't necessary.

Besides welfare issues, food buffs are quick to point out that intensively farmed pork is nearly always floppy, watery and tasteless.

What to buy

For a start, favour pig meat from the UK – a large proportion of what gets sold in Britain is imported from countries where welfare standards are lower. Secondly, look out for pork meat marked **free-range**. With a lack of legal definitions, this doesn't always mean exactly the same thing, but in most cases it implies a considerable improvement to the prevailing standards. At minimum, you'll know the pigs aren't kept permanently indoors. Note that **outdoor-reared** is better than **outdoor-bred** – the latter ensures that the pig was *born* in free-range conditions (so no farrowing crates), but the former also implies that it was *raised* outdoors.

Two extremes of pig farming: the worst of intensive and the best of organic
Photos: Compassion in World Farming

Organic pig meat – which is free-range but allows pigs to be kept indoors for a proportion of the time – offers further improvements. Farrowing crates are out; rooting and exercise areas are in; piglets are not removed from their mother so early; the diet is better; and medicines used must be approved by a certifying body. If you can't find free-range or organic pork in your supermarket, or if you want to buy directly from farmers, see pp.222–226 for pointers.

You might also see pork products marked with the **Little Red Tractor** or the RSPCA **Freedom Food** logos. These offer some basic animal welfare guarantees – especially Freedom Food – though fewer than organic.

Beef & veal

Meat from cows ranges widely, in terms of both animal welfare and its wastefulness (as already discussed, intensive beef farming requires remarkable quantities of crops and water). Much of the UK's beef comes from **suckler herds**, which spend most of their lives moseying around in fields, the calves staying with their mothers for up to a year. Compared with beef from intensively raised cattle, this is more animal-friendly, wastes less energy and crops, and is generally much better quality, because of the breeds favoured as well as the exercise the cows get. The animals' diets still leave a bit to be desired (despite post-BSE laws banning cows and other large animals in the feed, waste poultry and fish products are still permitted) and the cows may suffer stress during transportation. But compared with most pigs or dairy cows, these animals don't get a bad deal.

A growing proportion of our beef, however, comes from **intensive farms**, usually stocked with excess calves from the dairy industry, mostly removed from their mothers on day one. (Old worn-out milkers were also once used for meat but today, post-BSE, their carcasses are burned instead.) In these farms, the cows are kept mostly or entirely indoors, often in over-crowded concrete sheds, and have little chance to exercise or graze. As with most intensive farming, this increases the risk of many illnesses, which in turn heightens the need for antibiotics and other drugs.

Eating **veal** is not inherently different, ethically speaking, from eating lamb or any other young animal, but the way much of it is produced is cause for concern. In the worst cases, veal calves are reared in crates, in which they can't even turn around, packed into dark sheds. They suffer great distress, are very susceptible to disease – hence preventative antibiotics are often used – and are fed a poor all-liquid diet deliberately lacking in certain nutrients, to help create a white-coloured meat. The UK has already phased out veal crates and a recent law should see the same happen across the EU by 2007. But most veal will still be from all-indoor intensive or semi-intensive farms.

What to buy

Suckler-herd or **free-range** beef obviously makes for a more ethical choice and is very common, so look out for labels or ask your butcher. In the case of veal, suckler-herd meat from calves that have stayed with their mothers until slaughter is sometimes labelled using the French term *veau sous la mère*. Better still is buying **organic**, which ensures stricter animal-welfare standards, rules out routine antibiotics and shuns animal and fish products in the feed. Organic beef is widely available and less expensive than many organic meats, and organic veal (which is often *sous la mère*) is also available, though less ubiquitous. For pointers to suppliers, see pp.222–226. Whatever you buy, favour UK over continental veal.

Lamb & mutton

In terms of animal welfare, sheep get a pretty good deal compared to most farm animals. The overwhelming majority spend their lives freely grazing over extensive pastures, being brought inside only when the weather demands it. This is largely because, as yet, no one has worked out a way to make intensive sheep farming viable. But that's not to say the situation is perfect. There are some serious problems with the way in which sheep and lambs are transported and slaughtered, and neglect by some farmers means that around one in ten lambs dies of cold or hunger. Many are also castrated without anaesthetic.

To ensure the best guarantee of animal welfare, as well as respect for the environment, go for **organic** lamb and mutton, or buy directly from local farmers whom you can question about welfare issues (see pp.222–226).

Poultry & eggs
Factory fowl

The chicken industry is perhaps the most extreme example of modern farming methods. Governed by technology and market forces, this is a whole sector of agriculture carried out almost entirely behind closed doors, and mostly by large firms. Amazingly, just three companies – Aviagen, Cobb-Vantress and Hybro – provide nearly all the world's chicks, for both meat and egg-laying birds, which, during the last half decade, have been engineered into completely separate creatures. The chick companies are proud of their scientific approach, and make no back-to-nature pretence. Visit one of their websites – such as www.aviagen.com – and you'll be invited to check out the "features and benefits" or a "technical data sheet" for each of their "products". And if this sounds more like marketing for cars than hens, the names of the breeds – such as the Hybro PG+ and Cobb 500 – won't convince you otherwise.

Broilers: meat chickens

As we'll see, conditions for egg-laying hens are gradually improving, but the same cannot be said for meat chickens, or **broilers** as they're called. Like so many other foods, chicken meat was thought of as a luxury until relatively recently, when intensive farming methods allowed prices to be slashed. Unfortunately this happened at the expense of animal welfare.

A brave new chicken

The whole idea of a chicken bred solely for meat is only around fifty years old, but today intensive broiler farms in the UK account for nearly all of the roughly 800 million chickens we consume each year (that's around fourteen for each person in the country). To achieve this remarkable turnover, farms use chicks that have been specially bred to grow in the shortest possible time: a modern broiler can get to slaughter weight in just over **forty days**, twice as quickly as a few decades ago. And the technology is still quite young – some industry visionaries expect thirty days to be realistic in the near future.

Regrettably for the birds, however, while their breasts grow unnaturally quickly, the rest of the body cannot keep up, and millions of broilers each year develop **leg disorders** or die of **heart failure**. Indeed, the genetic selection is so rigorous that chickens kept for breeding broilers have to be severely underfed; if they weren't, their super-efficient ability to put on weight would kill them before they reached egg-laying age. But animal welfare is never really going to be a priority while the leading chick suppliers make such statements as "output of meat per breeder placed is the ultimate measure of performance".

It's not just the breeding process that focuses on a need for speed. Other elements of a broiler's life are controlled by the same bottom line, from sleep patterns (darkness is kept to a minimum as a sleeping bird won't eat) to its feed: maximum weight-gain, minimum excrement pellets.

Chickenshit

Most broilers live in flocks of tens of thousands in giant, windowless sheds, each bird getting about as much space as a piece of A4 paper. This is far less than either the EU or the British government recommends for basic levels of welfare, but there are no specific laws governing this industry. With such dense stocking, clearing out the **litter floor** is usually only possible once the birds are taken to slaughter, so they spend their short lives standing and sitting in their own filth, often leading to **ulcerous feet** and **skin disease**. Evidence of the latter was found in 2% of the chicken meat examined in a recent sample by *Which?* magazine.

When their days are up, the birds are transported by crowded truck to a slaughterhouse and processing plant, many of which can cope with more than 10,000 chickens per hour. After being hung upside-down by their feet, the birds have their heads dipped into an electrified pool and their throats cut by a spinning blade. A couple of hours, miles of conveyor belt and numerous machines later, they'll come out plucked, gutted, wrapped and packed – perhaps even marinated (or, more accurately, injected) – and ready for the restaurant or supermarket shelf. For more information about broilers, see the campaign sites of Compassion in World Farming (www.livefastdieyoung.org) or the RSPCA (chickens.rspca.org.uk).

As well as animal welfare concerns, industrially produced chicken is said by those in the know to be disastrous for taste and quality. The lack of exercise, poor diet and absorption of water during processing creates, according to none other than Delia Smith, "a coarse-grained, watery, limp chicken that has no flavour".

How free is free-range?

Various categories of chicken and poultry with higher welfare levels are available in the UK, but the labelling isn't as simple or strict as you might expect. Here's a rundown of the various labels you'll come across:

▶ **Extensive indoor or barn-reared** The same as standard intensive systems but with lower stocking densities and a slaughter age of at least 56 days.

▶ **Free-range** Basically the same as above but the birds have continuous daytime access to open-air runs for at least half their lifetime.

▶ **Traditional free-range** As above but with smaller flock sizes, a minimum slaughter age of 81 days, and access to open-air runs from six weeks of age at the latest.

▶ **Free-range total freedom** As above but with "open-air runs of unlimited area".

▶ **Organic** Organic standards require welfare at least as good as traditional free-range, but demand far smaller flock sizes, a better diet (mainly organic and free from animal protein), a slightly older minimum slaughter age and tighter pollution restrictions.

Even if free-range chicken isn't available, look out for the **RSPCA Freedom Food** label, and avoid fresh chickens with brown "hock burn" marks near the knee joints – these often imply that welfare standards have been low.

Eggs

The vast majority of laying hens in the UK – more than twenty million according to RSPCA estimates – are kept in cramped **battery cages**, stacked up high in vast buildings with little or no natural light. In most cases the hens have so little space that they cannot even turn around or stretch their wings, let alone follow their instincts to preen properly and dust-bathe. The cages lead not just to discomfort, but to **foot injury** and **weak bones**, so that by the end of their productive lives – usually about one year and a few hundred eggs – almost a third of the birds have broken bones, according to animal-welfare groups. And the other two-thirds are in such poor condition that after slaughter they are only used for processed food and animal food.

An egg-layer's **diet** contains not only grains, soya and nutrients, but often also fish products and even (in an odd twist on the chicken-and-egg question) waste chicken extracts. The hens are also given colorants, both artificial and natural, to ensure the consumer isn't faced with a perfectly harmless variety in yolk colour, and antibiotics are routinely administered. A study by the Soil Association showed that a large proportion of eggs contain traces of the toxic medicine lasalocid, known to be harmful to mammals but never tested on humans.

One advantage of cages is that they make it harder for crowded birds to peck each other, meaning that they don't necessarily need to be **debeaked** (the trimming of chicks' beaks with a red-hot blade). However, many battery hens are debeaked anyway, and most commentators agree that minimal debeaking is less cruel than battery conditions. Either way, the practice isn't necessary with a small flock size in better conditions, as is typical of hens which produce organic eggs.

A good egg?

Battery farming still accounts for around two-thirds of UK egg production, but things are starting to change. There are now various non-battery options and some food manufacturers have committed to using free-range eggs – which offer some improvement – in their prepared products, the best known being Marks & Spencer and McDonald's. Also, the UK is implementing an EU directive to replace the worst cages, by 2012, with marginally more spacious **enriched cages**, with a nest, perching space and scratching area. These developments are still a very long way from ruling out cruel practices, but they are at least a step in the right direction. In the meantime, a wide range of labels and descriptions are used. So here's how to read an egg box...

▶ **Farm, Fresh, Country, etc** Take no notice of terms such as these, which often appear next to pictures of rural cottages with birds pecking happily around outside. They mean nothing at all, with the exception of some descriptions like "Super Fresh", which relate simply to the delay between laying and packing.

▶ **The Lion Quality mark** appears on around 75% of UK eggs. The scheme was set up in the wake of the salmonella crisis, and it focuses on food safety rather than animal welfare or environmental practices.

Free-range may be better than battery or barn-reared, but – as this image from a modern free-range farm in Rotterdam shows – it's a long way from the traditional farmyard scene pictured on many egg boxes
Photo: Corbis

▶ **Four-grain eggs** come from hens fed on natural (non-animal) food, but this doesn't reflect on the welfare of the birds.

▶ **Barn eggs** are produced in similar indoor conditions to battery eggs but without the cages. This allows the chickens to move around, but conditions are usually still grossly overcrowded, leading to the birds attacking (and sometimes killing) each other, and even eating each others' droppings. Debeaking is necessary.

▶ **Freedom Food, RSPCA approved** requires basic welfare standards to be in place. The scheme rules out battery cages, but not crowded barns, colorants or debeaking – and doesn't necessarily mean free-range.

▶ **Free-range eggs** are from hens that have had continuous access to outdoor runs "mainly covered with vegetation". However, the sheds are still usually overcrowded – less than one square foot per bird is permitted – and the colony sizes are large, resulting in unnatural behaviour from the birds (sometimes including, ironically, a fear of going outside). Debeaking is standard.

▶ **Organic eggs**, which have become much easier to find in recent years, are the best option. Birds must have free access to organic pasture (so are necessarily free-range), be fed largely on organic food and be kept in smaller flocks. Debeaking, routine antibiotics and colorants are banned. However, note that organic hens are rarely bred on organic farms: they are delivered by one of the big chick-rearing companies at a few weeks old.

Non-chicken poultry & eggs

Most poultry – including **turkey, duck, quail** and **guinea fowl** – are intensively farmed in a similar way to chicken, so look out for better alternatives: the same multi-level free-range labelling systems apply. One exception is **geese**, which (so far at least) have not been able to survive the rigours of industrial farming, so are necessarily free-range. As for eggs, those from quails are commercially produced, intensively, but duck and geese eggs are generally not, so will mostly be from small-scale farms where animal welfare conditions are likely to be relatively high.

Dairy products
It's a cow's life

Many vegetarians shun meat primarily because of animal welfare concerns. But dairy products raise many of the same issues. The milk trade not only props up the veal industry but is also sometimes responsible for animal suffering itself. Dairy cows could easily live for two decades, but such is the strain put on them by modern breeding and milk-production techniques that many are slaughtered before they're five – exhausted, ill and, in the harsh light of profit margins, economically inefficient.

Modern dairy cattle have been **intensively bred** to yield the maximum quantities of milk. While a calf would naturally suckle a few litres a day from its mother, milking machines now extract up to fifty litres. The cows often have oversized udders, which create spinal problems, lameness and other damage, according to animal-rights groups. A significant proportion of dairy cows also develop mastitis, a painful infection of the udder. Breeding (mainly through artificial insemination and embryo transfer) has been so intense in the last few decades that many cows have grown too big for older milking parlours.

As with beef farms, dairy farms range from free-range setups, where the cows spend most of their time eating grass in fields, to more intensive operations, where the herds are often kept inside for more of the year than necessary, often in cramped and uncomfortable conditions. Besides the animal welfare issues, more intensive farms are also more ecologically problematic (for the reasons discussed earlier in this chapter) and are more likely to rely on preventative antibiotics.

To keep them milking, dairy cows are usually made to have calves each year, so for most of the year they're both pregnant and lactating. Newborn calves are taken from their mothers almost immediately – often within hours of birth – which is widely reported to cause great distress to both. Females wait in turn to replace their mothers, often spending their first few months in a cramped individual pen. Males are usually taken straight to the market to be sold for veal or are moved to intensive farms to be fattened up for low-quality beef.

Ethical dairy

Unless you happen to know a dairy farmer, the only way to guarantee your milk and cheese have been produced with a high standard of animal welfare, and have generated a minimum amount of pollution in the process, is to buy **organic**. In organic farms, cows get a better diet and living conditions, spend more time outside and have a lower incidence of lameness. Preventative antibiotics are banned. Calves stay with their mothers for longer and aren't weaned off milk for at least three months, or removed from the farm before six months.

Organic dairy products are in no short supply. So much organic milk is now produced, in fact, that a large proportion of it ends up being mixed with and sold as standard milk. However, for a full range of organic dairy products, see the specialist suppliers listed on pp.222–226.

You may also see organic milk branded as **White & Wild**. This is milk from the OMSCo Cooperative, which aims to give environmentally conscientious farmers a better deal. At the time of writing, for every twenty two-litre bottles purchased, a broad-leaved tree will be planted, both to soak up CO_2 and to create space for wildlife. For a family with a typical house and average milk consumption, that's enough to make your home carbon neutral. Find out more at:

White & Wild www.whiteandwild.co.uk

Fish & seafood
Plenty more in the sea?

The World Resources Institute estimates that fish consumption has risen more than fivefold in the last half century. In some ways this is a positive thing: fish provide a very healthy and important protein source for hundreds of millions of people around the world, and – unlike livestock – they don't require vast areas of crop land for feed. However, the massive global increase in fish consumption, which shows no sign of slowing down, has been made possible by two developments – **industrial fishing** and intensive **aquaculture** (fish farming) – both of which have come with environmental, and in some cases social, costs.

Sea-caught fish: tuna, cod, swordfish, etc

As fishing vessels have grown from small wooden boats to giant factory ships, the world's waters have been reaped so heavily that the proverb "plenty more fish in the sea" is starting to look distinctly tenuous. By the

"The one and only pure ocean machine, unflawed, navigating the waters of death", wrote Pablo Neruda of the bluefin tuna. Like many great ocean carnivores, its numbers have been decimated by both legal and illegal fishing and it's now critically endangered. Bluefin is most widely used in sushi but also served in steaks.

time industrial fishing came of age in the early 1980s, the global catch in two years was equivalent to all the fish caught in the nineteenth century. And today, according to UN figures, a quarter of the world's fisheries are either over-exploited or depleted, while another half are being fished to maximum safe levels. The best-known example is **cod** – which in some areas have gone from being richly plentiful to basically extinct – but this certainly isn't the only species to have suffered.

People have long argued about the extent and implications of over-fishing, but a recent groundbreaking study published in *Nature* suggested that the problem may be far worse than was previously expected. By scrutinizing early fishing records, Canadian academics reached the staggering conclusion that in the last half century 90% of all large fish – including halibut, marlin, swordfish, sharks and tuna – have been wiped out. And those that are left are tiny compared with their relatively recent ancestors.

The implications could be far-reaching, as over-fishing not only knocks out the target fish but also causes havoc in the wider food chain (partly indirectly, and partly because large numbers of non-target fish and other sea creatures are regularly killed in the nets). If these trends continue, the effect could be a "complete re-organization of ocean ecosystems, with unknown global consequences", in the words of one of the *Nature* report's

Tuna and dolphins

The various species of tuna sold in the UK are all being very heavily fished, some – such as the giant **bluefin**, which is mainly used in sushi – near to the point of extinction. **Skipjack** and **yellowfin**, which dominate the tinned market, are not in such a bad way, but their catching sometimes involves the killing of **dolphins**. The controversy relates primarily to yellowfin, which live in the Eastern Pacific and swim in large schools underneath groups of dolphins. Since around 1950 fishermen have exploited this relationship: find a group of the easily visible dolphins, surround them with large purse-seine nets, and pull in the tuna underneath, usually along with the dolphins, which are thrown back dead. This practice is thought to have killed many millions of dolphins, seriously depleting their numbers, which have not recovered since. Driftnets and other tuna-fishing techniques are also responsible for killing dolphins.

The issue came to the US public eye in the 1980s, resulting in a consumer boycott, improved fishing techniques, tighter regulations (in some countries) and the **Dolphin Safe** label from the Earth Island Institute (www.earthisland.org). All this has made a big difference and, though dolphins continue to die in tuna nets, only a tiny amount of the tuna on the European market now comes from so-called "dolphin-deadly" fisheries. In the UK, there hasn't yet been a consistent, legally binding definition of Dolphin Safe or Dolphin Friendly, but most of the major retailers and processors are now affiliated with the Earth Island Institute, so in general the dolphin-friendly claims that consumers come across can be trusted.

Still, the issues aren't quite cut and dried, because some tuna-fishing methods that avoid dolphins altogether – attracting them with floating logs or using baited hooks hanging off mile-long floating lines – can be problematic in other ways. They may be better for dolphins but worse for **sharks**, **turtles** and **non-target fish**, and they may risk damaging tuna stocks by yielding younger fish that haven't yet reproduced. Further, some claim that the inspection system is very weak and the tuna supply chain so convoluted that it's almost impossible to know where your fish has actually come from.

While tuna has got most of the attention, other species such as sea bass and swordfish are also widely associated with dolphin deaths.

authors. And global warming may compound the problem, since changing sea temperatures are also starting to affect marine eco systems.

Currently, many of the most over-fished areas are around Europe and North America. Europe has implemented a quota system to limit the damage and allow replenishment. But even if this is sufficient (which many experts doubt) and the rules are implemented properly (which so far they haven't always been), other areas are feeling the pressure in the meantime. The EU, for example, has already purchased fishing rights from a number of African countries. This may provide income for countries that definitely need it, but some commentators predict that a lack of regulation will soon see stocks in these regions depleted, resulting in dwindling catches for local people who rely on fishing to survive.

Bycatch and sea-bed damage

Fishermen have always hauled in a certain amount of **bycatch** – non-target fish and other marine life. But as fishing has become more industrial, the problem has become much more serious. The relationship between tuna fishing and dead dolphins is relatively common knowledge (see box opposite), but the problem actually is much wider, with turtles, sea birds, seals, whales and sharks routinely getting caught, not to mention huge quantities of small fish, which are often just thrown back dead.

Driftnets, used to catch tuna, swordfish, sardines, herring, albacore and other species, are one major culprit. Despite recent legislation, these nets are often many miles long and have earned the nickname "walls of death" for good reason. But **bottom trawling**, which entails dragging a fine net over the sea bed, can be even worse. This technique – widely used for prawns, scallops, plaice, clam, snapper and other species – can result in more bycatch than target and can also cause serious damage to the sea bed. In biologically diverse areas around underwater "seamounts", *New Scientist* recently reported, trawling is wiping out scores of species before they can even be identified.

Farmed fish: salmon, plaice, trout et al

With the seas suffering from depleted stocks, fish farming seems like the obvious solution. And, indeed, an increasing proportion of our fish is reared in farms – around a third of the global total – making aquaculture the fastest growing of all food sectors. For years the lochs of Scotland and the fjords of Norway have been gradually filling up with the **salmon** industry's giant plastic nets, with farms now accounting for more than 99% of the Scottish salmon on sale. **Trout** is also widely farmed and, with stock numbers low and financial potential high, the farming of **cod**, **sea bass** and **bream** is also on the rise.

Farms certainly get around the problem of bycatch and satisfy consumer demand for cheap fish, but instead of alleviating the over-exploitation of the sea they very often exacerbate it. After all, to farm carnivorous fish like salmon, cod and haddock, you need to catch a huge quantity of smaller fish to feed them. For each kilo of salmon you buy in a shop, for example, up to five kilos of fish will have been caught, transported and turned into fish food. By the end of this decade, some estimate, around 90% of the world's fish oil will be used to make aquaculture feed.

The problems of fish farming can go beyond this wastefulness: green and anti-poverty groups claim the farms can also be problematic in terms of **pollution**, **animal welfare** and – in the case of tropical prawns (see box opposite) – **human rights**.

Environmental impacts of aquaculture

One environmental problem with aquaculture is that millions of fish churn out a lot of **mineral-rich faeces**. Scottish salmon, for example, excrete twice as much phosphorus as the country's human population according to the World Wildlife Fund. This goes straight into the surrounding waters, suffocating sea-bed life and possibly creating the toxic algal blooms that have left much of Scotland closed to shellfishing. Besides minerals, the waste – not to mention the fish – also contains a cocktail of antibiotics, uneaten food and dyes (farmed salmon would be grey, not pink, if dye wasn't added). Various illegal chemicals and hormones, banned for their environmental and health impact, have also often shown up in spot checks.

Another potential impact of fish farms is a reduction in **wild stocks** nearby. Sometimes this happens through the inevitable spreading of the diseases and lice that thrive in intensive farms, but there may also be a more sinister mechanism at play. Farmed salmon, for example, regularly escape in huge numbers (the WWF estimates that 630,000 salmon escaped from Norwegian farms in 2002 alone) and if these fish, not adapted for life in the natural world, breed with wild salmon, a kind of negative evolution takes place, with wild fish becoming less and less able to cope with their natural conditions.

Prawns

Prawns fall into two categories. There are the small cold-water ones frequently used in sandwiches, and the larger tropical ones – also known as "tiger" or "king" prawns – which have become favourites in restaurants and supermarkets in the last decade or so. According to campaign groups such as Christian Aid (www.christianaid.org) and the Environmental Justice Foundation (www.ejfoundation.org), tiger prawns are about as unethical a crustacean as you can consume, their cultivation involving the very worst practices of both farmed and caught seafood.

The majority of the tigers that reach the UK have been farmed in Asian countries such as **Bangladesh** and the **Philippines**. Tropical prawn farming has a long history as a sustainable aquaculture, but the large-scale modern methods stand accused of being highly destructive. According to critics, the prawn farms' man-made pools drain local water sources, requiring an estimated 50,000 litres of water for each kilo of prawns produced, and can become a major source of pollution. **Salt** is added to the water in large quantities, as well as fishmeal food, antibiotics to limit the risks of overcrowding, growth stimulants to make the process faster, and lime to regulate the acidity. This saline cocktail inevitably filters back into nearby **agricultural land**, rendering it unproductive, and pollutes local drinking water sources.

Nearby fishing areas also get hit, according to anti-prawn campaigners, both by direct pollution and by aggressive industrial fishing for potential prawn-feed (like salmon, prawns consume far more food than they produce). Moreover, the farms have been responsible for massive destruction of **mangrove swamps**, which are essential to tropical coastal ecosystems. Amazingly, around 25% of the mangrove forest lost each year is due to prawn farming, according to the Marine Stewardship Council. In many cases the ponds end up so toxic or virus-ridden that they have to be abandoned, the companies that own them moving on to new locations and leaving local people with impure water, a damaged ability to feed themselves and few, if any, real benefits. There have even been numerous reports of people being **violently displaced** from prospective pond sites, as well as murder and rape in some cases.

In December 2004, the BBC broadcast a documentary focusing on the ethics of prawn farming in Honduras and concluded that the problems were being exaggerated by the likes of the Environmental Justice Foundation. The EJF, in turn, accused the BBC of poor journalism, not least because the film focused on a single farm. (You can read the film director's comments by searching the BBC website for "the price of prawns" and find the EJF response at www.ejfoundation.org/page104.html). Whatever the truth, the UN was concerned enough about the shrimp industry by August 2006 to publish a set of International Principles for Responsible Shrimp Farming. It remains to be seen if these will bring about a major change.

Not all tiger prawns are farmed: others are **sea-caught**. But these aren't necessarily better, since prawn trawlers are associated with problems of their own. The technique used – dragging a fine net over the sea-bed – is completely unselective. As well as seriously damaging the sea-bed itself, the nets bring in, by weight, as much as twenty times more bycatch than prawns, endangering turtles and other sea life and diminishing the catch of subsistence fishermen. According to the EJF, prawn trawling accounts for a third of the world's bycatch but produces only a fiftieth of its seafood.

Finally there's the issue of animal welfare. Few people find it easy to empathize with fish, but keeping creatures that are naturally migratory and/or solitary in cramped spaces with 50,000 others certainly raises some ethical questions. So do practices such as allowing fish to suffocate as a way of killing them, and stocking them in such high density that their fins are regularly damaged – two things reported to be common practice on trout farms.

Fish: the green options

The problems described above are serious, but they don't necessarily mean that we should stop eating fish and seafood. There are various measures you can take to minimize the negative impacts of what you buy. One option is to look out for the logo of the **Marine Stewardship Council** (see p.194). However, as yet supplies aren't huge and the range is small – a good sign for the integrity of the scheme, perhaps, but not great for choice.

Another option is to **be picky** about which types of fish and seafood you choose. The quandaries of tropical prawns, farmed salmon and sea-caught cod have already been discussed, but there are many other species endangered by over-fishing or caught in destructive ways, and others still which are relatively unproblematic. For an in-depth view, get *The Good Fish Guide*, a book by Bernadette Clarke of the Marine Conservation Society. You can order it directly from them (www.mcsuk. org ▷ 01989 566 017), but a taster is provided opposite in the form of the Society's top species for consumers to avoid or eat with a clear conscience. For more information on the fish in these lists, see the MCS's site:

FishOnline www.fishonline.org

Also, as a rule, try to avoid young, undersized fish, as catching these can exacerbate pressure on stocks.

Marine Stewardship Council

MSC-certified New Zealand Hoki

Good fish, bad fish

Do eat...

Alaska or walleye pollock
Bib or pouting (line-caught)
Black bream or porgy or seabream
(line-caught)
Clams (sustainably harvested)
Cockle (MSC certified or sustainably
harvested)
Coley or saithe (from North Sea)
Common dolphinfish (line-caught)
Cuttlefish (trap-caught)
Dab (line-caught or seine netted)
Dover sole (from Eastern channel)
Dublin Bay prawn (MSC certified or
pot- or creel-caught)
Flounder
Grey gurnard
Herring or sild (MSC certified or line-
caught from North Sea)
Hoki (MSC certified)
King scallop (sustainably harvested)
Lythe or pollack (line-caught)
Mackerel (MSC certified or line-
caught)
Mussels (sustainably harvested)
Oysters (farmed Native & Pacific)
Pacific halibut (line-caught)
Pacific salmon (MSC certified)
Red gurnard
Red mullet
Salmon (from organic or Freedom
Food-certified farms)
Spider crab
Sprat (from the North Sea, dolphin-
friendly)
Whiting (from the English Channel)
Winkle (sustainably harvested)
Witch (line-caught)

Don't eat...

Alfonsinos or golden eye perch
American plaice
Silver smelt (Argentine or greater)
Cod (except from Iceland)
Atlantic halibut
Atlantic salmon (wild-caught)
Blue ling
**Chilean seabass or Patagonian
  toothfish**
Dogfish (inc. catshark, nursehound)
European Hake
Greater forkbeard
Grouper
Haddock (except from North Sea,
West of Scotland, Skaggerak,
Kattegat and Iceland)
Ling
Marlin (blue, Indo-Pacific & white)
Monkfish
Orange roughy
Plaice (except from Irish Sea)
Rat or rabbit fish
Red or blackspot seabream
Redfish or ocean perch
Roundnose grenadier
Seabass (trawl-caught only)
Shark
Skates & rays
Snapper
Sturgeon
Swordfish
Tiger prawn (except organic)
Tuna (except dolphin-friendly,
pole- and line-caught yellowfin and
skipjack)
Tusk
Wolfish

The Marine Stewardship Council

Any seafood bearing this blue tick/fish label has been caught according to sustainable criteria set out by the **Marine Stewardship Council** (MSC). Initially set up by Unilever and the WWF, but now an independent organization, the MSC both promotes a responsible approach to fishing and monitors practices. To be awarded the mark, fisheries need to be able to demonstrate their commitment to:

▶ **The maintenance and re-establishment of healthy populations** of targeted species, and the integrity of ecosystems

▶ **Effective management systems**, considering biological, technological, economic, social, environmental and commercial aspects

▶ **Following relevant local, national and international laws**, standards, understandings and agreements

A small but growing number of fisheries are accredited and stocked in the supermarket, including pollock and salmon from Alaska; hoki from New Zealand; hake from South Africa; mackerel, herring and Dover sole from the UK; halibut, sablefish and toothfish from the US, and rock lobster from Australia (pictured) and the US. For more information, including where to buy, visit:

MSC www.msc.org

Marine Stewardship Council

A final option is to buy **organic fish**. These are, by default, farmed (nothing caught in the wild can qualify as organic, since you don't know where it has been or what it has eaten), but in much less intensive conditions, with no antibiotics or colorants and better protection for the environment. Devotees also swear that organic fish taste much better, as their diet is superior and the lower density of stocks allows them to exercise properly. If your local shops don't sell organic fish, try the delivery services listed on pp.222–226.

Bear in mind, though, that even when farmed organically, salmon, trout and other carnivorous fish are nonetheless fed on fishmeal from sea-caught fish, so you're not entirely sidestepping the problem of the oceans' ever-depleting fish stocks.

Fruit & vegetables
What to buy, where to buy

Fruit and vegetables tie together many of the issues discussed at the beginning of this chapter and the first section of this book, including organic versus conventional agriculture (see p.145) and the environmental burden of food transport (see p.156). Worker pay and conditions is another area of concern. The most shocking labour abuse in the fruit and veg sector has occurred in the developing world, such as on the **banana plantations** of Latin America (see p.198). However, a number of recent exposés – such as those in Felicity Lawrence's book, *Not On The Label* – have shown that many European farms, including those in Britain, rely on temporary, non-resident workers subcontracted through gangmasters and paid sub-minimum-wage rates.

Then there's the question of *where* we should buy our fruit and vegetables. The **supermarkets** (see p.216), which have become the unrivalled superpowers of the fresh-produce supply chain, are regularly accused of using their size to squeeze suppliers – both at home and abroad – so hard that it becomes almost impossible for them to stick to any serious labour and environmental standards. In the case of fruit and veg, they are also resented for causing waste, and increased agrochemical use, by refusing to accept anything that doesn't fulfil their famously strict specifications of size, shape and colour. The degree of conformity required – with carrot length, for example, specified in millimetres – would be entertaining were it not so disturbing.

Another concern is **genetic diversity**. Though we're now offered starfruit and guava at every turn, green commentators often lament the loss – in many cases permanently – of the literally thousands of varieties of apples, potatoes, squashes and other produce which once flourished in Britain. As Andrew Kimbrell wrote in *The Ecologist*, "monoculture industrial agriculture not only limits what we can eat today, it also reduces the choices of future generations ... the UN Food and Agriculture

Organisation (FAO) estimates that more than three quarters of agricultural genetic diversity was lost in this past century". Again, the blame for this is usually jointly pinned onto industrial farming and the supermarkets, which farmers and greens accuse of favouring shelf life and profit margins over and above everything else.

Two final issues, though more to do with health concerns than ethics, are worth touching on briefly: the question of **pesticide residue** on our fruit and veg (see box) and the possibility that non-local fresh produce

Pesticide residues

With thousands of farm workers killed every year by poisoning, and wildlife and the environment suffering in numerous ways, pesticides unequivocally pose certain threats to people and planet. But what about the residues on our fruit and veg? Green campaigners link pesticide residues to skin and eye irritation, mental and nervous problems, breast cancer and other conditions, and point out that little is known about the long-term effects of many of these substances (some of which are hormone disrupters), especially their combined "cocktail effect".

But most toxicologists seem less convinced that the quantities in question are big enough to be a worry. A major government study published in 1998 tested more than 2000 fruit and vegetable samples and found that around 73% were residue-free, 26% had residues below the MRL ("maximum recommended limit") and 1.3% contained residues above the limit. Some people were up in arms about the 1.3%, yet the report's authors concluded that – even in the case of those foods that slightly exceeded the limits – "food is safe from the point of view of pesticide residues".

Still, those who are concerned about pesticide residues – especially those who don't feel that they can justify the expense of buying organic for all their fresh produce – may be interested to know which fruit and veg tend to contain higher residues than others. The following lists of the fruit and veg at the top and bottom of the residue scales were prepared by the US's Environmental Working Group. They relate specifically to the levels of residues found in food as typically prepared – *not* the amount used in growing. So banana, for example, because of its thick, inedible skin, comes on the low-residues list despite being associated with massive pesticide use and worker exploitation. These lists, then, are not equivalent to the "most ethical" fruit and veg.

Highest levels Apple ▷ Bell Pepper ▷ Celery ▷ Cherry ▷ Grape ▷ Nectarine ▷ Peach ▷ Pear ▷ Potato ▷ Raspberry ▷ Spinach ▷ Strawberry

Lowest levels Asparagus ▷ Avocado ▷ Banana ▷ Broccoli ▷ Cauliflower ▷ Sweetcorn ▷ Kiwi ▷ Mango ▷ Onion ▷ Papaya ▷ Pea ▷ Pineapple

For more information, and methodology, see www.foodnews.org. Or to read more about the pesticide issue, see:

Pesticide Action Network www.pan-uk.org

may lose **nutrients** en route from its source. Studies by the Austrian Consumers Association, for example, found that "fresh" out-of-season fruit and vegetables are often significantly lower in vitamins and higher in harmful nitrates than genuinely fresh ones (or, indeed, frozen ones, which are usually put in the freezer within hours of being picked).

Ethical fruit & veg

With all the above in mind, the most common ethical advice is, first, to favour **organic** fruit and veg. And, second, to avoid supermarkets where possible and favour **seasonal**, **locally produced** fruit and veg from alternative outlets such as box schemes and farmers' markets – for more on these, see p.222. Conversely, supermarkets are about the only places where you're likely to find **Fairtrade**-certified fruit…

Fairtrade fruit

The success of the Fairtrade banana has led to an ever-growing range of fruit bearing the Fairtrade Mark. Like other such goods, these are sourced from the developing world according to rules which guarantee that the producers receive: a higher proportion of the price we pay for their crops,

WHERE TO BUY FAIRTRADE FRUIT	ASDA	Booths	Budgens	Co-op	M&S	Morrisons	Sainsbury's	Somerfield	Tesco	Waitrose
Apples	✓	✓	✓						✓	✓
Avocados	✓	✓		✓	✓		✓		✓	✓
Bananas	✓	✓	✓	✓	✓	✓	✓	✓	✓	✓
Clementines	✓	✓	✓	✓			✓		✓	✓
Coconuts							✓			
Grapes	✓	✓	✓	✓	✓		✓		✓	✓
Lemons	✓	✓	✓	✓					✓	✓
Lychees	✓	✓								
Mangoes	✓	✓		✓	✓		✓		✓	✓
Oranges	✓	✓	✓	✓			✓		✓	✓
Pears	✓	✓	✓				✓			
Pineapples	✓	✓		✓	✓		✓		✓	✓
Plums			✓				✓			
Satsumas, etc	✓	✓	✓	✓			✓		✓	✓

Bananas: globalization in a slippery skin

The world's most widely consumed fruit provides a perfect illustration of many of the most pressing debates about world trade and intensive farming. There are hundreds of varieties of banana grown around the world, most of them in India and other countries where they are cultivated for domestic consumption. But the export market, almost entirely driven by the US and Europe, is largely dominated by just one variety and a handful of giant companies. Roughly 60% of banana exports are controlled by just three multinationals – **Chiquita**, **Dole Food** and **Del Monte** – which produce primarily in Central and South America, the world of the so-called "dollar banana".

Banana farming was once dominated by the **United Fruit Company**, which controlled much of Central America and was instrumental in bringing about the 1954 CIA-orchestrated coup in Guatemala, which overthrew the country's elected government and led to half a century of conflict and bloodshed. Today, the big banana firms don't stand accused of starting "real" wars, but they were behind the trade war which saw the US, Ecuador and various American countries battling with the EU at the World Trade Organization in the late 1990s. The point in question was the legality of the EU's banana import policy, which to a certain extent shunned "dollar bananas" in favour of those grown in ex-European colonies in Africa, the Caribbean and the Pacific (the "ACP" countries).

Pro-free-trade commentators claimed that Ecuador and other poor dollar-banana countries were suffering due to their restricted access to European markets. But the EU claimed that small ACP family farms – and in some cases whole countries' economies – would be unable to survive without preferential treatment, so the human consequences of leaving everything to the free market would be huge. Anti-globalization protesters agreed, describing the situation as a classic case of big companies trying to use global trade rules to profit from a "race to the bottom". They pointed out that the Latin American producers were only able to undercut small farmers in the ACP countries because their plantations depended on terrible exploitation of workers and the environment.

It's true that the big banana producers have long been dogged by allegations about their low ethical standards. First, there's the question of **wages**: in the dollar-banana plantations, the workers who actually grow the bananas receive only 1–3% of the final price, or, put another way, as little as a dollar a day, in return for twelve or more hours of hard labour (according to figures from the Fairtrade Foundation). Child labour has been shown to be widespread, as has the intimidation, firing or even murder of would-be union organizers. Moreover, health and safety has often been seriously compromised by the use of **agrochemicals**.

Required in vast quantities due to the single-crop nature of the plantations, fungicides and other pesticides are often sprayed from planes, and though there are rules to ensure that workers are not put in danger, these have not always been observed. As well as directly breathing in the chemicals, the workers, many of whom live on or next to the plantations, have often ended up drinking and bathing in contaminated water, with sometimes catastrophic results. In the last few decades thousands of workers have died, been made seriously ill or given birth to deformed babies. According to a Fairtrade Foundation report from 2000, "some 20% of the male banana workers in

A banana worker from the Chinandega, Nicaragua, where widespread genetic illnesses, ranging from skin disorders to a babies, are blamed on decades of pesticide use
Photo: Corbis

Costa Rica were left sterile after handling toxic chemicals", while women working in the pack houses had twice the normal incidence of leukemia. The ecological damage of the big plantations has also been severe, including soil degradation, lost biodiversity, toxic run-off and forest clearance. None of this was deemed relevant to the WTO case, however, since international trade rules don't take social and environmental issues into account.

Partly as a result of the "banana wars" – which the EU eventually lost – two things happened. The first was the extension of Fairtrade labelling to bananas. Sourced from small-producer co-operatives in the ACP countries, fairly traded bananas provide all the standard ethical guarantees of the Fairtrade Mark, including improved health and safety and a higher proportion of the price going to the farmers.

The second was that the big banana firms started trying to redefine themselves as socially responsible companies, publishing codes of conduct relating to health and safety, pesticide use and union representation. Chiquita even joined the UK's Ethical Trading Initiative (see p.61) and launched a partnership with the Rainforest Alliance. As with all such big-business initiatives, however, the degree to which these aims are benefiting the workers on the ground is open to debate.

Where Fairtrade bananas aren't available, you may want to favour those from the ex-British colonies in the Caribbean – usually given a **Windward Isles** label – as they are generally grown by smaller-scale farms with better workers' rights, fewer chemicals and a slightly higher percentage of the profits heading back to the workers. For more on the banana trade, see:

Banana Link www.bananalink.org.uk

The Fairtrade Foundation

Sorting mangoes in a Fairtrade-certified plantation in Chacras, Ecuador

a premium for social and environmental improvement, advance payment opportunities, and reliable long-term trading relationships. For more on how the Fairtrade scheme works, see p.24.

The range of Fairtrade fruits ranges from avocados to satsumas – in addition to green beans – but each item is only available from certain shops, according to **market availability** and **seasonality**. For more on Fairtrade fruit, see:

Fairtrade Foundation www.fairtrade.org.uk

Local vs. organic vs. Fairtrade

One common ethical conundrum is whether it's better to buy organic produce or local produce. Very often it's possible to do both at once, but in some cases you have to pick between one or the other. Environmental groups tend to advise consumers to favour local over organic food, if it comes down to a choice between the two, but obviously it depends on how far the organic produce has travelled and whether it's been transported by ship, road or plane (see p.156).

Fairtrade fresh produce can also present some difficult choices. There's an increasing amount of fruit available that's organic *and* Fairtrade, but you sometimes have to plump for one or the other. In this case, there's a strong argument for favouring the Fairtrade option, since the certification process keeps a check on environmental sustainability and the responsible use of agrochemicals in addition to social and economic matters. But if the environment is firmly at the top of your priority list, then organic may be the way to go.

The Fairtrade versus local dilemma doesn't come up as frequently, since most fairly traded fresh produce consists of tropical fruits that couldn't be grown in the UK anyway. But since 2003, Fairtrade apples, shipped from South Africa, have been available, creating a slight tension between the Fairtrade movement, on the one hand, and environmentalists and UK farmers on the other. The apples from South Africa support empowerment projects, through which landless workers can become co-owners of fruit farms – a scheme praised by Nelson Mandela among others. Whether such unquestionably positive schemes justify shipping the apples from the southern hemisphere at a time when many British orchards are being abandoned is for each consumer to decide.

Soil Association Ethical Trade

For a brief while it looked as if the Fairtrade Mark was going to start appearing on certain British-grown organic foods. This was an attempt to deal with the fact that, even in comparatively wealthy countries such as the UK, ecologically friendly growers sometimes struggle to cover the cost of production. In the event, the idea was dropped, because Fairtrade consumers tended to believe the scheme should prioritize the extreme poverty of the developing world.

In response, the Soil Association launched its own **Ethical Trade** label, with the aim of introducing a Fairtrade-style certification system – focusing on "fairness, mutual respect and transparency" – into the UK organic market. The key principles are:

▶ A fair price for the farmer and others in the supply chain

▶ Fair treatment of workers

▶ Involvement in the local community

It's still relatively early days for the scheme, so you may not come across the label on many goods. For the latest information, including more details on the criteria, see:

Soil Association www.soilassociation.org.uk ▷ 0117 314 5000

Coffee & tea

...and other storecupboard fair trade products

Coffee

The ethics of the coffee trade are perhaps more widely discussed than those of any other sector. And it's not hard to understand why. First, there's the sheer scale of the industry. Literally billions of cups of coffee are consumed around the world every day, a colossal demand that has made coffee, in terms of total value, the most traded commodity in the world after oil and illegal drugs. It's thought that around 100 million people work in the coffee trade – more than double the entire working population of the UK – including more than twenty million farmers, the vast majority of whom are small-scale growers with less than ten acres of land.

The second reason we hear so much about coffee is that the world is in the midst of a so-called **coffee crisis**, with the prices received by farmers having dropped to their lowest levels in decades. In the last couple of years, prices have picked up a little, but they're still extremely low.

Coffee farmers have never been a wealthy bunch. For reasons ranging from their lack of capital to Western trade rules that slap huge import tariffs on processed goods, it's long been the case that the vast majority of the profits from each jar of coffee we buy goes to the retailers and packagers – with the farmers receiving as little as 2%. But as farm-gate prices have

Growing coffee

The coffee "tree" is an evergreen tropical shrub that only flourishes within a couple of thousand miles of the Equator. Especially in the case of the high-quality **Arabica** species – as opposed to the **Robusta** or **Liberica** used for lower-quality and instant coffees – it's an incredibly high-maintenance crop. After an initial four or five years bearing no fruit, each bush produces an annual crop of a few thousand "beans" (actually the seeds of the cherry-like fruit) – enough for only around 1kg of roasted coffee. The plants require constant attention, and the cherries usually have to be picked by hand, as they ripen at different times. Much highland coffee is grown on slopes so steep and remote that horses or mules, let alone motor vehicles, cannot be used.

plummeted, millions have been pushed from poverty into extreme poverty. This has resulted in massive suffering in many areas, and has been especially catastrophic in countries such as Ethiopia and Burundi, where coffee is central to the wider economy. As wages have dropped, many farmers have had to take their children out of school, forego medical treatment, or accumulate unpayable debt just to keep things ticking over. Others have abandoned coffee growing completely, in some cases finding themselves with no viable option but to turn to the production of illegal crops such as coca and marijuana. In some countries, such as Nicaragua, thousands of children have starved as a result of the crisis, according to the United Nations World Food Programme.

The coffee crisis – what happened?

The main cause of the price crisis faced by millions of coffee growers is massive **oversupply**: there's simply far more coffee being produced than consumers want to drink. On and off until 1989, coffee production and prices were regulated by quotas set by the International Coffee Organisation (ICO) – a group of producer and consumer countries that aimed to keep supply and demand in line with each other.

However, at the end of the 1980s, disagreement between producer and consumer countries, and a prevailing economic ethos of trade liberalization, led to the dismantling of the quota system. Production patterns soon started to change, with **Vietnam** – following advice from the World Bank – investing heavily in the coffee sector and becoming a major new supplier. Vietnam certainly needed the income and jobs, but its emergence as a serious player in the coffee market, along with other factors such as new processing technologies that allowed lower-quality beans to be substantially improved, soon led to a massive rise in the production of usable coffee. This was accompanied by a drop in the price that farmers could get for their crops.

The crisis soon spiralled into a vicious circle. Since many coffee farmers lack the experience, circumstances or capital to produce other crops, many have tried to deal with the price drop by working as hard as possible to produce even more coffee. But this, of course, only helps to build up the stockpiles and drive prices down even further.

The shifting dynamics of the coffee industry are also having **environmental impacts**, with traditional "shaded coffee", grown under a native tree canopy, giving way to "sun coffee". Sun coffee yields more coffee more quickly, but the bushes last for only 10–15 years, as opposed to the 50 years of a shaded bush. They typically also require far more fertilizers and pesticides, which, combined with the forest clearance required to plant the bushes, endangers the delicate ecological balances of highland tropical areas. According to groups such as Conservation International, these farming methods are threatening whole ecosystems, from Latin America to Indonesia.

The coffee giants

Even greater than the supermarkets' stranglehold over food retail is the control wielded over the coffee market by a handful of giant roasters and packagers: **Nestlé** (producers of Nescafé), **Kraft** (owned by tobacco giant Philip Morris and behind Kenco, Maxwell House and Carte Noire), **Sara Lee Corp** (who own Douwe Egberts) and **Procter & Gamble** (who mainly sell in the US).

Since these firms make their money buying, processing and reselling coffee, the drop in farm-gate prices has been to their advantage. Hence Nestlé's Annual Management Report for 2000, in explaining their good profits for that year, pointed to "favourable commodity prices" – business terminology that obscures the people behind the product. The idea of giant companies getting richer while farmers suffer – and in some cases literally starve – has led to a huge amount of resentment.

Of course, the big coffee firms are only doing what companies always do: buying their raw products from the cheapest seller with the aim of maximizing shareholder value. And it's true that they can't really be blamed for the oversupply. But campaigners have long accused the Big Four of failing even to acknowledge the extent of the problem.

In the last couple of years, there have been some positive developments, with three of the big four launching at least one coffee made from Fairtrade beans – Nestlé in the UK and Kraft and P&G in the US. In the case of Nestlé, this raised plenty of eyebrows, since the company is still the target of a boycott over its alleged marketing of breast-milk substitutes (see p.214).

Fairtrade coffee

Fairtrade coffee is sourced directly from the grower according to ethical trading principles. These include a **minimum price guarantee**, which states that no matter what happens on the commodity markets, the Fairtrade coffee price will never go lower than a certain level. In 2003, for example, despite the fact that a jar of Fairtrade coffee was only marginally more expensive than the conventionally traded equivalent, the price

Starbucks and other cafés: an ethicino?

Some independent cafés have been offering Fairtrade coffee for some time (if those in your area don't, you could always ask them to start). But recently the trend has been boosted – ironically enough – by the kind of chain cafés which have themselves often been the target of campaigner anger. **Costa Coffee** was the first big player to get involved, offering any·drink with CaféDirect Fairtrade coffee for 10p extra. Then **Starbucks** caught on, adopting Fairtrade in the UK for filter coffee and – once a month – as "coffee of the day".

The Organic Consumers Association accused Starbucks of making only a token gesture, pointing out that only a tiny fraction of the company's coffees were Fairtrade, but, more recently, the company has been praised by none other than Oxfam, who wrote: "It is a welcome relief … to see Starbucks taking a lead amongst the major coffee companies in addressing the crisis in the coffee market … it is paying its suppliers around double the open market price and it has independent checks done to see that it carries out its own purchasing guidelines."

This leaves ethical consumers with yet another conundrum. The company's coffee buying policies are clearly progressive, but writers such as Naomi Klein have criticized Starbucks' aggressive expansion policies (forcing out local cafés), its questionable employment practices (keeping employees as temporary workers to avoid benefit and pension obligations), and its contribution to the homogenization of high streets globally (with everything from the design to the music prescribed by the Seattle HQ). Similarly, **Pret A Manger** offers Fairtrade coffee as an option, though the fact that they're part owned by McDonald's rules it out for many people.

More thoroughly ethical is **Progreso**, a café chain set up – and jointly owned – by two Honduran coffee co-operatives, Oxfam and the UK's leading independent coffee roaster. The idea is to combine first-rate organic, fairly traded coffee with a business plan that gives the producers a real stake in the business. There are already branches in London (Portobello Road and Covent Garden) and the plan is to open many more outlets in the next few years. For more information, see:

Progreso www.progreso.org.uk

received by the farmers was three times the international price for robustas and double for arabicas.

Fairtrade coffees are very widely available. The selection includes instants, ground and beans ranging from Kilimanjaro Mountain Special and Ethiopia Djimma to Sumatra Mandheling and Italian-style espresso blend. The range of brands is equally great, including supermarket own-labels and offerings from the coffee giants and Fairtrade specialists. One of the latter that deserves a special mention is **CaféDirect**, which has been central in bringing Fairtrade into the mainstream since being founded by Oxfam, Traidcraft, Equal Exchange and Twin Trading in 1991. The company exceeds the basic Fairtrade standards, feeding a percentage of its gross profits each year back to the farmer groups that supply it.

CaféDirect www.cafedirect.co.uk

For a full list of Fairtrade coffee brands, and where to buy them, try:

Fairtrade Coffee www.fairtrade.org.uk/products_coffee_buy.htm

And for background info about the coffee trade and crisis, visit:

ICO www.ico.org
Oxfam www.maketradefair.com

Fairtrade coffee: better left to the market?

Few people argue against fair trade aims, but some free-marketeers have made a case against one aspect of the system. They claim that, by offering a minimum-price guarantee to, say, coffee and cocoa farmers, fair traders are interfering with the market, and this, they argue, may do more harm than good. So is this true?

As touched on in chapter three, the idea that fair trade is anti-market is on one level quite odd: no one is forcing the consumers, traders or suppliers to play by these rules; no one is manipulating fair trade supply and demand. Indeed, in many ways you could see this as less of a distorted free market than the equivalent non-fairtrade goods: there is almost no fair trade advertising, after all, and the direct links with producers aim to cut out middlemen who can genuinely distort the operation of a fair market by exploiting a monopoly over delivery equipment – or even the straightforward use of force. What the people who make this case are promoting, then, is not exactly a free market, but a specific version of it in which low price is the only issue that consumers and traders consider.

That said, the argument does raise a legitimate question: if people buy a "fairly trad-ed" product, might this not reduce the demand for the non-fair-trade alternative, depressing prices and forcing uncertified producers to plumb even lower depths of bad working conditions to stay afloat?

In a market where supply and demand are pretty much balanced, this argument simply doesn't stand up: if half the shoppers start purchasing fairly traded man-goes, and half the producers start producing them, then the remaining half of the market still has the same balance of supply and demand as before, and hence the price they receive shouldn't be affected. However, things are different for products where supply *does* exceed demand, such as the market for coffee. Ultimately, if there is oversupply, the free-marketeers argue, there must be too many producers. So, unless consumers start altruistically doubling their caffeine intake, the problem will only really be resolved when some coffee farmers stop producing and start diversify-ing into other crops. Fair trade, they claim, can only get in the way of this essential market mechanism by propping up the inefficient producers.

Tea

Whereas coffee is grown mainly by small-scale independent farmers, tea is primarily a **plantation** crop. There are some small tea producers, but the sector is dominated by large estates, many of which include a factory in which the teas are processed and packed. As such, the most pressing issues are those of **workers' rights** – pay, hours, conditions, etc. As with many areas, unions are often discouraged, or disallowed, on tea plantations, leaving the pickers and packers, most of them women, with little bargaining power to demand better conditions. Health and safety is also important, especially the issue of pesticides, which are widely used on

But the issues are not quite as simple as the free-market fundamentalists make out. True, it's essential that more coffee farmers diversify into other crops to reduce oversupply. But which farmers are best equipped to do this? According to Harriet Lamb of the Fairtrade Foundation, diversification is often easier for those currently supplying Fairtrade coffee than for those who aren't: after all, they are likely to have access to more **capital, advice and support**.

There are ways, of course, to support marginalized farmers and encourage diversification without "interfering with the market" – namely through financial and other types of **support from governments** and individuals. But all these things require people to be aware of the issues, and there can be little doubt that the Fairtrade scheme has done an excellent job of getting Western consumers thinking about something as far removed from their lives as the plight of equatorial coffee farmers.

But even if this were not the case, there would be a more fundamental question: if some farmers are going to have to go out of business, which of them should we do our best to save from this unfortunate fate? Or, put another way, which trade model do we want to survive? The first one (non-fair-trade) offers the potential for the lowest price and cheapest production, but might mean poor wages and substandard health and safety for farmers and farm workers; child labour and even slave labour (such as the 1000 enslaved coffee farmers set free in Brazil in 2003); environmental and therefore also economic sustainability sacrificed to short-term crop maximization; and large companies winning over smaller players as their deep pockets allow them to support their operations through the economic winter. The other option is a system in which the market is allowed to play out but within a set of minimum standards: small farmers paid a minimum price upfront, allowing them to invest without relying on debt; importers audited to ensure no bullying or malpractice is going on; transparency and redistribution ensured; and the environment cared for. Fairtrade provides consumers with a free-market-style choice between these two options.

(non-organic) tea plantations, in some cases leading to health problems among the workers.

Fairtrade & organic tea

Tea bearing the Fairtrade Mark ensures decent minimum standards of pay, conditions and labour rights for tea workers. Its strictures also include some environmental policies, but tea that is both organic *and* Fairtrade ensures even stricter standards.

In the last few years, the range of Fairtrade teas has grown enormously, so even connoisseurs and fans of obscure flavours are likely to find something to their taste. Three companies with particularly broad ranges are:

▶ **Clipper** (available from supermarkets and independents, but for full range buy online at www.clipper-teas.com): Standard, Camomile, Peppermint, Black Chai, Green Chai, Earl Grey, English Breakfast, Irish Breakfast, Lapsang Souchong, Darjeeling, Assam, Ceylon, Sri Lanka Gold, Nilgiri Blue Mountain, Green Tea with Aloe Vera/Lemon/Echinacea/Ginkgo/Ginseng

▶ **Equal Exchange** (available at health food and independent shops): Standard, Assam, Breakfast, Darjeeling, Green, Earl Grey, Lemon Green, Masala Chai, Mint Green, Rooibos

▶ **Hampstead Tea & Coffee Company** (available at health food and independent shops): Organic Biochai Masala, First Flush, Makaibari Darjeeling, Green, Oolong Leaf, Earl Grey, Ginger Green, Green Verveine, White Leaf

The big brands

Most of the best-known tea brands – from **Tetley** to **Taylors** to **Twinings** – have signed up to an initiative called the **Tea Sourcing Partnership**, which aims to monitor and improve ethical standards in the supply chains of the participating companies. Very much a corporate affair (with PricewaterhouseCoopers responsible for the monitoring), the scheme is itself a member of the Ethical Trading Initiative (see box on p.61). It's certainly a welcome development – and unusual in the extent of its industry coverage – but doesn't offer anything like the same guarantees as Fairtrade.

Tea Sourcing Partnership www.teasourcingpartnership.org.uk

Other Fairtrade-certified food & drink

Though the Fairtrade Mark is primarily associated with coffee and tea, it can be found on a much wider range of products. A few of these – such as **Mexican honey** – raise the question discussed on p.200: is it more ethical to buy Fairtrade or to favour the locally produced equivalent on environmental grounds?

Others pose no such dilemmas. Fairtrade **chocolate**, for instance, is not only giving a living wage to small farmers who desperately need it. It's also helping to inject transparency and other ethical standards into an industry which is being increasingly associated with serious human rights abuses. Nearly half of the world's cocoa is grown in Côte d'Ivoire in West Africa, where, according to US government estimates, more than 100,000 child labourers work in hazardous conditions on cocoa farms. Many of these are slave labourers, taken from neighbouring Mali. To make matters worse, cocoa farmers – like coffee producers – are currently suffering a low market price for their crop.

Fairtrade **sugar**, on the other hand, allows consumers to support the more conscientious growers in the developing world – which may help them overcome the crippling effect of Europe's farm subsidies (see p.26).

What's available?

Here's a list of all the other Fairtrade foods and drinks available at the time of writing. These can be found in some supermarkets, but also try the fair trade specialist suppliers listed on p.225. For the most up-to-date range, see www.fairtrade.org.uk/products.htm

▶ **Chocolate and chocolates** by Chocaid, Co-op, The Day Chocolate Co., Green & Black's (Maya Gold only), Starbucks, Tesco, Traidcraft

▶ **Cocoa and drinking chocolate** from Caley's, Clipper, Cocodirect, Day Chocolate, Equal Exchange, Green & Black's, Traidcraft

▶ **Fruit juice**, including orange juice, breakfast juice and tropical juice by Fruit Passion, JP Juices and Tesco

▶ **Honey**, including set and clear, by Cotswold Speciality Foods, Equal Exchange, Rowse and Traidcraft

▶ **Herbs and spices**, including vanilla pods by Bart and Ndali and black peppercorns by Steenbergs

▶ **Muesli**, by Alara, the Co-op, Tesco

▶ **Preserves and condiments**, including strawberry jam, marmalade, mango chutney and chocolate hazelnut spread, by Traidcraft, Duerr's and Venture Foods

▶ **Rice and quinoa** by Sainsbury's, Suma, Infinity and Community

▶ **Snacks, biscuits and dried fruit** by the Co-op, Doves, Equal Exchange, Tesco, Traidcraft, Tropical Wholefoods, Village Bakery and others

▶ **Sugar**, including white, golden, raw cane and Demerara, by the Co-op, Equal Exchange, Traidcraft, Whitworths

▶ **Wine, beer and spirits**, including wines from chardonnay to shiraz (by Co-op, Vinfruco, Friarwood, Traidcraft, etc); rum (by Co-op and Sainsbury's), ginger wine (by Broughton Pastures) and beer (by Co-op and Meantime).

The Dubble from Day Chocolate company is the first "ethical" product to enter the market alongside Mars, Snickers and the like. Made from cocoa from the "Kuapa Kokoo" Fairtrade-certified co-operative in Ghana, it's widely available in supermarkets, newsagents and other outlets.

Fairly traded foods & drinks without the mark

It's quite common to see foods which don't bear the Fairtrade Mark, but which – according to the packaging or retailer – have been "fairly" or "ethically" traded. Sometimes these are products that aren't yet covered by the Fairtrade scheme, such as pasta, but which have been imported and packaged by long-established ethical trading organizations, such as Traidcraft. Many such foods can be found via online fair trade specialists (see p.225) or at organic supermarkets and health-food shops. In other cases, however, you might come across "unofficially" fairly traded foods in product areas that the Fairtrade scheme *does* cover – most notably in the case of coffee. Such claims are most commonly added in good faith by small firms that consider themselves to be responsible businesses. However, they don't offer any official guarantees, and arguably serve to harm the credibility of the Fairtrade system.

Food & drink: the big brands
Nestlé et al: who owns whom?

Food is an increasingly branded world. In the UK every day brings, on average, nearly thirty new "food products". That's 10,000 new crisp flavours, fizzy drinks – and, indeed, organic chutneys – each year. Of these, only around 10% will last twelve months; the other 90% – with all the ad campaigns, press releases and packaging that went with them – will be junked in the bulging trash can of food-marketing history.

Despite this extraordinary turnover of new products, however, the more popular and widely known food brands – such as Coca-Cola, Nescafé and Flora – are remarkably enduring. There are hundreds of such household names, but the number of major companies actually producing them is surprisingly small. Just as food retail is increasingly controlled by just a few giant supermarkets, and pesticides by a few huge agrochemicals firms, branded, packaged food and drink is increasingly dominated by a handful of multinational corporations, each the result of many mergers and takeovers.

These big firms are a highly controversial bunch. Besides specific controversy surrounding the individual companies, the sector as a whole is associated with the unethical promotion – including advertising to children – of salty, fatty and otherwise harmful foods that are leading to a massive rise in obesity, diabetes and other nutrition-related diseases.

Whether these problems are the fault of the companies or cultural shifts, such as people doing less exercise, is an open question. But the situation is looking increasingly extreme – in rich and poor countries alike. In the UK, according to a 2004 House of Commons Health Committee report, "obesity has grown by almost 400% in the last 25 years", and in the future, "the sight of amputees will become much more familiar ... There will be many more blind people. There will be huge demand for kidney dialysis ... Indeed, this will be the first generation where children die before their parents as a consequence of childhood obesity."

The big food companies certainly aren't entirely to blame for the obesity boom, yet the firms do spend a lot of time and money lobbying governments *against* legislation that might do something to solve these problems – banning fizzy drinks in schools, or sweets at supermarket checkouts, for example, or enforcing compulsory health warnings on the packaging of certain products. Indeed, the major American food brands are A-list political donors, while in the UK – according to documents obtained by

The Guardian, "the food manufacturers' lobbying group, the Food and Drink Federation, on its own had over 2,000 contacts with ministers, MPs, lords, MEPs, MSPs and special advisers" in 2003 alone.

The big companies consistently describe themselves as being socially responsible corporations, yet their trade associations have a tendency simply to refuse to admit that unhealthy foods and drinks cause health problems. For example, the "Health and Diet" section of the British Soft Drinks Association website (www.britishsoftdrinks.com), with no hint of irony, claims that: "All soft drinks are healthy because they provide the vital fluids our bodies need with some also providing contributions to the various vitamins and minerals we need every day." Hmmm.

The industry line on fizzy drinks and fresh fruit

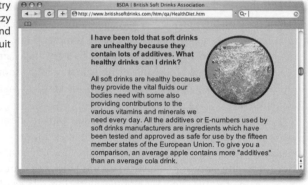

A few of the big players

It's well beyond the scope of this book to examine the ethical standards of every major food brand. But following is a quick summary of a few of the most controversial members of Big Food, with a list of the best-known brands owned by each. To find out more, try the online resources listed on pp.317–319, seek out the *Good Shopping Guide* (see p.321) or subscribe to *Ethical Consumer* magazine (see p.320).

Nestlé

With more than 230,000 employees and control of more than half of the international coffee market, Nestlé is easily the world's largest food company. The company's brands have been marred by two and a half decades of boycotting relating to its marketing of formula milk in the developing world (see box overleaf). And it came under fire in 2003 when it attempted to claim millions of dollars from the government of Ethiopia for assets seized by that country's military regime way back in the 1970s. Eleven million Ethiopians were facing starvation at the time, but Nestlé still saw fit to call it a "matter of principle", only dropping the claim after a public outcry. In 2005, Nestlé launched its first Fairtrade coffee – Partners' Blend – which has softened criticism from Oxfam and others campaigning on the coffee trade.

Nestlé brands

- Aero
- After Eight
- Black Magic
- Blue Riband
- Breakaway
- Buitoni
- Buxton
- Carnation
- Cheerios
- Dairy Box
- Drifter
- Golden Grahams
- Herta
- Jellytots
- Kit Kat
- Lion Bar
- Matchmakers
- Milkybar
- Minties
- Munch Bunch
- Munchies
- Nesquik
- Perrier
- Polo
- Quality Street
- Rolo
- Rowntree Fruit Pastilles/Gums
- San Pellegrino
- Santa Maria
- Shredded Wheat
- Shreddies
- Simply Double
- Ski
- Smarties
- Tip Top
- Toffee Crisp
- Valvert
- Vittel
- Walnut Whip
- Yorkie

Altria (Philip Morris)

Tobacco giant Philip Morris is best known for its Marlboro cigarettes. Less well known is the fact that the same corporation – recently renamed Altria – is among the world's biggest food companies, owning the majority of Kraft foods, among other things. Philip Morris's ethical record includes such highpoints as denying that smoking is addictive, being fined for failing to disclose political donations, and coming close to the top of the table of George W Bush campaign contributors (see p.64).

Altria brands

- Bird's
- Carte Noire
- Dairylea
- Dime
- Jacobs
- Kaffee HAG
- Kenco
- Kraft
- Lunchables
- Maxwell House
- Philadelphia
- RITZ
- Suchard
- Terry's
- Toblerone

Nestlé & infant formula

Since 1977, Nestlé, the world's largest food company, has been the target of the most global, long-standing and highly publicized of all consumer boycotts. The food giant has scores of brands (see p.213), but the controversy focuses on the product that launched the company right back in the 1860s: infant formula, also called breastmilk substitute, baby milk or bottle milk.

Where breastfeeding is impossible or impractical – as is often the case – infant formula can be a lifesaver, but it also comes with certain health risks. Even in rich countries, babies fed on formula milk during the first few months are more likely to suffer certain health problems, since breastmilk provides a perfect combination of nutrients and antibodies. But in developing countries the dangers are more acute. Formula milk needs to be prepared with water and served in sterilized bottles, which can be problematic if pure water or fuel are in short supply. And if parents find themselves stuck with it but unable to afford sufficient quantities (a real possibility, because moving back to breastfeeding is often impossible once formula milk has been used) they may over-dilute it, mix it with unsuitable solids or substitute it with cheaper but completely unsuitable alternatives, such as cows' milk or tea.

These risks have been known for decades. Right back in the 1930s pioneering paediatrician Dr Cicely Williams published and spoke about the hazards of inappropriate bottle feeding. But for much of the twentieth century the formula milk manufacturers – of which Nestlé was and is the biggest – aggressively promoted their products around the world. Pictures of plump "first-world" babies were used on tins and posters, and free samples (sometimes given out by marketing "nurses") were provided for hospitals and given out to new mothers, often making breastfeeding impossible and forcing mothers into months of purchasing. The result was a huge decline in the exclusive use of breastfeeding and the completely avoidable deaths of hundreds of thousands of babies each year around the world.

Things came to a head in the early 1970s, after exposés by *New Internationalist* magazine and War on Want. The latter's article was translated into German as "Nestlé Tötet Babies" (Nestlé Kills Babies) and Nestlé sued for libel. It won the court case on the grounds of this title, but it generated massive negative publicity for itself in the process. Things didn't really improve, so a few years later a consumer boycott began

– first in the US and then internationally – co-ordinated by the **International Baby Food Action Network** (IBFAN).

In 1981, the World Health Assembly drew up the International Code of Marketing of Breastmilk Substitutes, a set of recommended minimum standards relating to the promotion (or non-promotion) of formula milk. A few years later, Nestlé agreed to implement the Code voluntarily and the boycott was lifted. But four years after that, the campaign was revived, as IBFAN determined that Nestlé hadn't lived up to its promises and was still supplying cheap or free formula milk to hospitals.

A decade and a half on, the situation is still bad: the World Health Organization estimates that "some 1.5 million children still die every year because they are inappropriately fed ... less than 35% of infants worldwide are exclusively breastfed for the first four months of life". And though there have been many positive developments – explicit formula milk marketing has been almost stamped out, and breastfeeding rates in the developing world are rising – the question remains as to whether Nestlé, who have gone to great lengths to promote themselves as an ethical company, are acting responsibly.

According to IBFAN, the answer is no, since Nestlé and other firms are "continuing their unethical promotional activities whilst claiming to abide by the International Code". The campaigners continue to document some direct violations of the Code – which they display on their website – though their main accusations today relate to more subtle things such as Nestlé lobbying against regulation relating to infant formula, and refusing to accept that the Code should apply to *all* breastmilk substitutes – including those aimed at older babies – not just "infant formula".

Nestlé denies such allegations, pointing to its widespread promotion of breastfeeding, its regular audits, and its internal ombudsman for reporting bad practice. Peter Brabeck-Letmathe, the CEO, even claims to look personally into each reported breach of the Code, while acknowledging that – in a company of nearly a quarter of a million staff – slip-ups are bound to happen occasionally.

Nestlé also claims that formula milk products are "legitimate and useful", allowing mothers in poor countries the option of returning to work instead of staying at home – something which women in the West take for granted. And they claim that the only reason why they receive all the negative publicity is because they're the easiest target: while their food and drink brands are household names, the other baby milk firms are pharmaceutical companies, so couldn't easily be boycotted.

However, even in the last few years criticism of Nestlé's formula milk activities has kept coming – albeit less fierce than it once was – from sources as wide-ranging as UNICEF and, in 2003, the *British Medical Journal*. And the boycott continues. For both sides of the story, and more background on the breastfeeding issue, visit:

IBFAN www.ibfan.org
Nestlé www.babymilk.nestle.com
UNICEF www.unicef.org

Coca-Cola and PepsiCo

When the World Health Organization launched an offensive on the global health effects of sugary foods in 2003, fizzy drinks were at the top of their hit-list. To defend themselves against such attacks, and ensure that no one restricts their capability to sell fizzy drinks to kids, the market leaders of this sector – Coca-Cola and PepsiCo – have got the US government on their side through proactive lobbying and political donations (see www.opensecrets.org).

Coca-Cola, in particular, has courted controversy on many other levels. In the last few years, for example, they have faced public and shareholder criticism regarding their failure to address the murder of trade unionists in a Colombian bottling plant, and also for their factory in Kerala, India, where farmers have complained of their water reserves being bled dry and their fields polluted by dangerous waste which the factory allegedly sold to them as fertilizer.

Coca-Cola brands	PepsiCo brands	
▶ Capri-Sun	▶ Doritos	▶ Walkers
▶ Dr Pepper	▶ Pepsi	▶ Wotsits
▶ Fanta	▶ Quaker	
▶ Kia Ora	▶ 7UP	
▶ Lilt	▶ Smith's	
▶ Sprite	▶ Tropicana	

Supermarkets & alternatives
Where to shop?

The explosive growth of **supermarkets** in the last half century has completely revolutionized the food sector. If Britain ever was a nation of shopkeepers, it's certainly not any more. With the recent takeover of Safeway by Morrisons, just four companies – **Tesco**, **Sainsbury's**, **ASDA** and **Morrisons** – sell more than three-quarters of our food. Along with a handful of smaller players, including Marks & Spencer, Waitrose, the Co-op, Iceland and Budgens, the supermarkets – or "multiples" as they're known in the trade – account for the overwhelming majority of grocery sales. And it's not just retailing they've taken over: they've also displaced a huge number of businesses in the import, distribution and wholesale sectors.

Despite the supermarket stranglehold, however, some markets and local shops survive. And a number of alternatives with a distinctly ethical slant – such as **farmers' markets**, **organic box schemes** and **specialists** in Fairtrade products, free-range meat and so on – are starting to gain popularity across the country. Following is a brief look at the morals of supermarket shopping, followed by a small directory of these alternatives (from p.222).

Supermarkets

Perhaps more than any country in the world, the UK is addicted to supermarkets. Maybe it's their special offers or their dazzling choice. Or perhaps it's their all-under-one-roof convenience. But, whatever the reasons, few Britons buy much of their food anywhere else.

Compared with most giant companies, the big supermarkets have quite a lot on their ethical CVs. ASDA, Marks & Spencer, Sainsbury's and Tesco have all signed up to the **Ethical Trading Initiative**, which aims to improve labour standards among suppliers (see p.61). They quickly responded to consumer fears about **GM foods** by removing them from their stores. And they've been central in bringing certain ethical products – such as organic and Fairtrade goods – into the mainstream. As we'll see, the big supermarkets are currently positively battling to be the greenest.

But despite all this the supermarket sector is the subject of more resentment than almost any other, with criticism coming from consumers, environmentalists and farmers alike. Some of the objections are standard complaints about big businesses – political lobbying (which the supermarkets are famously good at), executive pay, and so on. And some relate to **quality**: food writers and gourmands accuse the big retailers of replacing the UK's base of knowledgeable fishmongers, butchers and greengrocers, and countless varieties of local fruit and veg, with a food non-culture devoid of expertise and variety. But there are also a number of more specific accusations, which fall into three categories…

Damaging communities and small businesses

The era of the supermarket has been the era of the **decline of the local shop**. According to a study published by the New Economics Foundation (www.neweconomics.org), in the five years to 2002 alone, "50 specialised stores like butchers, bakers, fishmongers and newsagents closed every week". That's 13,000 in total, before you add in milkmen and other food service providers who have found it impossible to compete.

Apart from obvious negative effects on town centres – and on people who for whatever reason are unable to drive to the supermarket – this has also led to a loss of decent **jobs**. Even according to research funded by the supermarkets, each new out-of-town store causes a net loss of 276 jobs. And those jobs which do get created are usually pretty unsatisfying: working as a check-out assistant can't exactly compare with running a greengrocer's.

One way in which the supermarkets have undercut local bakers, milkmen and grocers is by treating basics like milk, bread and tinned tomatoes as **loss leaders**, selling them at less than the wholesale cost and making up the profits from other products. On one level, this is good news, meaning that even people on very low incomes – if they can get to a supermarket – shouldn't struggle to afford the basics. However, since the supermarkets then overprice more healthy foods – and numerous reports have shown that they are significantly more expensive than greengrocers for many fruit and vegetables – then the overall effect may be negative. Indeed, loss leaders are illegal in many countries and a recent publication by the UK's Competition Commission declared these tactics worked against the public interest, but failed to suggest any rules to stop it. Some have put this down to the industry's strong links to government.

Commentators who worry about the effect of supermarkets on local communities also point out that the money spent in, say, a Tesco or Sainsbury's bypasses, rather than filters through, the **local economy**. The New Economics Foundation calculated that a pound spent on an organic box scheme generates nearly twice as much money for the local economy as a pound spent in the supermarket.

Exploiting farmers

It's widely accepted that the supermarkets have substantial power over the farmers that supply them. Indeed, as farmers' groups have said for years – and as food writer Joanna Blythman documented in her recent book, *Shopped* – the big chains are often in a position to dictate farm-gate prices and terms of trade. One result of this is that prices have been driven so low that many small farmers have gone out of business, and bigger ones have been forced to cut corners on labour and environmental standards. According to NFU figures, from a food basket costing £37 in the supermarket, farmers today receive only £11, while campaign group Corporate Watch noted in 2003 that "Tesco's profits, at £1.4 billion, are more than half the entire UK income from farming, £2.36 billion".

But it's not just prices. Farmers claim that the supermarkets' buying power has allowed them to get away with **avoiding long-term contracts** (hence shifting much of their business risk onto their suppliers), **delaying payments**, refusing perfectly good fruit and veg on minor cosmetic grounds, and even making farmers absorb the cost of **special offers** such as two-for-the-price-of-one promotions.

Despite all this, however, farmers find it very difficult to complain, for fear that the supermarket will simply refuse to continue stocking their products – something that, in many cases, would be enough to spell financial ruin. According to Joanna Blythman's investigations, many farmers "lay awake at night, dreading that phonecall from supermarket HQ saying 'Sorry, but we're going to de-list you'".

A counterargument might be that supermarkets negotiate hard on behalf of consumers – including the poorest members of society. But given that the average income of a UK farmer is below the national average, and that their produce sells for more in a supermarket than it would in a typical market or greengrocer's, this isn't a particularly convincing case.

Harming the environment

Though the supermarkets claim to be committed to the environment, there's no escaping the fact that they create a number of environmental burdens. They contribute to global warming, for example, by increasing the distance from plough to plate on three different levels: locally (by encouraging out-of-town-centre shopping), nationally (since produce gets delivered to stores via few-and-far-between centralized distribution centres) and internationally (by sourcing goods from abroad when British produce is available).

The supermarkets are also notorious for refusing to accept fruit and veg on pernickety cosmetic grounds, something that leads to a great deal of waste, and also to farmers increasing their agrochemical inputs to ensure that their carrots, for example, have "crowns" with diameters of within the specified range of millimetres. Joanna Blythman examined supermarket specifications and compiled a list of "faults" that would "almost certainly" cause a consignment of tomatoes to be rejected:

▶ More than 5% of the tomatoes not uniform in size (to within 5mm circumference)
▶ Light scarring or blemishes
▶ Ribbed, angular or misshapen tomatoes

▶ A colour of 0, 1, 2 or 7 on the supermarket's colour chart
▶ Slightly chewy skin
▶ Soft, tender tomatoes
▶ Tomatoes at different colour stages in the same box

Another criticism made by environmentalists is that supermarkets profiteer from the organic movement while ignoring its eco principles – by wrapping organic fruit and veg in unnecessary plastic packaging, for example, and failing to favour local growers wherever possible.

Which supermarkets are the most responsible?

Over the last few years, as consumers have become more concerned with the types of issues discussed in this chapter, the major supermarkets have responded with a wide range of measures designed to win ethical hearts and minds. To give just a few examples, Tesco recently started offering Clubcard points to those who bring their own bags, while ASDA have initiated a trial scheme in Cornwall and Devon whereby farmers will deliver produce directly to their nearest branches (rather than its being trucked via a distribution centre). Waitrose now has a dedicated local food section in each store, Sainsbury's have cut food miles by 5% in a year and Morrisons have started selling bio-ethanol fuel for green cars. Most of the big players are also members of the **Ethical Trading Initiative** (see p.61) and have promised to cut down on carbon emissions, waste and the use of non-sustainable palm oil (see p.252) over the next few years.

With such varied initiatives, it's not easy to rank the supermarkets in terms of their overall ethical standards. It *ought* to be, however, thanks to **Race to the Top**, a project launched in 2000 by the International Institute for Environment and Development. The idea was to work with the top ten UK supermarkets, measuring and helping to improve their standards on everything from developing-world labour conditions to animal welfare. Three years in, though, the project was wound up, the closing press release headed: "How ethical are our supermarkets? We can't tell you." All the big players had jumped ship after Tesco and ASDA refused to participate.

It's not too surprising that it was these two supermarkets who put a spanner in the works. **ASDA**, after all, is owned by the world's biggest and arguably least popular company: Wal-Mart, a famously anti-union, political-lobbying, sweat-shop-exploiting, gun-selling multinational whose predatory, expansionist policies are the stuff of corporate legend. China's *People's Daily* once looked into why no unions were recognized among

Supermarkets and animal welfare

When it comes to animal welfare, the general trend is simple: the posher the super-market, the better the policies. Hence in one recent survey the RSPCA congratulated "Marks & Spencer, Selfridges and Harvey Nichols" as the only supermarkets to ban battery eggs completely. However, it's not quite that straightforward. The best research into supermarkets and animal welfare is done by Compassion in World Farming (www.ciwf.org.uk), which compares the big retailers on the full range of relevant issues each year. The 2005 report ranked the main supermarkets as follows, out of a possible 60 points:

1 Waitrose 49.3

2 Marks & Spencer 48.0

3 The Co-operative Group 45.0

4 Tesco 35.1

5 Sainsbury's 29.3

6 Somerfield 23.5

7 ASDA 20.8

Wal-Mart's Chinese suppliers, but the company soon cleared up the confusion: "A Wal-Mart spokesman explained that there are no trade unions in its branches in other parts of the world either." **Tesco** is not in the same league as Wal-Mart, but shares its aggressive, global-expansion business model and has faced criticism from groups ranging from the Environment Agency (who named it a "significant repeat offender") to the WWF (who kicked it out of an initiative to stop sourcing endangered hardwood for garden furniture).

Sainsbury's fares slightly better – and has been praised for its extensive environmental reporting by Innovest and others in the corporate social responsibility circles – while **Somerfield** and **Safeway** (now Morrisons) at least demonstrated transparency by staying involved in the Race to the Top scheme when others had dropped out. But, in most respects – and especially in the area of animal welfare – all of the above trail behind the more up-market players such as **Waitrose** and **Marks & Spencer**, both of which have wide-ranging progressive policies.

Overall, however, the most ethical supermarket is probably the demo-cratically run **Co-op**. Also the UK's biggest farmer, the Co-op shows how much room for improvement there is among its competitors. It has thrown an incomparable weight behind Fairtrade – all its own-brand coffee and chocolate, for example, now bears the Mark. Its labour-rights audits are verified by an external company. It's started voluntarily phasing out certain pesticides. Its cleaning products are certified as animal-test-ing free. It's happy to reveal which companies manufacture its own-brand products. The list goes on.

Farmers' markets and farm shops

Though they still only account for a fraction of a percent of UK food sales, farmers' markets are on the up. The concept is simple: "farmers, growers or producers from a defined local area are present in person to sell their own produce, direct to the public. All products sold should have been grown, reared, caught, brewed, pickled, baked, smoked or processed by the stallholder."

This way, the farmers get a better deal than they would get via a retailer, environmentally harmful food transport is kept to a minimum, big business is cut out of the equation, and consumers get fresher produce and the chance to put questions directly to the producers.

To ensure these aims are kept pure, the National Farmers' Retail & Markets Association has developed a set of standards which farmers' markets must adhere to in order to gain official FARMA certification:

▶ **Local produce** "Primary produce" sold must be grown, reared or caught by the stall holder within the defined local area: usually a 30 mile radius around the market, though up to 50 miles is acceptable for larger cities and coastal or remote towns and villages. "Secondary" (prepared) produce must be brewed, pickled, baked, smoked or processed by the stall holder using at least one ingredient of origin from within the defined local area.

Reconnecting field and city: a farmers' market in central London

▶ **The principal producer** or a representative directly involved in the production process must attend the stall.

▶ **Information** should be available to customers about farmers' markets standards and the production methods of the producers.

Farm shops apply the same philosophy on a smaller scale, typically offering the produce of just one farm. To find farmers' markets and farm shops near you, visit:

Farmers' Markets www.farmersmarkets.net ▷ 01225 787 914
London Farmers' Markets www.lfm.org.uk
FARMA www.farma.org.uk

Organic delivery

Even if there weren't other arguments against the supermarkets, they're not an ideal place to buy **organic** food. In most supermarkets, organic produce is overpriced, over-packaged in plastic, often poor quality and – in some cases – imported by environmentally burdensome air freight. Farmers' markets are one alternative. **Box schemes** are another.

For a weekly fee, you'll get a mixed box or bag of local, seasonal fruit and veg – perhaps bolstered by foreign goods imported by ship – either delivered to your door or left somewhere ready for you to pick up. Most box-scheme companies also offer all sorts of other foods and goods, from bread to washing-up liquid, so it's perfectly possible to save yourself ever going to the supermarket. Even when you factor in the delivery van, the overall pollution and energy use will in most cases be much smaller than driving to and buying from the supermarket.

The Soil Association is the best source of information about box schemes. Their annual *Organic Directory* lists thousands, as well as everything from restaurants to organic textile suppliers and fish delivery. The guide is available both in paper form (order by phone) and on their website (you have to register before accessing it, but it's free):

Soil Association www.soilassociation.org ▷ 0117 914 2446

You could also try the smaller but more user-friendly lists at:

A Lot of Organics www.alotoforganics.co.uk
About Organics www.aboutorganics.co.uk
Links Organic www.linksorganic.com

If you can't find any local schemes, or if those you've tried aren't very good, you could try one of the bigger box scheme companies, some of which will deliver to nearly anywhere in the UK. For example:

Fresh Food www.freshfood.co.uk ▷ 020 8749 8778
Simply Organic www.simplyorganic.net ▷ 0870 760 6001

The South East is also well served by Organic Delivery (London only) and the award-winning Abel & Cole.

Organic Delivery www.organicdelivery.co.uk
▷ 020 7739 8181
Abel & Cole www.abel-cole.co.uk
▷ 020 7737 3648

A typical mixed box from Abel & Cole. Like most organic delivery services, they offer a wide range of fruit and veg options – from the Farmer's Choice Combi Bag (£8) to the Family Organic Box (£22) – as well as bread, fish, meat and store-cupboard goods.

Organic meat and fish specialists

Many of the above schemes will provide organic meat and fish products in addition to fruit and veg. But you may find a better selection as well as lower prices via a specialist – especially if you want to buy in bulk. For meat, try **Graig Farm Organics**, which offers everything from goat to wild boar (in addition to a full range of other groceries). For fish, another good option is **Hawkshead**, which sells organic salmon, trout, sea bass, prawns and mixed cases.

Graig Farm Organics www.graigfarm.co.uk ▷ 01597 851 655
Hawkshead Organic Fish www.organicfish.com ▷ 01539 436 541

Organic booze

A number of suppliers now offer **organic booze**, including a huge range of wines – some produced in the UK – and scores of traditional ales. Organic booze is usually also vegetarian-friendly (hardline veggies avoid many beers and most wines since fish derivatives are often used in their preparation). Three of the best suppliers are:

Organic Wine Company www.ecowine.com
Vinceremos www.vinceremos.co.uk
Vintage Roots www.vintageroots.co.uk

Fair trade specialists

The Fairtrade Foundation's website – www.fairtrade.org.uk – lists all the certified Fairtrade products available in the UK, along with details of which shops stock them. However, for the best selection at the lowest prices, try an online specialist such as the following.

Traidcraft

www.traidcraftshop.co.uk ▷ 0870 443 1018

Traidcraft sell a good range of fairly traded food, from basics (sugar, rice, pasta, nuts, jam, honey), via wine, teas and coffees, to a mouthwateringly rich list of chocolates and other sweet things. Many items are available in packs of six or more, allowing you to make savings when buying in bulk.

Goodness Direct

www.goodnessdirect.co.uk ▷ 0871 871 6611

Goodness Direct aims to sell "everything for your healthy eating, natural and ethical lifestyle". That includes a range of more than 150 Fairtrade-certified products in addition to various veggie, vegan and healthfood offerings and pet food. There is even a convenience food section, where the time-strapped can stock up on Organic Tofu Smoked Almond & Sesame Slices and the like.

Clipper Store

www.clipper-teas.com ▷ 01308 863 344

Probably the best way to buy Fairtrade-certified hot drinks is direct from Clipper, who offer an enormous range of teas (see p.208 for more information) as well as a decent number of coffees and hot chocolates. Most of what's available is also organic.

Other good sites and stores

Following are a few other sites and organizations that sell food relevant to the issues discussed in this chapter.

Big Barn

www.bigbarn.co.uk

A portal allowing you to search for your nearest local-food suppliers, find delivery services and order online. As they put it, it's a website that "gives consumers the opportunity to buy meat, game, fish, fruit and vegetables, cheese and dairy products,

drink, bakers' products and even nursery plants direct from the people who produce them". The site has recipes which use seasonal ingredients, and has a recipe archive to help you work out what to actually do with your local produce.

UK Food Online

www.ukfoodonline.co.uk

Though geared towards high-quality food, rather than ethical issues, this site includes plenty of relevant suppliers – for free-range veal and the like. Also, since they don't limit themselves to organic producers, they include many suppliers not found in the Soil Association list.

Farmgate Direct

www.farmgatedirect.com ▷ 0870 754 0014

Owned by the RSPCA, Farmgate Direct supply fresh chicken, beef, lamb, veal and salmon accredited under the Freedom Food scheme (see p.175). They aim to deliver within 72 hours of confirming your order.

Suma Wholefoods

www.suma.co.uk ▷ 0845 458 2295

Though they primarily supply to shops, this large wholesaler of green, organic and fairly traded foods (as well as other products) will deliver directly to customers who don't have access to a local retailer, subject to minimum orders. Suma is a co-operative with an equal-pay-for-all policy, allowing workers to "successfully manage their own businesses without an owner/manager elite".

HDRA Grow Your Own Organics

www.organicgardening.org.uk

A superb resource for anyone wanting to go organic in their own back yard. It's regularly updated, so it can give gardening and growing advice specific to whichever month it is. The site assures you that you don't need to have a huge garden to grow organic herbs, fruit or vegetables (although if there was advice on things to do with a windowbox, as one of the pages implies, it was impossible to find). Mushroom fans should also check out: www.fungi.com.

the organic organisation

Clothes, cosmetics & jewellery

Beauty may be only skin deep, but our clothes, make-up and jewellery raise issues that are less superficial. Besides garment sweatshops, the clothes and shoe industries are associated with certain environmental and (in the case of leather and fur) animal-rights issues. Cosmetics, meanwhile, are all too often the result of animal experiments, and the jewellery trade is only just starting to come to terms with problems such as child labour and conflicts funded by the illicit sale of diamonds. This chapter takes a quick look at these three industries, listing the most ethical companies in each.

Clothes & shoes
Fashion victims

Mention "ethical shopping" and the first thing many people think of is the boycotting of exploitative Asian sweatshops producing branded clothes for the West. It's certainly true that labour standards in the apparel sector are bad. But the factory isn't the first step in the making of clothes – and it's not the only one associated with social and environmental problems. First of all, the raw material needs to be grown, killed or manufactured, and dyed the right colour.

Clothing materials

Cotton

Cultivated by humans for more than 5000 years, and the basis of products ranging from T-shirts to US dollar bills, **cotton** is something of a natural wonder. But much has changed since the ancient Greek historian Herodotus first documented the existence of Indian "tree wool ... exceeding in beauty and goodness". Today, cotton lies at the heart of global debates on agrochemicals, GM versus organic farming, and ethical versus regular trade.

The agrochemical question relates to the fact that more **pesticides** are used on cotton than on any other crop. Indeed, despite covering only a few percent of the world's cultivable soils, cotton farms account for roughly 10% of all herbicide use and an astonishing 20–25% of insecticide use.

People argue about whether or not these chemicals – which include carcinogenic and otherwise nasty substances such as carbamates and organochlorines – are bad for the eventual wearer of the cotton. But the effects on farmers and the environment are much more pressing. There are no definitive global figures but anti-pesticide campaigners claim that thousands of cotton-farm workers are killed by agrochemicals each year. Research by Pesticide Action Network, for example, showed that in a single region within the small West African state of Benin "at least 61 men, women and children" were killed by cotton pesticides between 1999 and 2001. And, of course, for every one person who dies, hundreds of others have to put up with the ill effects of polluted air and water.

GM cotton: immoral fibre?

As with other areas of agriculture, the organic brigade are not alone in claiming they have the solution to the pesticide problem. The biotech companies – mainly Monsanto – have produced GM cotton engineered to be resistant to insects (with Bt toxin built into their leaves) and/or resistant to a powerful herbicide (which in theory allows less of other herbicides to be used). The technology is probably the most successful application of a GM crop and has, according to the UN, allowed farmers in China, India and elsewhere to reduce their pesticide use substantially and simultaneously increase yields. Critics aren't convinced, however, claiming that Bt-resistant insects will inevitably appear at some stage and that GM crops may prove damaging to biodiversity by killing non-target insects. They also point out that, as with any GM crop, releasing it into the environment could have any number of unforeseeable implications. More than half of the cotton on sale is now estimated to be GM, so anyone with an ideological problem with the technology should buy organic.

Some commentators also worry that the chemicals are entering the food chain, as the vast quantities of cottonseed harvested are fed to animals and made into cottonseed oil for human consumption.

There are two proposed solutions to all these problems. Biotechnologists advocate using **GM** cotton crops to cut back on pesticides (see box opposite), while greens advise consumers to opt out of pesticides *and* GM by choosing **organic cotton** or favouring alternatives such as hemp (see box overleaf). Just as with food, organic fibres can be grown using chemical-free alternatives to pesticides. In Uganda, for example, black ants are collected and set on the cotton fields to eat the pests.

Organic fabrics are also more eco-friendly in terms of processing. In the manufacture of conventional cotton cloth thousands of synthetic substances are used: chlorine **bleaches**, heavy-metal **dyes** and treatments such as formaldehyde to lessen creasability and minimise shrinking. Many of these are highly toxic, and can cause environmental and health problems if not handled and disposed of correctly.

The market for organic cotton is rocketing, thanks to orders from specialists and from a few big companies – including Nike and Levi – who buy a small proportion of their cotton from organic sources. The US used to be the biggest producer, but increasingly organic production is spreading to developing countries, which can undercut the West when it comes to low-chemical, labour-intensive production methods.

Organic cotton, then, may have some social as well as environmental benefits. But it doesn't directly address broader social issues such as the

US cotton subsidies

The single biggest problem faced by cotton farmers in the developing world is the massive subsidies given to giant cotton farms in wealthier countries. In the US, partly for historical reasons, and partly due to effective lobbying from farm groups, around 25,000 cotton farmers receive roughly $4 billion in support from the government – an average of £160,000 each. This allows them to sell below the cost of production, driving down international prices and making it extremely difficult for growers in poor countries to compete. In the words of Oxfam's Celine Charvariat, "American and European taxpayers are financing the destruction of the livelihoods of millions of cotton farmers in Africa … the cotton barons of Texas and Alabama are getting huge subsidies … and driving more efficient African farmers out of business."

In 2004, the World Trade Organization upheld Brazil's objection that US cotton subsidies are illegal. But the US government has resisted the decision, promising to "defend US agriculture in every forum we need to".

fact that millions of developing-world cotton growers – like coffee farmers – have to contend with fluctuating commodity markets and unscrupulous middlemen. There's also the question of **child labour**. According to a study by the India Committee of the Netherlands, 90% of all labour in the Indian cottonseed market is carried out by nearly half a million children, mostly girls aged between six and fourteen. It's these kinds of social issues that led to the emergence, in 2005, of **Fairtrade**-certified cotton. This works in a very similar way to Fairtrade coffee, guaranteeing the farmer a

Time for a hemp revival?

While some people advocate organic or GM cotton as the greenest of fabrics, others sing the praises of **hemp** – not the King Size Rizla variety, but its non-psychoactive industrial counterpart. The fact that most of hemp's rather evangelical advocates also seem to be keen smokers of their favourite plant doesn't do the campaign many favours. But with increasing numbers of governments and farmers examining its benefits, it seems they may have a point.

Cannabis sativa has a long and distinguished history, taking in at least 5000 years of use as a source of food, cloth, nets and countless other items. Many products have started out life as hemp, from proper paper – first created in Tibet at roughly the time of Christ – to Levi's jeans. Until the twentieth century, the plant was also the main source for ropes and sails (the word canvas is derived from the Latin *cannabis*), which made it so central to naval success that both Britain and the US once had laws requiring all farmers to dedicate a proportion of their land to it.

However, a couple of centuries after George Washington advised Americans to "make the most of hempseed and sow it everywhere", the wonderplant was on the decline, gradually being replaced by cotton for clothes, wood for paper and nylon for rope. Once the first round of the war on drugs got under way, things got even worse, with hemp officially or effectively banned in many countries.

Hemp fans claim that now is the time for a revival. Farmers would gain because the plant is unusually easy, quick, inexpensive and safe to grow, requiring (unlike cotton) very few agrochemicals. Consumers would benefit because hemp products, once produced in large quantities, would be cheaper than current materials, and because hemp cloth is many times stronger and more durable than cotton. The environment would benefit through reduced chemical use, improved soil structures (due to the plant's deep roots) and reduced felling of trees for paper and board, since hemp fibre is far quicker to produce at a sustainable rate than wood fibre and requires less energy input and chemical treatment. The plant could also potentially contribute to reduced fossil fuel use, as it's an ideal bio-fuel and can be used to make biodegradable alternatives to plastics and metals (in the 1940s Henry Ford famously produced a partly hemp-resin car powered by hemp-based fuel). To cap all this off, the plant's seeds are unusually nutritious, with a blend of amino acids close to perfect for humans.

minimum price in addition to a social premium to invest in community development projects (for more on how Fairtrade certification works, see p.26). The system also requires certain minimum labour standards of the factories that produce clothes from Fairtrade cotton, though the primary ethical focus is firmly on the cotton growers.

There are now a number of manufacturers and suppliers selling clothes that are both organic *and* Fairtrade. For a list of recommended shops and online retailers, turn to p.244.

Not everyone is entirely convinced of all hemp's supposed advantages, and fibre-processing technology will need to be developed before it becomes commercially advantageous. Still, few deny that the plant could offer some real long-term ecological benefits. So it's no wonder that "ethical clothes" suppliers often sell hemp products, sometimes sourced and produced according to fair trade principles (though it's worth pointing out that the world's biggest hemp producer is China, an oppressive regime by most measures).

If you fancy supporting the hemp movement and clothing yourself in cannabis, check out the specialist stores listed on p.248. If you really catch the hemp bug, a Google search will also reveal everything from ropes to varnishes and paints produced from the same plant.

Harvesting hemp in Russia, 1956

Silk

Silk thread is made by unravelling the cocoon of silk worms, each of which wraps itself up in a single continuous strand of up to a kilometre in length. Known as **sericulture**, the process of harvesting silk – cultivating the worms, harvesting the threads and winding them into thicker strands for making material – is a big industry in Asia, with China and India by far the biggest suppliers.

Millions of economically marginalized people make a living out of the silk trade but, in some regions including parts of India, the industry is rife with **child workers**, many as young as five and in bonded positions: essentially slaves paying off a family debt. A report from 2000 available from the Indian wing of UNDP, the UN's global development network (www.undp.org), makes for grim reading:

> Children are employed in almost all processes of the sericulture industry making it almost a child-based economy … they are required to work in filature units that are cramped, damp, dark, poorly ventilated … the handling of dead worms with bare hands, and the unbearable stench is also a cause for spreading infection and illness. Standing for 12–16 hours a day with hardly any break, concentrating on reeling the fine threads, leads to other health disorders. Vapours from the boiling cocoons and the diesel fumes from the machines also contribute to the poor conditions in the units … found responsible for retardation of the child's normal growth and development.

Other reports describe endemic bronchial ailments, coughs, back pains, asthma and TB among the child silk workers, as well as seriously damaged hands from checking the boiling cocoons.

This isn't true of all countries – nor the whole of India – and a blanket boycott of the sector would hurt millions of impoverished silk producers who don't exploit bonded child labour. Also, a real solution can probably only come from the relevant governments: "the problem", according to a 2003 Human Rights Watch study on bonded labour in the Indian silk industry, "is political will".

Still, consumers can opt for **fairly traded** silk products, which are available from companies such as Silken Dalliance and Traidcraft (listed later in this chapter). These not only have policies governing silk thread manufacture, but also aim to ensure that more of the profits head back to the people weaving the cloth and sewing the garments.

The West, curiously, pays much less attention to the children and adults working in the silk industry than to the **silk worms** themselves, though admittedly the latter do get a rather rough deal. If a worm eats its way out of its cocoon, the thread is broken, so the cocoons are boiled or baked while the worms are still inside (in some countries the worms are eaten afterwards). It is possible to make "raw"-style silk without killing the worm, and you may occasionally see this sold, usually labelled as vegetarian or vegan friendly.

Leather vs. veggie alternatives

Vegetarians object to leather for obvious reasons: though it might be described as a byproduct of the meat industry, the hide of an animal adds substantially to its slaughterhouse value, and so subsidizes the meat industry, including intensive farms. But leather – whether it be from cow, pig, sheep or goat – also raises another question: its **environmental impact**. Indeed, though animal skin may be a "natural" material, modern leather is the result of intensive chemical processing, including toxic carcinogenic substances such as salts of **chromium**. This not only makes it surprisingly energy-inefficient to produce but means that it generates massive quantities of waste: treating a ton of raw hide can result in 75,000 litres of waste water and 100kg of dried sludge. Anyone who has been within smelling range of a tannery will be unsurprised to learn that this waste, when not treated properly, can be extremely dangerous.

As environmental regulation has tightened up in the West, developing-world tanneries have seen their businesses expanding. This provides much-needed jobs and income, but the human and environmental costs can be high. A study by the Tokyo Institute of Technology found that 62% of the 2.4 million people in Kasur, Pakistan, suffer from ailments – including some as serious as cancer, tuberculosis and blindness – caused by industrial waste, with tanneries the major contributor. Similarly, in the Bangladeshi capital Dhaka, according to a report cited in the *World Health Organization Bulletin*, half a million residents are at risk of serious illness due to tannery pollution, with tannery workers there 50% more likely than their peers to die before the age of fifty. In other areas, large expanses of agricultural land have been rendered unusable by tannery pollution. Farmers in Tamil Nadu in Southern India have recently been compensated for the ruin of their land, but not everyone has been so lucky.

You may occasionally come across leathers tanned and dyed with natural substances – such as products by Eco Boudoir (see p.140) – but this is still something of a niche. Moreover, natural leather treatments may include palm oil, which is linked to rainforest destruction (see p.252).

Instead, some people advocate "vegetarian" **leather substitutes**. Being made of polyurethane and other plastics, these aren't exactly the most

Fur

Compared with most ethical shopping campaigns, the anti-fur movement of the 1980s and 90s was hugely successful. The majority of fur specialists shut down, and high-street shops phased out fur trims. But recently fur has bounced back somewhat, with sales rising as much as 35% per year in the UK, and claims from the industry that fur isn't as cruel as people think. The International Fur Trade Federation, for example, suggests that the farmed foxes and mink that supply around 85% of the world's pelts are "among the world's best cared for farm animals".

Animal rights campaigners aren't convinced, claiming that the fur farms (which are now banned in the UK) keep their minks and foxes in small cages equivalent to those used for battery chickens. And, for all the claims of respect for animal welfare, there is plenty of very disturbing footage – such as that filmed by People for the Ethical Treatment of Animals – showing caged fur animals apparently driven mad by their captivity, gnawing their own legs and running insanely round and round. Slaughtering methods, designed to protect the fur, are also contentious, in some cases allegedly including genital electrocution.

Trapping still provides some furs, and is often described as less cruel since animals get to live natural lives until capture. But most traps – such as the leghold models described as "inhumane" by the American Veterinary Medical Association – cause enormous suffering, with animals desperately trying to escape at first and being left exposed and in pain for anything from hours to days. Inevitably, non-target animals are also caught in the traps, adding to the death count for each coat – which, even in the case of minks or foxes, is around 30–40.

People for the Ethical Treatment of Animals www.furisdead.com • www.petatv.com
International Fur Trade Federation www.iftf.com

Compassion in World Farming

green products in the world themselves, but they're arguably a more ethical choice – especially if you don't want to support the meat industry. The best-known suppliers are listed on p.248.

Garment factories

The garment trade has long been associated with **sweatshops**. Way back in 1895, the *Standard Dictionary of the English Language* defined a "sweater" as an exploitative employer, "especially a contractor for piecework in the tailoring trade". There are various reasons for the link between clothes manufacture and labour abuse. One is the fact that the infrastructure costs of setting up a garment factory, or "shop", are relatively low, and the training needed to work there is minimal. So middlemen can afford to set up factories and compete for the business of clothes designers and retailers. Unlike the car sector, say, in which the big companies tend to own their own factories, and are therefore accountable to their own workers, the various layers of sub-contracting in the garment trade tend to diffuse and dissolve responsibility for workers' rights.

The subcontracted garment sweatshop was invented and first flourished in nineteenth-century Europe and America, but in the era of **globalization** the garment sector was one of the first to relocate to the developing world. It's not difficult to understand why. Clothes are big business, with British consumers spending on average around £400 per year on them – that's more than £23 billion in total. Yet, aside from materials, the only major production cost is **labour**, which is required in large quantities: taken together, the apparel and textile industries are the biggest industrial employers in the world, with a workforce of around 25 million.

For a UK firm, sourcing from a factory in Asia, Africa or Latin America doesn't just reduce this labour cost – it decimates it. For example, as journalist Seumas Milne reported, the women who make Littlewoods clothes at the Dressmen factory in Bangladesh get "less than a fiftieth of the hourly rate earned by their relatively low-paid British counterparts".

The collapse of the garment trade in the UK – where, according to some estimates, more than three-quarters of sewing jobs have disappeared in the last 25 years – has undoubtedly caused pain for many individuals who have found themselves out of work. But there's also no doubt that these kinds of jobs are desperately needed in poor countries, where millions have been created. The developing world now accounts for close to three-quarters of the world's clothing exports, with some economies relying almost entirely on the sector. In 2000, for example, textiles and clothing accounted for 84% of exports from Bangladesh (where around two million workers produce more than a billion garments for export each year) and 72% of Pakistan's.

This is all good news, many people argue. And, indeed, you might even see the transfer of European garment jobs to Asia as just deserts for Britain's systematic destruction of India's textile trade back in colonial days (a project aimed at creating a bigger market for British textiles). However, as Western clothing companies shop around for the best deal from suppliers (just as we do on the high street), countries and factories end up competing to offer the cheapest, most "flexible" workforce. Combine this with individual factory owners hell-bent on extracting every last drop of profit at the expense of their workers, and the result, in all too many cases, is abysmal working conditions.

Regardless of whether you see these conditions as a never-ending race to the bottom, or the first mile of a poor country's road to greater prosperity (for more on this debate, see p.294), there's little doubt that conditions are often extreme. True, some campaigners simplify or exaggerate the situation: jobs in export garment factories are clearly in demand and, with the exception of some cases where workers are locked into their positions through debt to their employer, they're clearly seen as a better option than the alternatives. Yet a range of sources – from workers' accounts to audits commissioned by the clothes companies themselves – have shown that, in return for the privilege of having a position, the mostly female workforce has to put up with inhumanely long hours, widespread suppression of unions, abusive managers and demeaning treatment.

Perhaps the biggest issue in most people's eyes is **child labour** – many Western shoppers have an image in their heads of rooms full of eight-year-olds sewing our branded clothes and trainers. The problem does exist, often with young teenagers being considered to be "apprentices" or "helpers" and earning even less than the adults, but arguably this problem *is* slightly exaggerated. In countries associated with bad sweatshops, such as China, there is little documented child labour in export manufacturing. Child workers are much more common in less-discussed industries, such as silk (see p.232) and rugs (see p.135), than in clothes factories.

A more pressing problem is **health and safety**, both in terms of workers getting injured by machines (due to lack of training or unsafe equipment) and the risk of **fires**. Despite minimal coverage in the mainstream media, hundreds of garment workers have been killed by fires in factories producing for export to the UK. In late 2000, for example, around fifty died in a garment factory near Dhaka, Bangladesh, where most clothes factories are rented properties not designed for the purpose. Most were killed by fumes and flames, but some were impaled on a fence when they tried to jump from fourth-floor windows: it was reported by local journalists that the exits were locked. Two years later, in an almost identical incident, forty died in a fire at the Shree Jee footwear plant in Agra, India, which was allegedly contracted via an agent to make shoes for British firms such as Stylo (Barratts), Peacocks, Stead & Simpson and Jacobson. Again, doors and windows were said to be locked. There are many such examples.

Fumes and dust are another serious problem in some factories. Many apparel workers have been made ill through exposure to toxic glues (for shoe soles), while airborne fibres can lead to lung damage in the absence of proper ventilation and masks. In a report on Gap factories produced by the Unite union, for instance, one African worker is quoted as complaining that "we can't escape breathing in the fibres and particles from the air. When we cough, if the T-shirt we were working on was made of blue fabric, then our mucus would be full of blue fibres." But the fact that it was Gap was immaterial: according to a "provincial task force" report quoted in the *Washington Post*, 96% of businesses in China's Guangdong province – a centre of clothes manufacturing – were in violation of health standards. The number of workers getting sick there is rising 70% per year, with more than 2500 deaths from occupational illnesses since 1989.

Perhaps the most pressing issue of all, however, is the **suppression of unions**. A report on the Asian garment industry by CAFOD (the Catholic

Home-grown sweat

While the majority of garment factories worthy of the "sweatshop" label are in the developing world, such employers haven't vanished in the West. According to the Smithsonian Institute, conditions for garment workers in rich countries improved during the mid-twentieth century, but almost universally fell in the 1980s. By 1996, the US government estimated that at least half of the country's 22,000 garment factories were in "serious violation of wage and safety laws". The UK is not quite as bad, though serious violations – especially in London's East End – are not uncommon.

While the term sweatshop usually refers to factories, exploitative subcontracting is just as big an issue in the homeworking sector, which is also important to the rag trade. The National Group on Homeworking (www.homeworking.gn.apc. org) estimates that there are around one million homeworkers sewing, packing, assembling and manufacturing in the UK. Many of them earn significantly less than the minimum wage, and some – usually those from ethnic minorities – receive less than 50p per hour.

Agency for Overseas Development) pointed out that efforts by local workers, NGOs and trade unions "are the most important factor in trying to improve wages and working conditions in Asia". The report noted that "in some countries, such as the Philippines and Sri Lanka, a history of active trade unionism, and state support for some degree of labour rights, have established expectations about acceptable labour standards. In others, such as China, Vietnam and Bangladesh, the floor is often set by physical endurance; how many hours a day, over how many years, can one ill-nourished human body continue to function."

Despite this, many Western clothes and shoe firms have been slow to demand union recognition in the factories they source from, and organizers continue to be harassed or assaulted. One Bangladeshi woman interviewed by CAFOD, for example, had been attacked and slashed with razor blades for being a union activist at a clothes factory. Sadly, this kind of assault and intimidation seems to be relatively common.

Clothes & shoes: the big brands

So what efforts have clothes companies made to deal with the social and environmental issues discussed above? Despite the focus on American superbrands such as Gap and Nike (see box), this is a question that applies to the entire sector.

When it comes to materials certified as Fairtrade or organic, it's easy to see how committed companies are, as you can be sure that any garments made of Fairtrade or organic cotton will be clearly labelled. Such products have traditionally been the realm of the specialist ethical brands listed later in this chapter, but in 2006 both Top Shop and Marks & Spencer introduced Fairtrade lines.

Things are a bit more cloudy when it comes to workers' rights. Due to increasing pressure from consumers, most of the big brands have at least recognized the sweatshops problem and drawn up **codes of conduct** that they request their suppliers adhere to. It's been a long time coming, but today most high-street names have a code based on key labour standards, including the **right to organize** (join a union).

Worker groups and sweatshop campaigners agree that these codes are very useful: they can help inform workers of their rights, make it more difficult for factory owners to claim they didn't know the rules and provide a yardstick by which to measure a company's progress and failings. But they also shouldn't be taken at face value: as discussed in chapter three, voluntary codes of conduct are not necessarily enforced. And it's often very difficult to tell, because the mainstream companies treat the names and addresses of their supplier factories as a closely guarded corporate secret. If the case of Nike vs. Kasky (see box overleaf) is anything to go by, the big companies also sometimes simply lie about their ethical standards.

The gap between professed policy and enforced action leads many commentators to conclude that most of the big firms are basically the same. **War on Want**, for example, interviewed Bangladeshi garment workers and concluded: "It didn't matter which factory they worked in, who owned it, or whom they supplied – the conditions were always bad."

Nike and Gap: demons or demonized?

In the UK, the sweatshop issue is associated almost exclusively with trainers by **Nike** and clothes by **Gap**. Both companies have been linked to some extremely exploitative factories and bad practice, from Nike allegedly petitioning the Indonesian government for exemption from the minimum wage and lying about labour conditions at its contractor factories (see p.240) to Gap's exploits at Saipan (see p.242). And the comparison between what Nike spends on advertising and what it spends on workers is a frightening and depressing indictment both of world inequality and the power of advertising in modern Western society. According to Sweatshop Watch, an average Nike worker would need to put in no fewer than 72,000 years of work to receive what Tiger Woods got for one five-year sponsorship contract. (To put that in context, if he or she had worked a seven-day week since Homo sapiens first arrived in East Asia, they might be nearly finished today.)

But are these companies qualitatively different from the industry as a whole in terms of labour and environmental standards? According to most people working to improve garment sweatshops, the answer is no. In fact, due to the threat of campaigns and boycotts, these two major brands have done more to improve things than many of the less-high-profile retailers. Indeed, in a 2006 interview with Rough Guides, campaign group Labour Behind the Label named Gap as one of the most progressive of the big clothes companies (albeit with much further to go). Nike, meanwhile, is part of the FLA (see p.241) and has, among other things, improved health and safety by phasing out dangerous solvent-based glue (as well as environmentally problematic PVC).

So why the focus on Nike and Gap? Part of the reason is that they're both huge companies which were early adopters of the global outsourcing model. And part of the reason is that they're very much marketing-led firms, whose lifestyle advertising clashes sharply with the daily life of the people who actually cut, stitch and glue their products. But another part of the reason is simply that, as major US firms, they've been subjected to the scrutiny of that country's tireless anti-sweatshop movement. Many other American clothes manufacturers, from Wal-Mart to Liz Claiborne, have also felt the pressure, but they don't make the headlines in the UK, since they're not familiar high-street names.

Likewise, according to pressure group Labour Behind the Label: "much as we would like to recommend good companies over bad ones, we have not come across a single company which we feel comfortable recommending."

This seems like pretty good grounds for avoiding the high-street names wherever possible and favouring fair trade specialists such as those listed from p.244. In reality, however, the range of ethical clothes is still pretty small. So what efforts have the individual brands made?

One level up from drawing up a code of conduct is joining an ethical trade group, such as the UK's **Ethical Trading Initiative** (see p.61). Membership certainly doesn't guarantee best practice, but it's a good start. **Littlewoods** controversially dropped out in 2003, but nearly all the major clothes companies are still involved. The big-name members include:

▶ **Debenhams**
▶ **Gap**
▶ **Levi Strauss**
▶ **Marks & Spencer**
▶ **Monsoon**

▶ **Mothercare**
▶ **Next**
▶ **New Look**
▶ **Pentland Group:**
Berghaus, Brasher,

Ellesse, KangaROOS,
Kickers, Lacoste, Mitre,
Red or Dead, Speedo,
Ted Baker

Among all of these names, special mention should go to **Marks & Spencer**, who since 2005 have launched a series of ethical projects – from phasing out toxic dyes to offering the UK's first Fairtrade-certified jeans.

Don't believe all you read: Nike vs. Kasky

In 1998, Californian activist Marc Kasky filed a law suit in the US, claiming that Nike had made misleading claims in response to accusations regarding conditions at one of its Vietnamese factories (accusations partly based on Nike's own research). Instead of defending its statements as true – presumably because it couldn't – Nike argued it could claim whatever it liked under US free speech law. In 2003, after various rounds of appeals, the state's supreme court decided, as Kasky contended, that free speech didn't apply, as Nike's statements were "commercial speech", intended to increase sales. The case was sent back to the lower courts, to try to determine whether the statements were lies, which are illegal in commercial speech. But Nike finally settled out of court by agreeing to contribute $2 million to the Fair Labor Association and worker education initiatives.

The folks at Reebok, meanwhile, have gone beyond claiming to be a reasonable employer and reinvented themselves as defenders of human rights, instigating the annual Reebok Human Rights Awards. The view that this was a cynical effort to cash in on the bad publicity surrounding Nike was bolstered in 2002 when prominent labour-rights activist Dita Indah Sari rejected the $50,000 prize in protest at the "low pay and exploitation" of Reebok employees in Indonesia and elsewhere.

Corbis

Young women applying glue to sport shoes at a Reebok factory in Zhongshan, China. Companies like Reebok – which today is one of the slightly more progressive of the big sportwear firms – have helped create massive economic growth in China. But many people question whether it can ever be ethical to source from a country with an appalling human rights record, widespread labour abuse and no recognition of independent trade unions.

However, even these positive developments have a downside: M&S reportedly demanded a discount from all its suppliers – including the fair trade ones – in order to fund its ethical marketing campaign.

Similar to the ETA but focusing primarily on sportswear is the US-based **Fair Labor Association** (FLA), which was set up by Bill Clinton's administration in response to growing concern about sweatshops among American consumers. The group aims to enforce an "industry-wide workplace code of conduct ... based on the core labor standards of the International Labour Organization". In 2003, the FLA broke ground by making the results of company factory audits – code-breaches, warts and all – available to the public (see www.fairlabor.org). However, questions have been raised regarding the number and quality of the factory audits. One insider told Rough Guides that some of the FLA auditing firms had little experience of interviewing workers and had a financial interest in not offending the company whose factory they were examining. Still, the initiative is certainly better than nothing. Members include:

▶ Adidas   ▶ Liz Claiborne   ▶ Reebok
▶ Asics   ▶ Nike   ▶ Van Heusen
▶ Gildan Activewear   ▶ Patagonia
▶ H&M   ▶ PUMA

So what about the rest? Many of the remaining UK retailers are controlled by entrepreneur **Philip Green**, who owns **BHS** as well as the giant Arcadia group, which includes **Burton, Dorothy Perkins, Evans, Miss Selfridge, Outfit, Top Shop, Top Man** and **Wallis**. Green, a famously fast-living Monaco-based billionaire, is described by the T&G Union's textile division as "extremely ruthless" in his dealings with suppliers and has been criticized for paying no tax in the UK. Arcadia has a decent code of conduct but has consistently ignored requests to join the Ethical Trading Initiative and was criticized in 2006 by Labour Behind The Label as being "way behind its major high street competitors when it comes to addressing the problems faced by workers making its products".

Upmarketness doesn't necessarily correlate with better or worse behaviour. Of the smaller, classier retailers, **Timberland** has been cited as something of a shining example, fully committed to improving standards

Made in the USA? The Saipan Debacle

Saipan is part of the Northern Mariana Islands in the western Pacific Ocean. Having been previously held by Spain, Germany and Japan, it was captured by the US in World War II and later given US territorial status. That makes it basically part of the States – so items produced there for the US market are free from import tariffs and quotas. And yet the minimum wage is lower, customs duties are said to be slacker and foreign workers can be granted renewable one-year work permits. Companies soon realized that they could benefit from these favourable conditions and still write "Made in the USA" on their labels. Trade soared and before long the temporary foreign workers – mainly from East Asia – outnumbered the locals by around 50%.

Stories of labour abuse in the islands' many garment factories didn't take long to surface. There were reports of effective indentured labour (with workers unable to leave their jobs due to debts imposed by their employers), withheld wages, workers being forced to "donate" unpaid hours on top of their normal shifts, and union organizers facing sacking and deportation. Finally, in 1999, a collection of workers, human rights groups and others sued some factory owners and more than twenty major retailers and manufacturers, including **Abercrombie & Fitch**, **Calvin Klein**, **Gap**, **Polo Ralph Lauren** and **Tommy Hilfiger USA**, over the alleged labour abuses. Eventually, all the companies except **Levi Strauss** (which claimed the allegations against them were false) were part of a $20 million settlement to pay withheld wages and set up a monitoring organization co-ordinated with the International Labour Organization.

and auditing not only its factories but also leather tanneries and other suppliers. **French Connection**, on the other hand, has what campaigners have described as a feeble code, with no reference to monitoring. Labour Behind the Label wrote with reasonable indignation in 2002 that the company "has never, in the course of five years of letter-writing by consumers and LBL, acknowledged our letters and concerns". Fcukers.

To keep abreast of issues surrounding brands and workers' rights in the rag trade, visit:

Clean Clothes Campaign www.cleanclothes.org
Sweatshop Watch www.sweatshopwatch.org

Shoes

Compared with clothes production, shoe manufacture tends to be more industrial and hi-tech – something that usually means longer-term contracts and more leverage over labour conditions for brands and retailers. However, aside from the trainer companies discussed above, the shoe sector has shown comparatively little interest in ethical issues.

There is still not a single shoe company in the Ethical Trading Initiative and in a survey of fourteen high-street shoe shops by *Ethical Consumer* magazine (see p.220), only **Clarks** and **Ecco** responded to the request for a code of conduct – and even those didn't make any reference to external monitoring of factories. So this industry clearly has a long way to go. Right now, just about the only shoe shops that seem concerned with ethical matters are specialists producing non-leather shoes (see p.248).

One contentious shoe company is **CAT**, whose bulldozers have become a favourite tool of the Israeli army. As the *Business Respect* newsletter noted in November 2003, the company "celebrated its inclusion for the third year in the Dow Jones Sustainability World Index, just as protesters in Iowa slammed the company for selling equipment to Israel that would allegedly be used 'to bulldoze Palestinian homes'".

China & Burma

Regardless of the codes and promises of clothes companies, another ethical question is *where* they do business. The international trade in shoes and clothes is increasingly dominated by just one country: China. Usually defined as an oppressive regime, China has no recognition of independent trade unions and its sweatshops are notorious. Yet nearly every clothes company is shifting its production to China – "to stay competitive", in the words of Gap. Indeed, as of mid-2006, China accounts for slightly over

50% of global production in both the clothes and shoe sectors. Some campaigners call on consumers to avoid Chinese-made clothes – and other goods – wherever possible (see p.44).

A more extreme case is Burma (p.310), whose abhorrent military dictatorship directly profits from the clothes export industry. Most of the major brands that were importing from Burma, or Myanmar as it may appear on clothes labels, have pulled out, but many companies have failed to assure the Burma Campaign UK that they don't still import from the country (the UK government knows which, if any, of them are still sourcing from Burma but refuses to reveal this information). For the most up-to-date list, see:

Burma Campaign UK www.burmacampaign.org.uk

Unfortunately, recent EU law means that clothes companies don't have to specify the country of origin on the label, so choosing garments on the grounds of where they were produced isn't always easy.

Clothes & shoes: the ethical specialists

As the issues covered in this chapter become more widely discussed, a growing number of **fairly traded** and **organic** clothes are appearing on the market. Traditionally, this section of the clothes industry tends towards flowing dresses, flowery patterns and "ethnic" styles. There's still quite a lot of that around, but there are now also many stylish and modern options too – as evidenced by the shops and sites listed below.

Standards for organic materials are precise and legally binding, just as with food (see p.148). But with fair trade, consumers should understand the distinction between certified clothes bearing the Fairtrade Mark and other, uncertified, items. For more on this distinction, turn to p.24. The following listings include fair trade clothes in both categories.

Most of the following sell online and/or via a catalogue.

Fair trade clothes

Epona

www.eponasport.com ▷ 0191 415 1201

A small but reasonably priced range of T-shirts and hoodies in Fairtrade-certified, organic cotton.

Ganesha

www.ganesha.co.uk ▷ 020 7928 3444 ▷ 3 Gabriel's Wharf, 56 Upper Ground, London

Stylish skirts, kurtars (for men and women), scarves, T-shirts and more, mainly in colourful Indian materials and produced by members of IFAT (see p.30). Ganesha also stock designer flip-flops from West Bengal (made by a multinational company, but from a factory certified to the ISO 9002 standard for employer and environmental safety) and various categories of cool bags: "Street India", "Kitsch", "Leather" and the very stylish "A Bit Fancy".

From Ganesha: handloom cotton shirt with handworked mother-of-pearl buttons (£25) from a small IFAT-registered Bangladeshi company, and a pink floral bag (£15) from a social enterprise in South India

Gossypium

www.gossypium.co.uk ▷ 0800 085 6549 ▷ Abinger Place, Lewes

Elegant, simple T-shirts, tops, night-wear and knickers – plus yoga and kids' clothes – in Fairtrade-certified organic cotton from India. The kimono-style hoody is one of the more stylish items you'll find in the world of fair trade threads. Gossypium (who take their name from the Latin term for the cotton-plant genus) are fully transparent about their products' origins, from field to shop.

Hug

www.hug.co.uk ▷ 0845 130 1525

Nicely cut T-shirts, tops ("hugs") and jeans for men, women and children. The style is quite similar to what you might find at Gap, but these garments are made with Fairtrade-certified cotton and high-tech, eco-friendly dyes. Order online and your item will arrive in a letter-box-friendly parcel; if you don't like it, simply send it back freepost.

People Tree

www.ptree.co.uk ▷ 0845 450 4595

Selling via the Web, phone, fax or their catalogue/magazine (and with a part of the range available in Top Shop), People Tree offers one of the biggest ranges of fair trade clothes, mostly in organic cotton. There are some simple clothes for all genders and ages, plus bags, baskets and other accessories. In addition to its fair trade policy, the company uses its profits to support a school in Bangladesh.

Tonic T-shirts

www.tonictshirts.com

Tonic's "ethical and organic streetwear" comprises a mix of printed and embroidered T-shirts, both plain and buttoned, in Fairtrade-certified cotton. The designs are a postmodern mix of ironic and retro-cool.

Traidcraft

www.traidcraftshop.co.uk ▷ 0191 491 1001

Traidcraft offer a varied range of fair trade clothes for women – from silk ties, shawls and dressy tops to alpaca scarves and jumpers – plus a couple of items for men. Available via their mail order catalogue, their website and some fair trade shops (see p.139).

Organic and eco clothes

Eco Clothworks

www.clothworks.co.uk ▷ 01225 309 218

Prices aren't low – the pin-tucked pure silk shirt, dyed with madder and oak galls, is a cool £160 – but the Eco Clothworks range of organic cotton, silk and hemp clothes is as designer as ethical fashion gets. It currently only offers clothing for women and children, but does so in a variety of stylish and sometimes slightly retro looks.

Greenfibres

www.greenfibres.com ▷ 01803 868 001 ▷ 99 High St, Totnes

Among the best-known organic textile companies, Greenfibres sells clothes for men, women and children – underwear, casual wear and even suits – as well as towels and sheets, etc. It describes itself as "non exploitative", though not explicitly fair trade.

Howies

www.howies.co.uk ▷ 01239 615 988

Fashionable clothes in a surfer/skater style. The fabrics are organic, the T-shirt messages subversive and their well-designed, interactive website full of "truths" – facts and stats – on everything from fish farms to food packaging.

Howies girl's jumper, in 100% recycled cotton

Patagonia

www.patagonia.com/europe ▷
01629 583 800

High-quality fleeces, jackets and other outdoor pursuits gear made from organic cotton by a company with good environmental credentials. Use the details above to find your nearest stockist or order a catalogue.

Natural Collection

www.naturalcollection.com ▷ 0870 331 3333

A full range of men's and women's clothes – casual wear, sportswear, knitwear, underwear and more – in organic cotton and hemp. The selection includes that rare thing in the ethical world: a nicely cut men's shirt (Italian-designed and in hemp).

Ralper

www.ralper.co.uk

Launched in mid-2004, Ralper aims to become "the brand that gave the young fashionable dresser the ability to buy ethical clothes". Their range – T-shirts with and without screenprints, plus socks – is designed in Britain and branded to appeal to a young market. But the clothes are made by developing-world producer groups registered with IFAT (see p.30). Ralper is a member of the British Association of Fair Trade Shops (see p.139).

Organic wool

There may not be much organic leather available, but there's no shortage of organic wool. Though sheep aren't the worst-treated of farm animals, buying organic wool supports small-scale, ecologically friendly farms. Suppliers include:

Ford Barton www.fordbarton.co.uk ▷ 01398 351 139 ▷ Stoodleigh, Tiverton, Devon
Hebridean Woolhouse www.hebrideanwoolhouse.com ▷ 01932 254 855
Lower Turley Farm 0188 432 234 ▷ Cullompton, Devon
Organic Pure Wool www.organicpurewool.co.uk ▷ 01570 493 374 ▷ Ceredigion, Wales
Organic Wool Company www.organicwool.co.uk ▷ 01239 821 171
Rosuick Organic www.rosuick.co.uk ▷ 01326 231 302 ▷ Helston, Cornwall

Silken Dalliance

01993 810 008 ▷ 25 Oxford St, Woodstock

A specialist retailer of fairly traded silk products, mostly sourced from Vietnam, Thailand and Bangladesh. Stocks dresses, skirts, tops, shirts, trousers and suits as well as beaded bags, scarves, hats and silver jewellery.

Spirit of Nature

www.spiritofnature.co.uk ▷ 0870 725 9885

Despite a cringeworthy strapline ("Fill your life with happiness … capture the spirit of nature"), this company sells an extensive range of organic cotton and hemp clothes for adults and children, including jeans.

Hemp clothes

Hemp Store

www.thehempstore.co.uk ▷ 01223 309 993 ▷ 90 Windsor Rd, Cambridge

Stocks a wide range of hemp clothes, plus bags and wallets – the owners also claim to be committed to fair trade, sourcing most of their own-brand goods from a trusted Nepalese importer.

Inbi Hemp

www.inbi-hemp.co.uk ▷ 0870 333 1858

Though the strapline "clothing for the inner you" suggests relaxation tapes and did-geridoos, the hemp range at this Brighton-based supplier is actually quite sharp.

Leather substitutes

Beyond Skin

www.beyondskin.co.uk

High-end non-leather shoes for female fashionistas (customers include the likes of Natalie Portman). The almond-toe kitten heels pictured cost a cool £267.

Ethical Wares

www.ethicalwares.com ▷ 01570 471 155

Leather-substitute footwear – from Black Cat stilettos to steel-toe-cap boots – as well as some fair trade clothes, bags and jewellery (in a rather hippyish style).

Freerangers

www.freerangers.co.uk ▷ 01207 565 957

English-made non-animal Birkenstock-esque shoes, plus bags, briefcases, belts, wallets and even cases for your palm pilot.

Vegan Store

www.veganstore.co.uk ▷ 01273 302 979

Sells a range of "fabulously fake jackets" (very realistic and good value, too) as well as shoes, belts and other vegan essentials (such as non-animal-derived marshmallows).

Vegetarian Shoes

www.vegetarian-shoes.co.uk ▷ 01273 691 913 ▷ 12 Gardner St, Brighton

A wide range of stylish non-animal footwear including boots, smart shoes, trainers and camper-style day-to-day wear – some of them produced in Britain's oldest co-operative (established 1881).

More alt.clothes...

In addition to the suppliers listed above, there are a few ethical specialists offering the sorts of clothes more traditionally associated with green

Traid

Traid was launched in 1999 with the twin aims of promoting recycling and raising money for good causes (the name stands for Textile Recycling for Aid and International Development). It's something like a cross between a charity shop and an exclusive boutique. Unwanted clothes are donated to the shops, and then "redesigned and reconstructed" by Traid designers to make unique and fashionable garments. Prices are similar to high-street stores, but the garments are one-offs and the profits go to charity.

Traid www.traid.org.uk ▷ 020 8733 2580

London 61 Westbourne Grove, W2 · 69–71 Kilburn High Rd, NW6
2 Acre Lane, SW2 · 119 King Street, W6 · 375 Holloway Rd, N7
Brighton 39 Duke St
Wembley Unit 12–13, Central Square

shopping. Some focus on vibrant, flowing clothes made of fairly traded silks and hand-loomed materials...

Bishopston Trading www.bishopstontrading.co.uk
Chandni Chowk www.chandnichowk.co.uk

...while others are closer to the stalls you might find at Glastonbury, complete with dolphin T-shirts and yin-yang jumpers:

Siesta www.siestacrafts.co.uk
One World Is Enough www.one-world-is-enough.net

There are also a few companies specializing in just one product – such as Pachacuti, which can meet all your needs for fairly traded Panama hats:

Pachacuti www.panamas.co.uk ▷ 01335 300 485

The high fashion world, if you can afford it, has at least one designer with a social and environmental conscience in **Katherine Hamnett**, and there are also a few companies producing ethical versions of merchandise such as T-shirts for bands. Look out for the **Ethical Threads** label – which sources from unionized producers and is spearheaded by Billy Bragg – or **T-shirt and Sons**, whose garments are in organic cotton.

Even **Adbusters**, the ultimate anti-consumerists famed for tweaking billboard ads to reverse their meaning, have started selling their own non-sweatshop trainers. The first offering was designed specifically with Nike founder Phil Knight in mind: "Phil Knight had a dream. He'd sell shoes. He'd sell dreams. He'd get rich. He'd use sweatshops if he had to. Then along came a new shoe. Plain. Simple. Cheap. Fair. Designed for only one thing: kicking Phil's ass."

Whether garment workers of the developing world are impressed by Adbusters helping their plight by producing trainers in Portugal is an open question, but the idea of a trainer from an "anti-corporation" undoubtedly has a certain appeal.

Blackspot Sneakers www.blackspotsneaker.org

In the US – perhaps because of the country's numerous non-union-ized garment factories – another type of company has evolved, selling clothes made domestically but under guaranteed union conditions. These include:

American Apparel www.americanapparel.net
No Sweat Apparel www.nosweatapparel.com

For a near-comprehensive list of organic clothes suppliers, check out the directory at the Soil Association website: www.soilassociation.org

Cosmetics & toiletries
Because you (and the bunny) are worth it

When it comes to cosmetics, toiletries and perfumes, the major worry for most consumers is **animal testing**. We cover this below, but first it's worth running through a few less-discussed issues. One is the ethical standards of the giant businesses that dominate the "health and beauty" market. There isn't room here for a proper profile of each, but suffice to say that they're very politically active. According to Open Secrets (www.opensecrets. org), George Bush's Republican party has received substantial cash dona-tions from **Bristol Myers Squibb** and **Revlon**. And **Procter & Gamble**, **Colgate-Palmolive** and **Johnson & Johnson** are, among other things, on the board of the National Foreign Trade Council, a lobby group which has actively opposed legislation to stop trade with Burma (and whose website opens with a quote of gratitude and approval from none other than Dick Cheney). To see the many brands these companies own, see the box on p.253.

Another issue is the degree to which cosmetics manufacturers use needlessly risky **chemicals**, such as persistent toxins that may accumulate in the human body or the wider environment, posing risks to health and wildlife. As with paint (see p.132), there is little evidence to suggest that standard exposure to cosmetics chemicals causes anything more serious than occasional allergic reactions, though intensive long-term exposure does seem to present risks. In 2002, for instance, researchers from Lund University in Sweden found that female hairdressers were one-third more likely than a control group to give birth to babies with malformations or other serious physical defects (especially heart defects). Extended exposure to everyday hair sprays, dyes and the like seemed to be the most likely cause.

There are environmental concerns about the use of **"natural" products**, too. According to the WWF, as many as 10,000 plant species are threatened with extinction due to the demand for herbal remedies, and the natural ingredients used in certain toiletries and cosmetics inevitably pose similar threats. One particular concern is **palm oil**, derivatives of which are widely used in soaps, lipsticks and perfumes, among other products. According to environmental groups such as the World Rainforest Movement (see www.wrm.org.uy) these are helping to wipe out biodiversity and tacitly supporting the forced displacement of forest-based peoples in Indonesia and elsewhere.

Similarly, in 2003, a joint investigation by the Environmental Investigation Agency and Friends of the Earth revealed the extensive damage being done by illegal mining of soapstone for talcum powder (used in everything from lipstick to deodorant) in the nature reserves of Rajasthan, India. Subjecting workers to appalling health and safety risks, causing serious pollution, lowering the water table and generally causing environmental wipe-out, these mines have been identified as the single most serious threat to the survival of the endangered Indian Tiger (for more, see www.eia-international.org). Several multinationals were shown to be purchasing this talc – including Revlon, Johnson & Johnson, Cussons, Avon and Unilever – but, to be fair, many smaller companies were probably also benefiting from the destruction.

Other issues surrounding cosmetics include the human-rights standards of developing-world make-up factories (*New York Times* columnist Joseph Kahn recently reported slave labour conditions in a Chinese false-eyelash plant) and the question of whether ingredients such as cocoa butter are traded according to fair trade principles. Finally, vegans and strict vegetarians should be aware that many cosmetic items contain animal-derived products.

Animal testing

Animal testing for cosmetics and their ingredients has been heavily cut back in the last two decades, and the UK has banned such tests outright. However, testing does continue and the ban makes little difference since most of what's on sale in the UK is imported from, or contains ingredients imported from, abroad. According to animal-rights campaigners, around 40,000 animals in Europe and millions globally are subjected to tests each year, for products ranging from hair dyes to toothpastes. These include notorious experiments such as the **Lethal Dose 50% Test** (animals are gradually poisoned with increasing doses of a substance until half of them die) and the **Draize Eye Test** (in which chemicals are added to animals' eyes and the damage recorded over several days).

Who tests on animals?

As of summer 2004, the following companies were still conducting and/or commissioning animal tests for cosmetics, toiletries or ingredients, according to the British Union for the Abolition of Vivisection:

▶ **Unilever** All Clear, Cutex Denim, cK cosmetics, Cerutto 1881, Chloe, Escape, Eternity, Jean Louis Scherrer, Karl Lagerfeld, Narcisse, Obsession, Valentino; Procter & Gamble: Hugo Boss, Max Factor, Oil of Olay, Crest, Head & Shoulders, Pantene Pro-V, Clairol Herbal Essence, Nice n Easy, Aussie hair products, Camay soap, Cover Girl, Giorgio Beverly Hills, Old Spice, Sure, Vidal Sassoon, Clarion, Colorfast, Mary Quant, Maxi, Noxell, Noxzema, Outdoor Girl, SK-11, Biactol, Clearsil

▶ **Colgate Palmolive** Colgate, Palmolive, Soft Soap, Lady and Mennen Speed Sticks, Vel Beauty Bar; L'Oréal: Elvive, Elnett, Studio Line, Plenitude, Feria, Recital, L'Oréal, Colour Cosmetics, Garnier Fructis, Garnier Ambre Solaire, Garnier Nutralia, Garnier Belle Colour, Maybelline, Freestyle, Excellence, Castings, Anais Anais, La vie en rose, Biotherm, Giorgio Armani, Helena Rubenstein, Lancome, Ralph Lauren, Cacharel, Redken, Vichy, Matrix

▶ **Lever Faberge (part of Unilever)** Mentadent, Signal, Ponds, Vaseline Intensive Care skin products, Pears, Sure, Impulse, Addiction, Sunsilk, Timotei, Organics, Lynx, Brut, Aquatonic, Shield, Lux, Dove, Knights Castile, Salon Selectives, Physio Sport, Lifebuoy, Harmony

▶ **Bristol-Myers** Clairol Nice 'n' Easy, Natural Instincts, Glints, Herbal Essences, Lasting Colour, Loving Care, Born Blonde, Mum, Mum Botanicals, Hydrience

▶ **Schwarzkopf & Henkel** Gliss, Mont Saint Michel, Scorpio, La Perla, Sergio Tacchini, Krizia, Fiorucci

▶ **Bourjois Limited:** Bourjois

▶ **Wella** Vivality, Vosine, Shock Waves, Silvikrin

▶ **COTY** Rimmel, Adidas, Sensiq, Cutex

▶ **Beiersdorf** Nivia, La Prairie, Atrixo

The following claim not to conduct or commission animal tests but do buy newly animal tested ingredients:

▶ **Boots** Botanics, 17, no. 7, Summer Sun, Soltan

▶ **Estee Lauder** Aramis, Clinique, Prescriptives, Origins, M.A.C, Aveda, La Mer, Stila, Jo Malone, Bumble & Bumble, Bobby Brown

▶ **Gillette** Mach3, Venus, Sensor, Right Guard, Oral-B

▶ **Yves Rocher** Yves Rocher Revlon: Revlon, Ultima II, Almay, Charlie

After persistent public and campaigner pressure, an **EU-wide ban** on the sale of animal-tested cosmetics was finally agreed in 2003. However, it's not due to become effective until 2009 and there have already been at least two legal actions to try to have it overturned: one directly from a coalition of cosmetics companies, which refuse to reveal their identities, and one from the government of France, home to industry giants associated with animal testing such as L'Oréal. So it remains to be seen whether the legislation will survive.

In the meantime, tests are gradually being developed that don't require animals – often funded, it has to be said, by the same companies that are still conducting animal experiments. But until non-animal tests exist for all products and ingredients – which, as *New Scientist* has pointed out, is a matter less of ethics than of governments deciding "how much taxpayers money should be spent" – the argument really comes down to whether you believe intense animal suffering is a reasonable price to pay for the development of new make-up ingredients.

Clean cosmetics

According to survey after survey, nearly all consumers feel strongly that animal testing for cosmetics should be stopped. But the same people continue to give their support to companies that aren't on the animal-testing clean list. According to animal-rights groups, this is partly because many statements on the sides of bottles and tubes are misleading. "Against animal testing", for example, means basically nothing at all. Others, such as "we have not carried out animal testing since 1990", could mean that the manufacturers simply commissioned the animal testing from other companies. For the strictest standards, look out for the white-rabbit logo of the **Humane Cosmetics Standard** (HCS), a scheme supported by many animal-rights groups and administered in the UK by **BUAV** (the British Union for the Abolition of Vivisection).

To use the HCS logo, the company must exclude all ingredients tested on animals after a fixed **cut-off point** (usually a year in the 1980s or 90s) and prove this via independent audits. There are now more than 75 certified companies. For an up-to-the-minute list, or to request the wallet-sized *Little Book Of Cruelty Free*, visit:

BUAV www.buav.org/gocrueltyfree

The fact that a company isn't HCS-endorsed doesn't necessarily mean it uses or commissions animal testing. Handmade soap specialist Lush, for example, doesn't buy from any companies that currently test on animals, but it doesn't have a fixed cut-off point. According to the likes of BUAV, such policies are a step in the right direction, but since they don't eliminate all long- and short-term incentives for developing ingredients that require animal testing, they remain insufficient.

Alternative suppliers

Leaving aside the animal-testing question, there are a number of manufacturers trying to be ethical operators on a broader level. Often this doesn't go much further than shunning the plethora of synthetic chemicals used by the big firms. But many of these companies also use organic ingredients and recyclable plastic bottles, and shun animal-based ingredients. And, unlike the big boys, they are small businesses far removed from the ugly world of corporate lobbying and political donations.

Green People

www.greenpeople.co.uk ▷ 08702 401 444

Established in 1997, Green People sell more than one hundred organic (and veggie-friendly) toiletries and skin products, from sun creams to organic jojoba, hemp and rosehip oils. The website includes a useful questions and answers section, and the company donates 10% of its net profits to environmental charities.

Honesty Cosmetics

www.honestycosmetics.co.uk ▷ 01629 814 888

Admirably marketing their products "without unrealistic claims of emotional or physical benefit", Honesty Cosmetics sell a wide range of reasonably priced toiletries and cosmetics, including own-brands products that are non-animal-tested, petrochemical-free, vegan-friendly and made with natural oils sourced with an eye to environmental sustainability. Available online or via a catalogue, the range also includes organic tampons, lipsticks and nail varnishes by Beauty Without Cruelty, and green household cleaning products.

Neal's Yard

www.nealsyardremedies.com ▷ 020 7627 1949

You may need to take out a small second mortgage to become a regular, but Neal's Yard products – some organic, all non-petrochemical and minimally packaged – are as good as toiletries get. Available in many specialist stores (call for a local stockist) as well as online or via a catalogue.

The Body Shop

Founded by **Anita Roddick** in Brighton in 1976, the **Body Shop** is now a global company, with nearly 2000 shops in 50 countries and shares on the London Stock Exchange. But it claims to be unlike other big companies, placing human rights, environmental sustainability and animal welfare at the core of its operations. Dame Roddick, aka the "Queen of Green", has certainly been a tireless campaigner on a wide range of social justice and environmental issues, using her position at the Body Shop to bring numerous issues to the public's attention, from Amazonian rainforest destruction to Shell's activities in Nigeria. And the company has initiated various progressive projects, working with the likes of Amnesty International and creating a **fair trade** scheme, called "community trade", for some items, including various beauty-product ingredients.

However, the chain has also received its share of criticism. Sometimes the objections, such as those from London Greenpeace in the early 1990s, have focused on general chain-store complaints: the company's near-identical shops leading to homogenization of public spaces and its promotion of a "buy more" lifestyle fuelling the consumerism that's ravaging the planet. But other critics have been far more specific, notably American journalist **Jon Entine**, who throughout the 1990s made it a personal mission to expose Roddick and the Body Shop as ethical frauds. His allegations – covering everything from the "theft" of the Body Shop name to animal testing – were laid out in his social audit of the company (see www.jonentine.com). But Entine himself is a controversial figure. An "adjunct fellow" with the influential right-wing think tank the American Enterprise Institute, he's a keen defender of big businesses and critic of environmentalists. He recently gave a speech warning that we should be concerned about NGOs and social investors, whose leaders "are products of the activist community, yet they are different and more dangerous".

More recently, criticism of the Body Shop has come from a less likely source: Roddick herself. In 2001 she described the firm as a "dysfunctional coffin" driven too much by soulless market forces and shareholder profits. But that was nothing compared to the takeover of the company in March 2006 by L'Oréal. The French cosmetics giant promised to keep the Body Shop running as a separate company, with its ethical values "ring-fenced". But animal-rights campaigners weren't convinced. Within days of the sale, groups such as Naturewatch and Uncaged were calling for a boycott of the company, due to L'Oréal's animal-testing activities.

So where does all this leave the only "ethical" company most people could name? Tarnished, perhaps. Yet the Body Shop remains far more progressive than its high-street neighbours. It has expanded its fair trade efforts to dozens of suppliers; it is HCS-approved for being animal-testing free; it has been praised by Friends of the Earth for its policy on dangerous chemicals and by the WWF on sustainable wood; it has published far-reaching codes of conduct and done much social and environmental reporting; and it uses its stores to raise awareness of green electricity and other issues.

For more information, or to buy online, see:

Body Shop www.bodyshop.com

Culpeper www.culpeper.co.uk ▷ 0870 950 9001
Faith In Nature www.faithinnature.com ▷ 0161 764 2555
Weleda www.weleda.co.uk

Jewellery
How bad is your bling?

Compared with clothes, say, the ethics of the jewellery industry are rarely discussed – perhaps partly because, unlike T-shirts and jeans, jewellery tends to be non-branded, so there are no household-name corporations to hold to account. Yet in terms of both extraction of materials and manufacture, the production of jewellery is associated with a number of problems, including poverty wages, child labour, dangerous working conditions, environmental degradation and even war.

In some cases, there are obvious things that consumers can do. If you happen to be buying **diamonds**, for example, you can demand assurances that the stones haven't come from conflict zones (see box overleaf). And **coral** jewellery is a no-no: coral reefs are among the world's most fragile eco-systems, and they're already taking a severe beating from global warming, farm effluent and other pollution. Direct harvesting of coral for pendants can only make things worse.

For the more common materials, however, it's not immediately obvious how ethical shopping can improve standards. For instance, the majority of precious and semi-precious stones (though not diamonds) come from small-scale mines in remote regions of poor countries such as Brazil, Madagascar, Mali and India. Some of these mines are associated with desperate and dangerous conditions – with women and children "literally scratching for a living", in the words of campaigner and fair trade jewellery retailer Greg Valerio – as well as serious, and often avoidable, environmental impacts. But jewellery shops and importers aren't directly associated with the mines or their workers, so it's unlikely that consumer pressure will result in direct improvements. And, since the mines are very often the only source of employment in a region, simply avoiding precious stones is not going to help.

Similarly, the more industrial mines that most of our **gold and silver** comes from are linked to environmental hazards such as the contamination of groundwater through acid-rock drainage – a phenomenon that takes place when air reacts with sulphide minerals in the rocks. Yet, in most cases, there's no way to know the green credentials of the specific mines from which a bracelet, say, originated.

Finally, there's the question of the conditions under which the jewellery is manufactured. Much of the cheaper, mass-produced stuff is made in **sweatshop** conditions in East Asia. As ever, jobs in these factories are in demand, but the mostly non-unionized workforce is often exposed to serious health and safety risks. Many migrant workers in China, for example, have been left crippled by **silicosis** – also known as "dust lung" – after drilling beads or cutting semi-precious stones such as opal and topaz into hearts and other shapes for use in Western bangles, necklaces and earrings. And child labour is common throughout the smaller developing-world workshops that produce many of the higher-quality pieces on sale in the UK.

Ethical jewellery suppliers

A number of companies are now offering jewellery sourced according to fair trade principles. As with all uncertified fair trade, there are no rules and regulations governing exactly what this means, but in general it refers to the retailers working directly with manufacturers, ensuring they get safe working conditions, a decent slice of the profits and long-term trading agreements. Obviously, a few ethical jewellery suppliers can't immediately solve all the problems mentioned above, but in at least one case

– **Cred** – the fair traders are also doing their utmost to inject a dose of ethical awareness into the jewellery industry at large.

The main online/mail-order suppliers are listed overleaf. Many fair trade shops also sell some jewellery – see p.139 to find your nearest.

Conflict diamonds

Granted, diamonds aren't an everyday purchase. But if you're going to spend a fortune on an engagement ring, or treat yourself to a once-in-a-lifetime gift, it's worth bearing ethics in mind. The problem is that, like all valuable natural resources, diamonds have the potential to fuel corruption, land appropriation and even full-scale conflict in the countries in which they're found. Only a minority of diamonds come from war zones (an estimated 2%) but that minority has contributed to the drawing out of wars in which millions of innocent people have been murdered, mutilated or tortured. In the last decade or so, at least three brutal African conflicts – in **Sierra Leone**, **Angola** and the **Democratic Republic of Congo** – have been partly driven or funded by the exploitation of diamond mines by armed groups.

The victims aren't necessarily limited to those in the countries where diamonds are mined, however. According to Action Aid, the last couple of years have seen a boom in diamond sales – in part because the 9/11 terrorist attacks have reduced the demand for travel, leaving the affluent with more disposable income. But this is sadly ironic considering that **Al Qaeda** – believed to be behind the 9/11 attacks – are thought to have been partly funded by conflict diamonds.

After years of tireless campaigning from groups such as Global Witness, the international community has started to address the conflict-diamond problem through a global initiative called the **Kimberley Process**. Involving governments, NGOs and the diamond companies, it aims to "Stop conflict diamonds, Promote prosperity diamonds" by imposing a certification scheme that tracks all uncut stones from mining to cutting. Seventy producer, exporter and importer countries have now signed up.

For all its positive impacts, however, the Kimberley Process only tracks diamonds to the cutting stage, so it doesn't help jewellery shoppers to be sure about what they're buying. As such, some people have suggested avoiding African diamonds and opting instead, where possible, for Canadian stones, which are distinguishable through a minute etched hallmark of a polar bear. After all, even developing-world diamonds that *don't* come from war zones can raise ethical problems: the expulsion of the Gwi and Gana Bushmen from their lands in the Botswanan **Kalahari**, for example, is seen by many as inseparable from diamond prospecting.

But a boycott of African diamonds would hurt some very poor countries that are economically reliant on these precious stones – in Botswana, for example, diamonds contribute around a third of GDP. So probably a better option is to quiz your jewellers as to where their diamonds are from and whether their suppliers offer a guarantee that their stones are Kimberley certified. When Global Witness and Amnesty did a survey in late 2004, they found that only 18% of stores surveyed could provide a copy of their conflict diamond policy and 22% said they had no policy at all. If you get a blank look, suggest that the jeweller gets up to speed on the issue and shop elsewhere. If they show you some paperwork, check that it isn't a simple gemmological certificate, which relates purely to the diamond's authenticity, not its origins. For more information on conflict diamonds, see:

Global Witness www.globalwitness.org/buyconflictfree
Kimberley Process www.kimberleyprocess.com

Cred

www.cred.tv ▷ 01243 839 249

Cred, which is a charity as well as a business, sells silver chains, bangles, bracelets and rings – some plain, some with stones – traded according to their primary goal: "justice for the poor". Shop online or by phone, or visit their stockists in Chichester (01243 536 638), London's Wood Green (020 8888 4462) or Bradford-Upon-Avon (01225 868 888). Besides their own ethical sourcing efforts, Cred are causing something of a stir in the wider jewellery industry. They were recently behind the first major study on the ethics of jewellery supply chains, and they're looking into certifying small-scale mining activities in the developing world, exposing illegal large-scale mining operations that are causing harm, and setting up an Ethical Jewellery Initiative (a bit like a more specific version of the Ethical Trading Initiative; see p.61).

People Tree

www.ptree.co.uk ▷ 0845 450 4595

Though it focuses on clothes, the People Tree website/catalogue includes some delicate silver earrings and necklaces, as well as a wide selection of bead-based pieces from Thailand, Indonesia, India and elsewhere. Though it may not sound very pretty, the chain made from silver rings and recycled ring-pulls is surprisingly effective.

Silver Chilli

www.silverchilli.com

Online supplier of silver jewellery from Mexico, with much of the profits going back to local projects and communities and a fair trade policy seeking to overcome the "mafia-style" Mexican silver business, in which wealthy shop owners reap most of the rewards. The selection ranges from the chunky Tejida Plata Bangle (£33) to delicate necklaces, earrings and bracelets made with silver-grey freshwater pearls (£6–24).

Tearcraft

www.tearcraft.org ▷ 020 8977 9144

Some people may have misgivings about supporting an overtly evangelical Christian organization, but Tearcraft's fair trade catalogue and online shop includes a wide range of fairly traded necklaces, earrings, pendants, brooches and rings, mostly in silver but often with semi-precious stones.

Traidcraft

www.traidcraftshop.co.uk ▷ 0191 491 1001

Traidcraft's trusty fair trade catalogue and website includes a selection of mostly inexpensive jewellery, mainly sourced from South East Asia and India. Other than the East Timor Bangle (£28), most pieces are less than a tenner.

Money
matters

Most of us trust our money to institutions that attempt to increase its worth – for our gain and their own – by investing it in shares, bonds and property, loaning it to companies, countries or individuals, or gambling with it by speculating on future currency or commodity values. This goes not only for the cash in our bank accounts, but also for our pension contributions and our investments, as well as the essentially collective pools of money in the power of insurance companies.

Whether that's a problem depends on whether you care who your money is invested in or loaned to. Unless the financial institution in question has an investment policy stating otherwise, your cash could be supporting those linked to oppressive governments, arms sales, deforestation and the rest of the sin list. As for currency speculation, it's a way of making money that can wreak economic chaos in developing countries (see p.271).

These issues are particularly pertinent because financial institutions are so powerful. Pension funds and insurance companies control around 70% of the UK stock market, and the political influence of the financial sector is also immense. One director at the World Trade Organization, for instance, claimed that the hugely controversial GATS agreement (which opened up services such as healthcare to global markets) would never have happened "without the tremendous pressure exerted by the American financial services industry, particularly by companies like American Express and Citicorp".

In response to increasing public awareness of these kinds of issues, a growing number of banks, pension funds and other bodies are offering ethical financial services. But how does it all work? And does it have any effect? This chapter deals with these questions, then gives specific information about banks (p.269), pensions (p.277), insurance (p.281), mortgages (p.283), investments and financial advisers (p.285).

Ethical money: the basics
How does it work? *Does* it work?

In the world of money, as in any sector, the term ethical has no fixed meaning. But most commonly it refers to **socially responsible investment** (SRI), the practice of considering social and environmental factors when deciding which shares to buy and who to loan money to. This concept is nothing new – it's often traced back to Quakers and Methodists boycotting certain sections of the stock market around a hundred years ago. But in the last decade it has become a booming sector. There are now a number of banks, many pensions and more than fifty UK investment funds driven by SRI policies, plus numerous financial advisers specializing in the field. However, ethical investment policies vary widely, from the highly strict – usually dubbed "dark green" – to the more flexible, or "light green".

The green spectrum

Dark green investment policies are traditionally based on **negative screening**. This involves drawing up a list of unacceptable practices deemed to be harmful to people, the environment or animals and excluding any company found to be involved in these practices. An investment organization might decide upon its own criteria, or it could get some pointers from an external body such as EIRIS (see p.268), but either way the approach involves excluding entire industries – nuclear power, arms manufacture and tobacco being a few common examples – as well as any individual company associated with unethical behaviour.

Another dark green approach is so-called **cause-based** investment (also known as alternative investment, mission-based investment and socially directed investment). Practised by the more specialist ethical organizations such as Triodos Bank (see p.274), this involves investing directly in projects and companies deemed to have social and environmental worth, usually completely avoiding loans to big companies and investments on the stock market. Typical beneficiaries are charities, organic farms and community housing projects – the kinds of organizations that struggle to find the credit they need at affordable rates elsewhere.

Light-green investors take a different approach. They may rule out a few industries, such as arms manufacture, but generally they prefer **posi-**

tive screening: any company can qualify for investment as long as it fulfils a certain number of positive criteria, which may range from recycling waste to reporting openly on its own environmental impact – whatever that impact may be.

A variation on this approach is **best-of-sector** screening: investing only in the most ethical company in each sector. The logic is simple: if you accept that, say, nuclear power companies are inevitably going to exist, giving them all an incentive to be the best in the field may make a bigger difference than boycotting the whole sector.

Screening, however, is typically only one half of a light-green policy, the other being an **engagement** strategy, through which lenders and investors use their insider influence to push for better ethical standards. A bank might say, for example, "OK, we'll lend you the cash for your oil platform,

Common screening criteria

Here are the kinds of pluses and minuses that an ethical finance organization would be looking out for:

Negative

▶ **Industries** The blacklist often includes alcohol, animal experiments, arms, fur, gambling, genetic engineering, intensive farming, nuclear power, oil, pornography and tobacco.

▶ **Environment** Association with specific problems such as chemical pollution, CO_2 emissions or deforestation; or a straightforward lack of any kind of environmental policy.

▶ **Human rights** Lack of a code of conduct on workers' rights; association with human rights abuses of any kind; or links to oppressive governments.

▶ **Management** Excessive directors' pay; lack of financial transparency; political donations; conflicts of interest; use of tax havens.

Positive

▶ **Charity & community** Charitable donations; participation in and support for local events; sensitivity to the business's effect on local people.

▶ **Environment** Clear environmental policies; environmental auditing and reporting; recycling; minimizing pollution and avoidable energy use.

▶ **Staff** Clear codes of conduct on pay and labour conditions, equal opportunities and staff "development".

▶ **Management** Disclosure of payments to foreign governments; compliance with "corporate governance" protocols.

but only if you fit robust environmental protection." Or a pension fund which owns shares in a supermarket chain might threaten to cause a fuss at the annual general meeting unless it agrees to audit labour standards in the developing-world farms that supply it.

Dark green vs. light green

The dark green vs. light green argument largely comes down to the old question of idealism vs. pragmatism. Advocates of the dark-green approach think that it's morally unacceptable to profit from companies or industries whose activities may cause harm to others – regardless of whether the link is obvious (as with arms manufacturing) or more convoluted (oil consumption contributing towards global warming, for example). And they claim that the lighter-green banks and investment funds may actually do harm – by giving the thumbs up to dodgy firms, and in the process helping them create a veneer of social responsibility.

On the other hand, the pragmatists argue that working *with* companies – through engagement and positive screening – is far more likely to make a difference than simply avoiding their whole sector. It's better to have progressive bankers and investors involved in every industry, they claim, than to leave the most unscrupulous financial backers and most dodgy businesses to get on with wrecking the planet. After all, dark-green ethical banks, pensions and investment funds have a tiny market share (less than 2% in the UK), and there are plenty of other lenders and investors queuing up to finance or buy into even the murkiest companies.

Furthermore, light-green advocates point out that there's an odd logic to financially boycotting sectors which we continue to support as consumers and voters. Does it make sense, for example, to object to our money being invested in oil companies while we continue to drive cars? Or to shun arms firms unless we're committed to the total abolishment of the British armed forces?

These are all fair points. But does the pragmatic option actually work? Can investors and bankers really make a difference by "engaging" with companies? Exponents of this approach claim there have been numerous successes. Friends of the Earth point to **McDonald's** phasing out environmentally problematic polystyrene packaging, for example, and **Ford** pulling out of the Global Climate Coalition (a now-defunct pressure group which argued against the Kyoto treaty and other measures to combat climate change). Others point to the role that shareholders played in the fall of apartheid in South Africa. And British ethical fund managers claim to have made big impacts behind the scenes on a whole range of issues – including the introduction of codes of conduct governing labour abuses in overseas garment factories. But, despite all these examples, there are few cases where it can be said definitively that shareholders' ethical concerns have resulted in a company changing significantly for the better.

That's perhaps not too surprising, because the financial "engagers" are only likely to change a company's practices if they can show not just a moral case for improving behaviour, but also a financial one. Sometimes this may be possible, but very often it's simply not true that better corporate behaviour means more profits. As one city analyst told *The Observer* in 2002, "On current share trends it pays to be socially irresponsible all the way."

To really *force* a company to change requires the progressive investors – or **shareholder activists**, as the more extreme ones are known – to table a resolution at the company's AGM (annual general meeting). These are occasionally successful on some issues, such as the 2003 GlaxoSmithKline shareholders' protest against the outrageous pay awarded to the company's CEO. But specifically *ethical* resolutions are rare in the UK (unlike in the US; see www.iccr.org). And when they do happen, they don't generally achieve landslide support. The Greenpeace-led resolution against BP Amoco's Northstar project in Alaska, for example, was considered a major success when it achieved around 13.5% of the vote.

But that doesn't mean the engagement approach is worthless. Such resolutions can force issues not just into the AGM but also into the media. They can also play their part in wider protest. For instance, British construction company Balfour Beatty withdrew from the Ilisu Dam project in Turkey – which would allegedly have displaced thousands of people and have had potentially disastrous environmental consequences – after a wide-ranging campaign against the company. Shareholders were not solely responsible, but they played their part, delivering, in the words of Simon McRae from Friends of the Earth, "a big slap in the face" at the AGM.

The bigger the better

Ultimately, dark green and light green strategies are both valid, and in practice many ethical banks and investment funds favour a mixed approach: excluding certain industries and giving preference to companies with positive practices; but also taking the engagement path on some issues. Similarly, rather than boycotting a whole industry, an organiza-

The FTSE4GOOD series

Launched in 2001, the FTSE4Good is the world's first significant series of share indices (statistical tools which list companies and share prices) designed specifically for socially responsible investors. It's essentially a screened version of normal FTSE indices, in which tobacco, nuclear-power and arms industries are excluded. Other companies only qualify if they meet "globally recognised corporate responsibility standards". These standards, set out by FTSE and EIRIS (see p.268), focus on three areas:

FTSE4Good Index Series

▶ Working towards environmental sustainability

▶ Developing positive relationships with stakeholders

▶ Upholding and supporting universal human rights

There are two indices each for UK, US, Europe and Global: a "benchmark" index listing all the companies that qualify, and a "tradeable" index listing the current top 50 or 100 companies. Numerous ethical investors use the index as a reference tool – they pay a fee, which is donated to UNICEF (the UN's children's fund).

There's no doubt that the FTSE4Good has increased public awareness of corporate ethics. For example, when the index was launched, the exclusion of Tesco (for its failure to publish an environmental report) was widely reported in the mainstream press. But not everyone approves of the indices. Some critics see them as yet another tool for promoting corporate social responsibility – which they consider a hopeless substitute for proper regulation (see p.59) – while many in the ethical investment world have criticized the criteria they use for being too vague or loose. Presumably in response to these concerns, the requirements have been made more rigorous numerous times since the indices were first launched. But it's still towards the "light" end of the green spectrum, with oil firms and other controversial companies lurking on the list. For more information visit: www.ftse.com/ftse4good

A less-high-profile operation is the Corporate Responsibility Index, maintained by Business in the Community. It's aimed more at managers than investors: anyone can join and the members are ranked each year. For more information or to see how the members compare, visit: www.bitc.org.uk/programmes/key_initiatives

tion may be more selective – the Co-operative Bank policy, for instance, doesn't categorically rule out all companies involved in manufacturing armaments for defence, but it won't invest in any firm which produces torture devices, or any which exports arms of any kind to countries deemed to have oppressive regimes.

Regardless of the shade of green or the type of approach, the biggest determinant of the impact of ethical finance is simply the size and number of organizations involved. Indeed, when really major investors – such as

CalPERS, the Californian public pension fund worth more than $200 billion – start throwing their weight around, even governments start taking notice. According to journalist Jon Entine, when Thailand found itself on the CalPERS investment blacklist, "government officials pleaded for time, saying 'there should be sufficient channels in which we are given appropriate opportunities to show that Thailand has complied with good-practice standards, as we have every intention to do'". So even if ethical finance is not revolutionizing the world right now, its impact gets greater with each person who changes bank on ethical grounds, or signs up for an ethical pension or investment fund.

Ethical finance Q&A

Does "going ethical" mean getting less interest?

In the case of banks (see p.269), having an "ethical" account certainly doesn't need to mean you being poorer – quite the opposite. Most of the population get practically no interest on their high-street current account, and pay over the odds for services and overdrafts. Compare that with Smile, the Internet arm of the ethically progressive Co-operative Bank. At the time of writing it offers 3.04% interest and a free £500 overdraft.

Things are a bit more contentious when it comes to investments and pensions, but the evidence suggests that "screened" pension and investment funds are actually just as good a bet as non-ethical ones. Probably the most in-depth assessment of the issue is *Does Ethical Investment Pay?*, produced in 1999 by EIRIS (see p.268). The study examined the performance of fifteen leading ethical funds over a long period, and found that ethical investment generally involves marginally less risk, but offers marginally lower returns than conventional investment. The balance of risks and returns, it concludes, is "not materially different". In other words, you're less likely to see your savings rocket, but also less likely to see them plummet.

EIRIS's study also compared the impact of different "levels" of ethical-ness. They defined five "ethical indices", each of which excluded between one- and two-thirds of the FTSE All-Share Index; all five returned a risk–return balance "broadly similar" to the All-Share. If you're feeling really keen, you can download the 74-page study as a PDF document from www.eiris.org.

Some studies – such as a recent Australian survey carried out by AMP Henderson – have even suggested that ethical investment funds are actually *more* profitable than average. As SocialFunds.com reported, the survey found that ethical funds "outperformed the most relevant benchmark, the S&P/ASX 200, over the one-, two-, three- and five-year periods, through September 30, 2003", despite underperforming in 2002.

Who does the research?

Some banks and investment funds have their own research teams, but many ethical investors trust a research service to screen companies on their behalf. The UK's largest service is **EIRIS**, the **Ethical Investment Research Service**. Set up in 1983 – with the support of the Church of England, the Joseph Rowntree Trusts, Oxfam and the Society of Friends, among others – EIRIS has both commercial and charity wings, and keeps tabs on companies and oppressive governments for many institutional investors, as well as the FTSE4GOOD share indices (see p.266). The EIRIS website is a valuable resource, whether you want to find out more about responsible investing or locate an ethically minded financial adviser:

EIRIS www.eiris.org

Other organizations that provide screening research include **SIRI Group** (www.sirigroup.com) and **Ethical Screening** (www.ethicalscreening.com).

Who gets the money?

It is sometimes said that "ethical" banks, pension managers and investment funds do invest in dodgy companies – just slightly less dodgy companies than the alternatives. It's certainly true that most SRI funds, while they shun arms, tobacco and the like, nonetheless invest in a list of companies that you might not exactly think of as moral trailblazers. As the box opposite shows, the most popular shares in ethical portfolios include major banks, supermarkets and retailers that are themselves highly criticized from some corners.

This may not bother you, but if it does, bear in mind that not all ethical policies are alike. The Triodos Bank (p.274), for example, only finances schemes and companies "which add social, environmental and cultural value" to the world; and there are investment policies out there ranging

The ethical share chart

The following list, drawn up by EIRIS in 2002, shows the companies whose shares crop up in the biggest number of ethical investment funds – starting with the most popular. There isn't an up-to-date version, but while individual companies will have come and gone, the type of firms represented is likely to have changed relatively little.

1 Vodafone Group	17 Cable and Wireless
2 FirstGroup	18 mm02
3 National Express Group	19 Northern Rock
4 Prudential	20 CGNU
5 HBOS	21 Electrocomponents
6 Abbey National	22 The Sage Group
7 BG Group	23 Pearson
8 Centrica	24 Tesco
9 ARM Holdings	25 Xansa
10 Halma	26 Reed Elsevier
11 The Royal Bank of Scotland Group	27 Compass Group
12 Berkeley Group	28 Johnson Matthey
13 BT Group	29 Debenhams
14 Reuters Group	30 First Technology
15 RPS Group	31 Marks & Spencer Group
16 Nestor Healthcare Group	32 The Go-Ahead Group

from **vegan** (avoiding all forms of animal products and testing) to **Islamic** (ruling out alcohol and money-lending firms), so there's no reason why you shouldn't find one that suits you. Ask a financial adviser for more information (see p.286).

Banks & building societies
Your savings, your landmine

The major banks have got a pretty unimpressive ethical track record. This includes the Big Four – HSBC, Lloyds TSB, Barclays and Royal Bank of Scotland/NatWest – who between them account for around two-thirds of the UK current-account market. The most common criticisms they have faced over the years relate to who they lend to (and offer accounts to). Barclays and HSBC, for example, have been accused by Friends of the Earth of funding illegal deforestation in Indonesia by lending to companies such as Asia Pulp and Paper. And all the Big Four have been attacked at some stage by NGOs focusing on areas such as arms exports to – and natural-resource extraction from – countries with oppressive regimes.

Some progress has been made recently in the area of unethical lending, with three of the Big Four (minus Lloyds TSB at the time of writing) having signed up for the **Equator Principles**, a set of guidelines on socially and environmentally sound financing. However, as with most voluntary schemes, campaigners claim that the Equator framework hasn't stopped banks making irresponsible loans. For instance, in a report called *Principles, Profits, or Just PR?*, pressure group Bank Track noted that "despite the existence of the Principles, many controversial projects such as the Baku Ceyhan oil pipeline went ahead virtually unaltered while other, similarly disastrous projects, such as the Sakhalin II oil project in the Russian Far East and the Nam Theun dam in Laos are lined up for financing by the EP banks". For more info, see:

Equator Principles www.equator-principles.com
Bank Track www.banktrack.org

Corbis

A section of the Amazon razed to the ground. UK banks have long been criticized for lending money to companies involved in destruction of rainforests, which are home to at least half the world's plant and animal species. Besides the collection of valuable hardwood, deforestation is driven by mining, the claiming of farmland for animal feed and palm oil, urbanization and global warming. At current rates of deforestation, there would be no tropical rainforest left by 2100.

Another issue is **currency speculation**, which is linked to the destabilization of developing-world economies (see box). According to a report by War on Want, the UK's biggest currency gamblers include HSBC, Barclays and Royal Bank of Scotland/NatWest, with Lloyds TSB not too far behind.

Currency speculation

Every day, an estimated $1–2 trillion is traded on the international currency markets. To put this figure in perspective, imagine a couple of hundred pounds for every single person on the planet, or a stack of £50 notes reaching from the Earth to the Moon. Some of this is related to trade and long-term investment, but the vast majority – probably at least 90% – is the speculative "hot money" of banks, investment funds and super-rich individuals aiming to profit from short-term changes in exchange rates. Currency speculation is nothing new, but it has grown out of all proportion in the last decade.

The problem with this potentially lucrative activity is that it can harm economic stability, especially in developing countries whose governments lack the financial weight to protect themselves against the speculators. There isn't space here to go into the details but when there's a speculative "run" on a particular currency, the economy of that country can be left in tatters, with a devalued currency and a messed-up banking system. It is now widely accepted, for example, that currency speculation played a major role in the financial crises of East Asia, which resulted in massive job losses and increased poverty. For their part, the successful speculators pay no tax on their winnings, even though the sums involved are massive. According to ATTAC (the Association for the Taxation of Financial Transactions for the Aid of Citizens), NatWest made £432 million from currency trading in 1998, while HSBC made £2.3 million a day from it in 1997.

An increasing number of economists and anti-poverty campaigners are calling for the "caging" of hot money. One suggested means for doing this is the introduction of a minimal tax on all currency transactions, set at perhaps 0.1%: small enough to leave trade unaffected, but big enough to calm speculation, which relies on very marginal changes in exchange rates. According to its proponents, the would-be **Tobin Tax** – named after James Tobin, the Nobel Prize-winning economist who thought up the idea in the 1970s – could simultaneously stabilize global finance and raise huge sums of money either for the countries where transactions are occurring or for a global anti-poverty fund. Even after the shrinking effect it would have on the currency market, the tax's advocates estimate that a 0.1% tax could raise up to $300 billion each year – roughly six times the combined international aid budget. But many commentators see the whole idea as unworkable due to the practical problems of implementing any system of global taxation. For more information, visit the Stamp Out Poverty site (www.stampoutpoverty.org) or ATTAC (www.attac.org).

It remains to be seen whether the currency speculation issue will be resolved – by a Tobin tax or some other approach. In the meantime, consumers already have the option of switching to a bank, such as any of those recommended in this chapter, which makes a point of not taking part in aggressive currency speculation.

Most of the big names in banking have also yet to make much meaningful progress in areas such as drawing up regular reports on their social and environmental performance. One exception here is HSBC, which was one of the first global super-companies to commit to making its operations carbon-neutral by reducing its energy use, sourcing green electricity and investing in offsetting projects.

Profiteering from **third-world debt** was once another source of contention, but most UK banks have bowed to years of pressure to write off debts to the poorest countries, or "swap" them for commitments that governments spend the money they would be repaying on reducing poverty in their countries.

One final question is whether the banks are ethical in their treatment of their customers. Even the UK's Competition Commission – not known as the most zealously anti-corporate of watchdogs – has accused the Big Four of making too much profit, while a report commissioned by the Treasury, published in 2000, described them as holding a "complex monopoly". But then executive salaries of up to £10 million a year have to come from somewhere.

Banking options

Ethical specialists: current & savings accounts

The Co-operative Bank

www.co-operativebank.co.uk ▷ 08457 212 212

Set up in 1872 as the Loan and Deposit Department of the Co-operative Wholesale Society, the Co-operative Bank now has more than three million customer accounts and is the only UK Clearing Bank to publish an ethical investment policy – something it first did in 1992. The policy, which is determined through regular consultation with the bank's customers, addresses concerns about human rights, arms, corporate responsibility, genetic modification, social enterprise, ecological impact and animal welfare (see box opposite). A mix of negative and positive screening, it's a medium shade of green: companies that use animal tests are OK, for example, but only in the field of medicine; arms firms that export to oppressive regimes are no-go, but arms firms in general aren't explicitly ruled out. The bank also attempts to support charities and positive business ventures such as fair trade and research into alternatives to animal testing.

Practicalities More than 300 branches and Handybanks; pay in and withdraw at post offices; 30,000 Link cash machines; 24-hour phone and Internet banking. Accounts offered: current, numerous savings, ISAs, business, student.

The Co-operative Bank & Smile Ethical Policy

Following is a summary of the ethical policy of the Co-operative Bank and Smile at the time of writing, with crosses for those practices that the banks avoid investing in and ticks for those which they try actively to support. For more information, see www.co-operativebank.co.uk/ethics

Human rights

✘ Governments or businesses which fail to uphold basic human rights within their sphere of influence; businesses with "concerning links" to oppressive regimes

Arms trade

✘ Manufacture or transfer of armaments to oppressive regimes; manufacture of torture equipment or other equipment used to violate human rights

Corporate responsibility

✘ Multinational companies without a clear commitment to core labour standards; irresponsible marketing practices in developing countries; tobacco products

✔ Responsible position on fair trade; labour rights in their own operations and through their supply chains in developing countries

Genetic modification

✘ Uncontrolled release of GMOs into the environment; "terminator" technologies; patenting of indigenous knowledge; non-medical cloning

Social enterprise

✔ Charities and organizations involved in the "social enterprise" sector, including co-operatives, credit unions and community finance initiatives

Ecological impact

✘ Extraction/production of fossil fuels; environmentally persistent or harmful chemicals; unsustainable harvest of timber, fish and other natural resources

✔ Recycling; renewable energy and energy efficiency; sustainable products and services such as organic produce; the pursuit of ecological sustainability

Animal welfare

✘ Animal testing of cosmetic or household products; intensive farming; blood sports; the fur trade

✔ Development of alternatives to animal experimentation; farming methods which promote animal welfare

Smile

www.smile.co.uk ▷ 0870 (THE BANK) 843 2265

The UK's first Internet-only bank, Smile has been a huge success since it was launched by the Co-operative Bank in 1999. It shares the same ethical policy as its parent (see box), but as it has no branches it can offer better interest rates (currently 3.04% on current accounts, 4% on savings). It regularly scores highest in the country in banking customer-satisfaction surveys.

Practicalities No branches; excellent Internet banking with 24-hour backup phone line; postage-free envelopes provided for cheques; pay in/withdraw at post offices; 30,000 Link cash machines. Accounts offered: current, instant savings, ISAs, student.

The Ecology Building Society

www.ecology.co.uk ▷ 0845 674 5566

Established in 1981, the Ecology is a small mutual building society whose savings accounts are only used to fund mortgages considered to be "green" (renovation projects, energy-efficient construction and the like). It's perhaps the world's only financial organization that will enquire if you are a member of a green group before offering you an account. Interest rates depend on the withdrawal period and amount deposited, ranging at the time of writing from 1.5% to 3.5%.

Practicalities No branches; pay in/withdraw by cheque or transfer. Accounts offered: instant and 60-day-notice savings accounts; Cash Mini ISA.

Ethical specialists: savings only

The Triodos Bank

www.triodos.co.uk ▷ 0500 008 720

Established in Holland in 1980, with a British office opening in 1995, the Triodos Bank is a specialist ethical savings bank with a "cause-based" approach. It only invests in "organisations which create real social, environmental and cultural value" – charities, social businesses, community projects and environmental initiatives – but it still offers good rates of interest. Triodos doesn't offer a current account, but does offer a wide range of savings accounts, from the general Positive Saver account to those focusing on investment in a more specific area: Charity, Just Housing, Earth, Organic, etc. Notice periods are one, thirty or ninety days (you can use the savings calculator on their website to compare accounts and rates, which go up to 3.8% at the time of writing). A model of transparency, the bank publishes a full list of all the companies and organizations it invests in.

Practicalities No branches; pay in/withdraw by cheque or transfer. Accounts offered: ISAs, young saver, regular saver, social investor cheque, and others.

Charity Bank

www.charitybank.org ▷ 01732 520 029

Describing itself as "the world's first not-for-profit bank", Charity Bank was established in 2002 by the long-standing Charities Aid Foundation, an organization that provides credit to charities, who frequently find credit difficult to come by. The bank itself is a registered charity and its notice-period savings accounts (no current accounts are offered) are aimed at people more interested in knowing that their money is doing something useful than in earning huge returns. However, over and above the 2% interest on offer, customers can make substantial savings on their tax bill by investing money for a minimum of five years. For high-rate tax payers, the bank claims, this can work out at a return equivalent to more than 8%.

Practicalities No branches; pay in/withdraw by post. Accounts offered: various notice-period savings.

Credit cards

None of the major credit card providers – such as Visa and American Express – are known for being particularly ethical companies, but there are a wide range of **charity** (or "affinity") credit cards available, which support causes ranging from the RSPCA and NSPCC to your local football team.

Usually, when you sign up for such a card, the bank or other issuing company will make a lump payment (often in the region of £25) to the relevant charity. After that, they'll make a small donation each time you spend a certain amount on the card – for example, 10p donated for each £50 spent.

Most of these cards have no fixed charges and offer competitive rates, so if you use a credit card, there's no reason not to sign up. Many of the high-street banks offer charity-linked cards, though you're free to choose a more ethically minded supplier – such as the **Co-operative Bank**, whose Amnesty International card has already raised more than a million pounds for the human rights organization.

The highest-profile charity credit card at the time of writing is the American Express RED – part of the "(Product) Red" campaign, spearheaded by Bono of U2. At least 1% of what you spend via the card will be contributed to the fight against AIDS – a much higher rate than with most charity cards. Find out more at:

(Product) Red www.joinred.com

Mutual building societies

Though they don't really fit into the ethical specialists category, mutual building societies (ie those which haven't been turned into banks) are often described as a more ethical place to put your cash than the high-street banks. After all, they don't invest in anything other than people's mortgages and, since they don't take business accounts, they don't have any dubious multinationals as customers. Most mutuals also make significant policy decisions democratically, with each saver entitled to one vote, regardless of the amount in their account.

Despite all this, mutuals generally offer very good rates of **interest** – perhaps because they're not floated on the stock exchange, so have no shareholder dividends to pay, and perhaps because their focus on service rather than profits allows them to be much more efficient (running costs rise about 35% when mutuals turn into banks, according to the Building Society Association).

Building societies that are no longer mutuals include Abbey National, Alliance and Leicester, Bradford & Bingley and Halifax. For a full list of the remaining mutuals, and for more information, visit:

Building Society Association www.bsa.org.uk

Credit unions

Credit unions are co-operative-style alternatives to the savings accounts offered by standard banks and building societies. The idea is that a group of people who share a common bond – such as a residential area, employer, occupation or church – join together to form a union. They invest their savings into a pool, from which loans can be made to members.

Credit unions claim to offer ethical and financial benefits over conventional savings options. On the ethical level, the unions can help tackle **financial exclusion**. Banks often refuse finance to the poorest members of society due to their having a credit history tarnished long ago, but credit unions can make a case-by-case decision on who can borrow based on their current ability to repay and savings record with the union. Furthermore, since only members can borrow, there are no loans to dodgy businesses. On the financial level, savers can expect dividends of up to around 8% on their investment (largely because there are so few overheads to pay), and borrowers receive better terms on their loans than a bank would offer. For example, under UK law, interest on a loan from a credit union can't be set at more than 1% a month on the reducing balance; all loans are insured, at no cost to the borrower; and there are no fees for the arrangement of a loan, or for paying it off early.

Credit unions are owned by their members and are run democratically within a clear legal framework, including the obligatory training of people elected as officers. They've been around since the nineteenth century and have grown to include 100 million members in 35,000 unions in more than eighty countries (though the majority are in the US and Canada). For more information, or to locate a credit union, visit:

British Association of Credit Unions Limited www.abcul.coop

Credit unions have made an enormous impact in the **developing world**, where rural populations live many miles from the nearest bank, and the poor have few possessions to put down as security. To read more about this, see:

World Council of Credit Unions www.woccu.org/development

Pensions
Responsible retirement

It's difficult to overestimate the financial weight of pension funds. In the UK they're worth hundreds of billions of pounds and own around a third of the stock market. As such, they have the potential to put enormous pressure on companies to improve their ethical standards.

This potential is a very long way from being fully realized, but the last decade has seen a steady rise in the number of specialist ethical pension options. And, perhaps more importantly, the new millennium has seen a huge increase in the number of mainstream pensions taking ethical factors into consideration when investing. This is largely because the Labour government passed a law in July 2000 obliging trustees of stakeholder and occupational pensions (including local government schemes) to declare if and how "social, environmental or ethical considerations are taken into account in the selection, retention and realisation of investments". The trustees are not obliged to invest ethically, but they must at least state their position and make it available to all members in a document called a **Statement of Investment Principles** (SIP).

This is all good news, but research shows that there is still a huge gap between what pension-fund members want and what is actually happen-

Pension basics

In the UK, everyone is entitled to the basic state retirement pension. However, this offers no red carpet into retirement, so most people will want to take out a second pension to top it up. There are three main types:

▶ **Occupational pensions** Offered by employers, including local government, to employees. These generally offer the best deal, as the employer usually contributes.

▶ **Stakeholder pensions** Low-charge, flexible pensions available to everyone but designed for people who are not offered an occupational pension. Since 2001, all companies with more than five employees must offer a stakeholder pension, though you can also get them direct from financial services companies, trade unions and other organizations.

▶ **Personal pensions** These are bought from financial services companies, such as insurance companies, banks, investment companies and building societies. Since the emergence of stakeholder pensions, for most people there is little reason to choose a personal pension.

For more on pension types visit this government website: www.pensionguide.gov.uk

ing. Perhaps there's something about pensions that makes people feel more strongly about ethical issues: according to studies carried out by EIRIS and SustainAbility, the vast majority of people think their pension fund *should* operate an ethical policy, give members input into it and publish a list of companies invested in. Despite this, according to surveys carried out by Friends of the Earth in 2000 and Just Pensions in 2002, only "a handful" display good practice when it comes to ethical investment, even though most pension managers claim to consider SRI principles.

Campaign Against the Arms Trade highlighted this fact in 2002, when they published lists showing the number of shares in **arms companies** owned by the major pension schemes. NHS trusts, trade unions and nearly every local authority were all revealed to have defence firms in their investment portfolios. More recent research from Just Pensions suggests some improvement – with 30% of fund managers making some investment decisions on ethical grounds – but there's still a long way to go. For more background, see:

Campaign Against the Arms Trade www.caat.org.uk
EIRIS www.eiris.co.uk
Friends of the Earth www.foe.co.uk
Just Pensions www.justpensions.org
SustainAbility www.sustainability.com

Pension options

If you already pay into an occupational or stakeholder pension (see box on previous page), you can request the SIP from your fund managers, asking for clarification if the wording is unclear or noncommittal. It may also be worth doing some research online: some of the studies and sites mentioned above refer to many specific funds.

Once you have the information you need, if you're not satisfied with the stance of your scheme, **send your views** to the managers – and encourage like-minded colleagues to do the same. You may want to lobby for the introduction of a specific ethical plan, or request that social or environmental considerations are taken into account on the standard plan. If you want help working out what to ask and say, visit:

Fair Pensions www.fairpensions.org.uk

You may also want to direct the fund managers' attention to that site, and also to the research done by Just Pensions (www.justpensions.org),

Nice motor! Patriot missile launcher at 1997's IDEX Arms Show in Abu Dhabi, United Arab Emirates. Arms firms are widely invested in, or receive loans from, UK pension funds, retail funds, insurers and banks.
Photo: Corbis

who produce information specifically designed for pension managers and trustees interested in implementing SRI. If all else fails, you could ditch your employer's scheme and switch to a separate stakeholder or personal pension plan that reflects your ethical criteria. However, this may significantly reduce the amount you are able to save (you'll probably lose any employer contributions) so you'd be well advised to seek advice from a financial adviser before proceeding. See p.286 to find an ethically enlightened one.

If you currently have a **personal pension**, your fund isn't actually obliged to inform you of their angle on socially responsible investment. However, it is highly likely that they will be happy to reveal their position and also offer you the option of transferring to a specific ethical plan (though you may have to pay for the privilege).

If you're feeling particularly vigilant, you may also want to contact your **council**. As Martin Hogbin from Campaign Against the Arms Trade points out, council taxpayers also have the right to "question the investment policies of their local authority, as their taxes are used to top up existing pension funds".

Ethical stakeholder providers

If you want to start paying into a stakeholder or personal pension, you can buy one through a pension scheme provider, directly from a pension company or through an independent financial adviser. You'll pay for the services of an adviser, of course, but you'll also reduce the risk of making the wrong decision.

Stakeholder pensions tend to be a more popular ethical option with financial advisers than personal pensions, so that's what we've listed below (for information purposes only: this is not financial advice). Note, however, that many ethical personal pensions are also available and, because the companies selling them are able to charge higher costs than with stakeholder pensions (and therefore can employ more research staff), they may be more suitable if you have unusually specific concerns.

The following list of ethical stakeholder pension schemes was provided by the UK Social Investment Forum. For the most up-to-date version, visit www.uksif.co.uk.

Clerical Medical www.clericalmedical.co.uk ▷ 0870 602 2244
Friends Provident www.friendsprovident.com ▷ 0870 607 1352
Legal & General www.landg.com/pensions ▷ 0800 027 1818
Norwich Union www.your-pension.com ▷ 0800 056 2326
NPI Stakeholder www.npi.co.uk ▷ 0870 898 6961
Scottish Equitable www.scottishequitable.co.uk ▷ 08456 100 010
Scottish Life www.scottishlife.co.uk ▷ 0131 456 7777
Scottish Widows www.scottishwidows.co.uk ▷ 0131 456 7777
Standard Life www.standardlife.co.uk ▷ 0845 606 0012

It's the finding out that counts

So much of ethical consumerism comes down to information provided by the media. A good illustration of this is the pension fund for UK MPs. You might imagine that, of all people, MPs would have an idea about how the world works – including, for example, the fact that pension funds often invest in dubious businesses. However, it was only when *The Observer* newspaper specifically drew their attention to the fact that their retirement pool was being pumped into arms exporters and tobacco giants that the right honourable members took any action. Almost immediately after the article was published in 2001, MPs tabled a motion to establish an ethical pension option.

Insurance
Not the most enlightened of sectors

Like pension companies, insurers have huge assets – it is estimated that at any one time the industry controls roughly 10% of the world's capital flows. Technically speaking this isn't consumers' money, but to all intents and purposes insurance funds are collectively owned by their policyholders – and, since the money is widely invested, that makes taking out insurance a bit like any other form of investing.

You might expect, therefore, that there would be a range of ethical insurance schemes on offer, from companies operating screened investment policies (see p.262). This is true of the side of the industry that deals with life assurance and pensions but when it comes to the other side – the one that insures homes, contents, travel and the like – the options are surprisingly limited. Some companies claim to use their power as shareholders as a force for good, but investment screening is still non-existent in the sector.

One reason for this is the interrelated structure of the industry. To be an actual insurer – rather than a small insurance firm selling policies underwritten by an insurer – requires an enormous amount of money. Even if you did have the required cash, you'd rely on a **re-insurer** to underwrite you, and there aren't any re-insurers with serious ethical investment policies. Also, according to some insiders in the industry, the culture of the whole sector is inherently at odds with the idea of anything beyond profits – even more so than in other financial industries.

Quite apart from what your insurance company is investing in, another issue is who and what insurance companies are willing to cover. Indeed, since many environmentally harmful projects wouldn't be feasible without insurance, the big companies collectively wield major influence over what does and doesn't go ahead. As such, they could be a force for good if they imposed industry-wide ethical standards.

In 1995, some in the industry made moves towards recognizing their responsibilities by signing up to the UN's *Statement of Environmental Commitment by the Insurance Industry*, also referred to as **UNEP III**. This focuses on sustainable development and includes the statement "we will seek to include environmental considerations in our asset management". However, as with many non-binding agreements, the document has allegedly been largely ignored by many of its signatories. Friends of the Earth's report *Capital Punishment* (2000) emphasized this, listing some of the environmentally damaging companies, mainly within the oil industry, that big-name insurers continue to invest in.

Insurance options

Despite the failings of UNEP III, it's better than nothing, so as a first step you may want to ask your insurer if they've signed up. On the next ethical level up, a few of the big insurance firms claim to encourage high social and environmental standards via their activities as shareholders. These include Aviva, which owns Norwich Union, but the insurer which has gone furthest is the Co-operative Bank's sister organization, **CIS** (Co-operative Insurance Society). There's also one small ethical specialist in the sector: **Naturesave**.

CIS

www.cis.co.uk ▷ 08457 464 646

CIS have had a "Responsible Shareholder" approach for some time and in 2005 became the first major insurance company to launch a fully fledged ethical policy. The principles in the policy largely match those of the Co-op Bank (see p.273), though CIS only promises to promote those principles through engagement with companies rather than shunning certain sectors. On a broader level, CIS is flaunting its green credentials by cladding its enormous office block in solar panels. Animal-rights activists will probably never forgive the insurer for the stake it used to own in Huntingdon Life Sciences, but CIS is the most ethically progressive of the big insurers nonetheless.

Naturesave Policies

www.naturesave.co.uk ▷ 01803 864 390

This small insurance intermediary covering home, contents, travel and business sells policies underwritten by Lloyd's of London. It claims to be deeply committed to sustainable development, and 10% of the premium made from each policy sold is put towards the Naturesave Trust, which funds environmental and conservation projects (this is taken from the profits rather than added to the policy price). The company also lobbies the insurance industry to spend money on dealing with environmental risks at their roots instead of paying out compensation once disasters happen.

Animal Friends Insurance

www.animalfriends.org.uk ▷ 0870 403 0300

This small firm, which sells pet insurance only, promises to devote its profits to animal welfare charities. It also claims to try to influence the investment policies of underwriters.

Mortgages
From eco-warriors to eco-borrowers

Whereas it's quite clear what makes a bank or investment fund ethical (it attempts to exert an influence somewhere by selectively investing or by being an active shareholder), an "ethical mortgage" seems to mean different things to different people.

Overall, however, there are two main considerations. The first is the ethical credentials of the lender. After all, during the lifespan of a mortgage you'll potentially be handing over tens of thousands of pounds' worth of profit to whoever lent you the money in the first place. So if, for example, you don't trust the ethical standards of the major banks (see p.269), it would certainly be a logical step to avoid them for mortgages as well as for current accounts.

The second consideration relates to **interest-only** mortgages. With these, instead of paying off part of the loan and part of the interest each month, you only pay back part of the interest – the rest of your payments being used to invest in a package, such as an **endowment** or **ISA**, that at the end of a fixed term will be used to pay off the mortgage (assuming the investment grows enough). This is roughly the same as any other kind of investment, so the same ethical screening processes can be applied. Many companies now offer ethical endowments and the like.

Mortgage options

The standard ethical advice is to favour mutual building societies over demutualized ones and banks, since a mutual is unlikely to do anything more dodgy with your money than lend it out as mortgages. Happily, mutuals very often offer a better deal anyway, so favouring them needn't mean bigger charges or monthly payments.

One exception to the rule is the ethically renowned **Co-operative Bank**. Like those of the **Norwich & Peterborough** (listed overleaf), their "ethical" mortgages are really just standard mortgage packages in which the free extras are aimed at eco-conscious people. But in taking out a mortgage plan with them, you are at least supporting an ethics-led organization.

For more comprehensive information on mortgages, seek the help of a clued-up financial adviser. One company that specializes in mortgages is the **Ethical Investors Group**. For others see p.286.

Co-operative Bank

www.co-operativebank.co.uk ▷ 08457 212 212

As well as offering good rates on its CAT-standard mortgages, the Co-operative Bank, for each year that your mortgage with them exists, will offset a fifth of a typical home's greenhouse emissions via projects with Climate Care (see p.13). Also, along with each valuation, they'll provide a free Home Energy Rating, detailing a building's energy efficiency and potential energy- and money-saving measures.

The Ecology Building Society

www.ecology.co.uk ▷ 0845 674 5566

This small mutual building society lends on the grounds of the building rather than the individual, giving mortgages to fund energy-efficient housing, renovation of derelict and dilapidated properties, small-scale and ecologically driven enterprise, and "low-impact lifestyles". Many lenders refuse to touch derelict properties, but the Ecology, being small, can work one-to-one with borrowers to make sure their renovation project is financially sound. And if renovation is going well, and the building gaining value, the society may offer further funds for more improvements.

Ethical Investors Group

www.ethicalmortgage.co.uk ▷ 01242 539 848

Formed in 1989, this Cheltenham-based company (which donates half of its profits to charity) offers financial advice on ethical borrowing. It has grouped mortgage lenders into five categories according to their ethical positions and promises to help you find "the very best mortgage rate from the lender that you feel most comfortable with".

Norwich & Peterborough Building Society

www.npbs.co.uk ▷ 0845 300 6727

Norwich & Peterborough, another mutual building society, offers two "environmental" mortgages. For each of its Green Mortgages sold, it will plant eight trees a year for five years, enough in theory to absorb the carbon dioxide produced by the property, while its Brown Mortgage offers a good deal for people intending to convert or restore a building.

Investing directly

Occasionally, ethically focused organizations issue shares, allowing people an opportunity to invest in them directly. For example, Traidcraft and the Ethical Property Company had share issues in 2000, and CaféDirect in 2003. The only problem is that such offers come up only sporadically and aren't announced anywhere specific, so it's very easy to miss the boat. The best place to keep an eye out is in ethical living magazines (see p.320).

Stocks, shares & advisers
Retail funds and IFAs

There are more than fifty SRIFs – socially responsible investment funds – in the UK. They run the gamut of ethical investment strategies described at the start of this chapter and offer products ranging from unit trusts and OEICs to investment trusts and ISAs. All told, they have an estimated total value of more than £6 billion (up from just a few hundred million pounds at the beginning of the 1990s).

With so many options out there, and new players entering the market all the time, a list of funds here would be of little use. Instead we've provided links to resources where you can find information, and some tips on how to locate an independent financial adviser with experience in the ethical investment field.

EIRIS Guide to Ethical Funds

www.eiris.org ▷ 020 7840 5703

Published by the Ethical Investment Research and Information Service, *The Guide to Ethical Funds* contains summaries of each fund's policies and gives their top ten holdings. It's available to purchase directly from EIRIS.

Ethical Investors Group

www.ethicalinvestors.com ▷ 01242 539 848

The Ethical Funds Directory on the website of this IFA group provides information about the policies of many UK ethical funds. The site also covers general issues about ethical finance and provides some information on mortgages, pensions and other areas.

SocialFunds.com

www.socialfunds.com

This is a US site, so not all the information is relevant to UK readers. But it constitutes a massive resource – including news on global SRI developments – so is certainly worth a visit.

Trustnet

www.trustnet.com

This massive, free-to-access website is updated daily, and contains information about all kinds of investment funds – ethical and otherwise. It maintains two specific ethical lists (Unit Trust & OEICs and Conventional Investment Trusts), and provides full information about each fund's performance, size, charges, etc. The ethical lists can be quite hard to find, but you should be able to go straight to them via this address: www.trustnet.com/help/focus.asp?ethical

UK Social Investment Forum

www.uksif.org ▷ 020 7405 0040

Established in 1991, the UK Social Investment Forum is a "membership network" for promoting socially responsible investment. The Member Directory provides links to nearly all the main companies and organizations involved in ethical investment, and the homepage covers recent news and developments.

Independent financial advisers

An increasing number of financial advisers, or IFAs, are developing expertise in the ethical sector, so finding advice shouldn't be difficult. The best way to locate an ethical specialist near you is via the Ethical Investment Association, the UK Social Investment Forum or the Ethical Investment Research Service.

Ethical Investment Association www.ethicalinvestment.org.uk
UK Social Investment Forum www.uksif.org ▷ 020 7405 0040
Ethical Investment Research Service www.eiris.org ▷ 020 7840 5703

For more information about IFAs in general, contact IFAP, the UK association that promotes the profession. Their website lets you search for advisers in your area, and they can give some information about specialists in ethical matters:

IFAP www.ifap.org.uk ▷ 0117 971 1177

Transport & travel

Both at home and abroad, we travel further today than ever before. According to the Department for Transport, every year we manage on average 7000 miles each within Great Britain, most of them by car. And, as the price of air travel drops, we also leave the country with growing frequency: the British take foreign holidays around 250% more often than we did just twenty years ago. This chapter explains how we can minimize the harm done by all this travel and transport and also examines some of the other issues surrounding our foreign holidays.

Cars & fuel
What are you driving?

When it comes to cars, the single biggest ethical issue is climate change. Our motors account for around a fifth of the UK's greenhouse gases, with a typical vehicle producing its own weight in CO_2 for every 6000 miles driven. But cars raise other issues besides. For instance, their emissions include a cocktail of carcinogens and otherwise noxious fumes which, according to the government, are largely responsible for the airborne pollution that causes around 25,000 premature deaths and as many hospitalizations each year in the UK alone.

Road accidents, of course, are responsible for thousands more deaths and hundreds of thousands of injuries annually, as well as costing the economy tens of billions of pounds. More Brits have died on roads since 1945 than were killed in World War II – and many of the victims have been

Planes, trains & automobiles...

Comparing the impact on climate change of different forms of transport is not simple, as it's necessary to factor in, among other things, occupancy levels (a car with four people in it is almost four times less polluting, per passenger, than the same car with one person in it), speed (driving at 80mph can burn 30% more fuel than driving at 50mph) and the specific vehicle (a diesel train is far more polluting than an electric train). There's also the fact that planes, though not necessarily *much* worse than cars in terms of emissions per passenger mile, allow us to travel incomparably further. Despite all this confusion, the following diagram should give you a rough sense of how the various forms of transport compare. Climate aside, riding from London to Edinburgh with two people on a Vespa is not recommended...

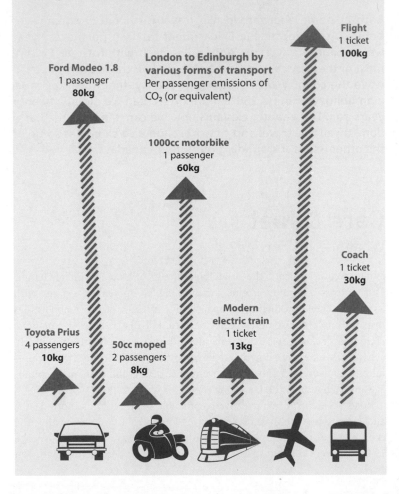

London to Edinburgh by various forms of transport
Per passenger emissions of CO_2 (or equivalent)

Flight
1 ticket
100kg

Ford Modeo 1.8
1 passenger
80kg

1000cc motorbike
1 passenger
60kg

Coach
1 ticket
30kg

Modern electric train
1 ticket
13kg

Toyota Prius
4 passengers
10kg

50cc moped
2 passengers
8kg

children, pedestrians, cyclists and other non-drivers. You can, alarmingly, watch the human and financial costs increasing in real time at:

Accident Count www.uk-roadsafety.co.uk/Rs_Documents/accident_count.htm

And that's not all. New roads eat ever further into the countryside and consume huge amounts of resources; buying petrol supports the activities of oil companies and oppressive governments; and many of the big car manufacturers have highly questionable records on everything from political donations to workers' rights.

Thankfully, there are many steps we can take to reduce the harm done by our cars – from making a few changes to the way we drive to choosing a more efficient, lower-emissions vehicle.

Lower-carbon driving

Even if your vehicle's a gas-guzzler, you could cut its fuel usage by as much as 30% by tweaking your driving practices. Here's how. Some of the following tips are already incorporated into the driving test.

▶ **Drive at the right speed** Most cars achieve maximum fuel efficiency when travelling at speeds of around 30–50mph. As speeds edge above 55mph, fuel consumption goes up as much as 15% for every additional 10mph. So simply driving on the motorway at 60mph rather than 80mph can cut emissions and fuel costs by almost a third.

▶ **Lighten the load** Keep heavy items out of the car unless you need them – you'll typically lose a percent or two in efficiency for every 50kg you haul. Also keep an eye on tyre pressure: rolling resistance goes up and efficiency goes down by as much as 1% for every PSI (pound per square inch) below the recommended pressure range. However, there's no benefit, and some risk, to driving with over-inflated tyres.

▶ **Avoid idling** Except when it's required (such as in stop-and-go traffic), idling is wasteful – and it doesn't benefit your car, except perhaps in extremely cold conditions. Even five minutes of idling can throw half a kilo of greenhouse gas into the air, and anything more than about ten seconds of idling generates more global-warming pollution than stopping and restarting.

▶ **Starting and stopping** Jack-rabbit starts and stops not only put wear and tear on your car, but they also drain fuel economy. Accelerate gradually, and anticipate stops by starting to brake well in advance. If you have a manual transmission, the best time to change gears is between 1500 and 2500 rpm.

▶ **Cut back on air-con** Running air conditioning typically cuts down a vehicle's efficiency by a few percent. That said, if it's a choice between driving with the windows down and running the A/C, there may be little difference in fuel usage, according to some studies. That's because wide-open windows can increase the car's aerodynamic drag, especially at high speeds. If outside temperatures are comfortable, try using the vents and fan but leaving the A/C off.

The rules are a bit different for **hybrid cars** (see p.292), which has led to some confusion. In 2005, *The New York Times* and *Consumer Reports* magazine declared that hybrids fall far short of their advertised miles per gallon. However, according to energy expert Amory Lovins of the Rocky Mountain Institute, this is because the tests employed by both publications didn't take into account the different driving style needed for hybrids,

Breakdown organizations

If you use a car but have misgivings about it – for example, you feel that public transport should be prioritized over the needs of drivers – then consider which company you use for roadside rescue. The **AA** (part of energy group Centrica) and the **RAC** (part of the RAC Group, which also includes Hyundai cars and a giant vehicle leasing firm) may not be the most disagreeable companies in the world, but they do have a long history of lobbying for road expansion and drivers' rights through groups like the British Road Federation.

The **ETA** (Environmental Transport Association) was set up specifically as an environmentally sound alternative to the big roadside rescue companies. It offers a similar service at a similar cost, boasting a 35-minute average callout time, an 80% success rate in fixing cars by the roadside, and very high customer satisfaction. While it's not anti-car as such, it "conducts and commissions research into environmental transport issues and lobbies the government to encourage its support of alternatives to the car". It even organizes Green Transport Week and Car Free Day, and also offers roadside rescue for cyclists.

Environmental Transport Association www.eta.co.uk ▷ 0800 212 810

which typically call on the electric motor at low speeds and the petrol engine at higher speeds. With a standard engine, you're best off accelerating lightly no matter what the speed. In a hybrid, you should accelerate briskly until you get to the optimal in-between speed, around 30–40mph, where the car is at its most efficient. A technique called "pulse and glide" driving – basically, hovering in that optimal speed range through small accelerations and decelerations – can further boost a hybrid car's efficiency. When it's time to slow down, brake slowly at first, then increase the pressure: this ensures that the maximum energy goes into recharging the battery versus creating unusable heat in the brakes themselves.

How to buy a greener vehicle

On the whole, cars are gradually getting greener. This applies both to their fuel efficiency (and therefore their contribution to climate change) and to their emissions of poisonous gases (such as carbon monoxide) and particulates (tiny solid particles that can lead to lung and heart disease, among other health problems). However, some cars are *far* greener than others, so if you're in the market for a new vehicle, it makes sense to seek out the lowest-emissions model that fits your needs and budget. Even if it means spending a bit more up front, you may save money in the long run thanks to lower fuel costs.

Unfortunately, the UK government's PowerShift scheme – which offered grants to help individuals buy an alternative car type or convert their current car to a greener fuel – has come to an end. But it's worth keeping your eyes open for other grants via the following website, which is also a useful source of information about greener vehicles.

Energy Saving Trust www.est.org.uk/fleet

"Standard" petrol and diesel cars

Unless you opt for an electric or electric-hybrid vehicle (discussed later on), the first question is diesel versus petrol. Both have their pros and cons. Standard diesel fuel is worse than petrol in terms of poisonous emissions and yet diesel engines are significantly more fuel-efficient and hence better in terms of global warming. In terms of alternative fuels, diesel engines leave you the option of using biodiesel (see p.296), while petrol engines are cheaper and easier to convert to LPG (see p.301). Overall, a diesel car is generally the greenest choice for people who live in the

Good cars, bad cars

Following are the greenest and least green cars (excluding electric models) available in the UK at the time of writing, as determined by the ETA. As the lists show, the most eco-friendly cars are light and have comparatively small engines. The most climate-frying and air-polluting cars tend be heavy, un-aerodynamic and/or super-powerful – either boy-racer vehicles or hulking 4WDs.

The ten best...
Honda Civic 1.4 IMA Executive
Toyota Prius 1.5 VVT-i Hybrid
Citroen C1 1.0i
Toyota Yaris 1.0 VVT-i
Daihatsu New Sirion M300 1.0L EFi
Suzuki Swift 1.3 GLZ 3 door DDiS
Vauxhall Corsa 1.3CDTi 16v SXI 5 door
Peugeot 107 1.0 (65bhp)
Toyota Aygo 1.0 VVT-i 3 & 5 door
Ford Fiesta 1.4 Duratorq TDCi

...and the ten worst
Lamborghini Diablo 132
Bentley Arnage RL
Aston Martin Lagonda V12 Vanquish S
Aston Martin Lagonda DB9
Bentley Continental Flying Spur
Rolls-Royce Phantom
Chrysler Jeep New Grand Cherokee 5.71
Porsche Cayenne S 6 Speed
Corvette C6 7.0 V8
Volkswagen Phaeton 6.0 4Motion

countryside, but city dwellers concerned about urban air quality might prefer to plump for petrol.

Whether you go for petrol or diesel, it's not hard to find information about the relative greenness of the various models. The ETA's online Car Buyer's Guide provides emissions and efficiency data – plus an overall environmental star rating – for most of the cars on the UK market. The VCA CarFuelData site is equally comprehensive.

ETA Car Buyer's Guide www.eta.co.uk
VCA CarFuelData www.vcacarfueldata.org.uk

Electric hybrid cars

Electric "hybrid" cars, such as the **Toyota Prius**, **Honda Insight** and **Lexus Hybrid Synergy Drive**, look and drive just like normal cars, yet their semi-electric engines are as much as twice as efficient as their straight petrol equivalents. Unlike "proper" electric cars (discussed overleaf), hybrids never need to be plugged in and charged up. Instead, the car charges its own battery when the brakes are applied (converting the car's kinetic energy into electrical energy) and also when the petrol-powered part of the engine is powering the car along at high speeds. The battery's energy is then automatically used when lower speeds are required. The result is that hybrid cars can achieve over 60 miles per gallon – and with exceptionally low levels of harmful emissions.

The main problem with hybrids is that they're currently quite expensive. If buying new, you can expect to pay around 10–20% more than you would for an equivalent non-hybrid model. And the fuel consumption won't necessarily be lower than that of a small, super-efficient, non-hybrid diesel such as the Toyota Yaris. That said, hybrids only cost £40 per year in road tax and are exempt from London congestion charging.

The Honda Insight's hybrid petrol–electric engine
makes it one of the greenest "normal" cars on the market

Which car companies are most ethical?

Fuel efficiency and emissions are the most obvious ethical considerations involved in buying a car, but you may also want to consider the ethical record of the company in question. This can be tricky, since many smaller car firms are partly or completely owned by bigger corporations such as **Ford** (Aston Martin, Jaguar, Land Rover, Mazda and Volvo), **General Motors** (Saab and Vauxhall), **DaimlerChrysler** (Jeep, Mercedes and Smart) and **Volkswagen** (Audi, Seat and Skoda). Added to this is the fact that any single car is likely to be the result of many different factories in as many different countries – seat covers from Indonesia, say, body panels from Italy and wheel nuts from Mexico.

Of the various manufacturers, the US giants Ford, GM and DaimlerChrysler (the first two of which are among the biggest five corporations in the world) have arguably the worst ethical records. For one thing, they're big political donors: all three ranked among George Bush's top benefactors in 2000. For another, they were all key members of the influential **Global Climate Coalition** (see p.298), which worked to stop the US government ratifying the Kyoto Protocol. The same companies have also lobbied – through groups such as the **Coalition for Vehicle Choice** – to block proposed laws imposing minimum fuel efficiency standards in the US. Their efforts have helped ensure that fuel efficiency in the US has actually *dropped* over the past quarter of a century, despite shooting up in Europe and Japan.

Though none are squeaky clean, the European and East Asian firms have typically courted less controversy. Two exceptions are **Suzuki** and **Daewoo**, both accused at the time of writing of being involved in projects with direct financial links to the Burmese military government. It is beyond the scope of this book to do a full comparison of every brand available in the UK, but the most recent in-depth report in *Ethical Consumer* magazine put **Peugeot**, **Citroen**, **Rover**, **MG** and the various **VW** companies at the top of their list (see p.320 for subscription and back-issue details for the magazine).

Electric cars

Recharged via a standard **mains socket**, electric cars are the greenest vehicles on four wheels. Like most battery-powered devices, they have literally no harmful emissions, and, if charged up with electricity from renewable sources, their use creates practically no carbon dioxide. Even if charged up with electricity generated from fossil fuels, they're much more eco-friendly than petrol cars, due to their high levels of energy efficiency.

Unfortunately, there are a few catches. Most electric cars don't go very fast and they need to be recharged after a certain number of miles (usually between 30 and 120, depending on the model). Moreover, you need a parking space near a plug socket.

At the time of writing, the only electric car widely available in the UK is the **G-Wiz**. Designed for two adults plus either two children *or* shopping, and capable of 40mph, the G-Wiz will do roughly 40 miles before requiring a recharge (which takes a few hours). At the time of writing, they cost around £7000, but by the manufacturer's calculations you could potentially save more than that every year in fuel (a G-Wiz achieves the equivalent of 600mpg), tax (eco-friendly cars are exempt) and, in central London, parking and the Congestion Charge (both free). You'll also save money on maintenance, since electric cars have very few moving parts. For more information, see:

G-Wiz www.goingreen.co.uk

Electric cars with more room, a longer range and a faster top speed do exist. These range from serious sports cars (see www.acpropulsion.com) to vans (such as the Renault Kangoo Electric, which can manage around 70mph). However, none of these are available in Britain at the time of writing. Hopefully this will change over the next few years.

A truly carbon-neutral vehicle? G-wiz!

For more information on electric cars, try:

Electric Vehicles UK www.evuk.co.uk

Motorbikes and mopeds

As the diagram on p.288 shows, motorbikes are relatively green when it comes to CO_2 emissions. Indeed, a modern moped can be almost twice as climate friendly as a train. Obviously, motorcycles with bigger engines release more CO_2, but only very powerful performance bikes emit as much as a typical family car.

If you live in a city, however, it's worth knowing that motorbikes have comparatively *bad* emissions of poisonous gases and particulates. A recent Swiss study found that even a 1997 Vespa scooter was far worse than a typical modern car in terms of poisonous emissions per kilometre travelled. More recent bikes tend to have slightly lower harmful emissions, but they're still worse than cars in this respect.

Even more climate-friendly than a typical moped is an **electric** model. Unlike electric cars, these are widely available, with decent models starting at around £1500. In terms of climate change (and cost), driving a decent e-scooter for thirty miles is equivalent to leaving a 100W light bulb on for just a few hours. Moreover, such vehicles produce zero poisonous emissions. Some models – such as the EVT168 (pictured) – even look flashy, too. The downside is that most current e-scooters can only manage about 30mph and need to be recharged every thirty miles or so. For more information, visit:

Scoot Electric www.scootelectric.co.uk

By 2007, the UK's first **fuel-cell** motorbike should also be available – the space-age-looking ENV by Intelligent Energy. These will retail for around £5000 but offer considerably greater range and power than an e-scooter. Find out more at:

ENV Bike www.envbike.com

Fuel-cell cars

Instead of being charged up, fuel-cell vehicles generate electrical energy on-board via a catalytic process – generally the combination of oxygen (from the air) with **hydrogen**. The hydrogen can be made on the fly from petrol or methanol, or, more commonly, generated elsewhere using electricity and then stored on board in replaceable canisters.

Like other electric cars, fuel-cell vehicles help reduce air-borne pollution in towns and cities (water vapour is often the only emission) and they're extremely efficient in terms of CO_2 per mile. Trials using taxis and buses have already successfully demonstrated that the fuel cell can work well, and commercial models – such as the **Necar**, designed by DaimlerChrysler, Ford and Ballard – may be available to consumers within the next few years.

It's questionable whether hydrogen vehicles will be the environmental panacea that their advocates describe. The main problem is that it takes a lot of energy (most of which currently comes from fossil fuels) to make the hydrogen in the first place. So it's unclear whether the creation of a hydrogen infrastructure – production plants, distribution channels and re-filling stations – would be a major benefit in terms of global warming without a concurrent growth in renewable energy.

Buying fuel: petrol, diesel & alternatives

Even if you don't upgrade to a greener vehicle, you may want to consider what you put in your existing one. That might mean using a more eco-logically friendly alternative to petrol (such as LPG) or diesel (such as biodiesel). Or it might simply mean favouring certain petrol brands over others (see p.298).

Biodiesel and vegetable oil

The term diesel, by definition, simply means a fuel for powering a diesel engine. Today it generally refers to a type of petroleum, but when Rudolph Diesel invented his super-efficient combustion engine at the end of the nineteenth century, he envisaged the fuel of the future coming from plants; he famously ran his prototypes on peanut oil. Today, with climate-change kicking in, so-called **biodiesel** – essentially vegetable oil treated with ethanol – is making a comeback, contributing power to everything from US bus fleets to Indian trains.

When burned, biodiesel churns out plenty of CO_2 but most of this will be soaked up from the atmosphere by the plants grown to produce the next batch of fuel – and so on. This elegant cycle isn't entirely carbon neutral, since energy (usually from fossil fuels) goes into preparing and distributing the stuff. Still, pure biodiesel reduces greenhouse emissions by around half compared with standard diesel, and it also cuts down on various exhaust-pipe poisons. It's not really a large-scale, long-term sub-stitute for oil, due to a lack of agricultural land: even if half of Britain's farms produced nothing but crops for biodiesel, they probably wouldn't be able to provide enough fuel to match the UK's current car use. That said, most of the biodiesel currently available in the UK is recycled from oil used in chip-shops, schools and food factories, so this doesn't require any new growing.

Biodiesel can be used in many recent diesel cars without any modification and, when purchased from a legitimate vendor, of which there are hundreds around the country, it's completely legal. In 2002 the government finally start encouraging its use with a 20p-per-litre tax cut, meaning it's now usually cheaper to buy than its mineral equivalent (though still far more expensive than in much of Europe, where it's completely tax-free). It's usually available either neat or in a mix with 95% normal diesel, which is obviously nowhere near as good from a carbon perspective but still reduces certain harmful emissions (and makes an engine run more efficiently).

Daniel Blackburn

Before filling up, check with the manufacturer of your car whether they approve the use of neat or mixed biodiesel, otherwise you could invalidate your engine warranty. And only buy fuel that conforms to government standards EN14214/EN590. For a list of filling stations that meet these criteria, try:

EST www.est.org.uk/fleet
▷ 0845 602 1425

Biodiesel is one thing, but what about all those stories in the press about people filling up with plain old vegetable oil in supermarket car parks – such as Welshman Daniel Blackburn, who made the headlines in 2003 by using veg oil to motor all the way from John O'Groats to Land's End? It's true that, after a conversion costing around £500–

Daniel Blackburn just couldn't get enough of that eco-friendly veg oil on his way from John O'Groats to Land's End

Oil companies

In a world threatened by climate change, there perhaps isn't any such thing as ethical petrol, but you may at least want to be selective about which brands you give your money to. As a whole, the oil industry has an extremely poor ethical record, but in the last decade there's been at least some divergence between the big companies in terms of their position on climate change and other social and political issues.

Back in the 1990s, BP (now part of BP Amoco), Shell (of Royal Dutch/Shell) and Exxon (Esso in the UK) were all key players in the **Global Climate Coalition**, a lobby group formed in 1989 as the prospect of global diplomatic action on climate change appeared on the horizon. Along with lobbying at UN meetings, the coalition became an oft-quoted presence in US news reports and financed anti-Kyoto commercials warning that "Americans would pay the price" for the treaty. The GCC began to fracture with the departure of BP in 1997 and Shell in 1998. By 2001, it was history, though arguably it had served its purpose and was no longer necessary. A 2001 memo written to Exxon by the US under-secretary of state, Paula Dobriansky, and later obtained by Greenpeace, states that George Bush rejected Kyoto "partly based on input from you [the GCC]".

Since the days of the GCC, some of the major oil companies have shifted towards public acknowledgement of climate change, but **Exxon** – the largest of them all – has continued to sow seeds of doubt. From 2000 to 2003, according to an exposé by Chris Mooney in *Mother Jones* magazine, the company poured more than $8 million into more than forty organizations aligned with climate-change scepticism. And these contributions seem to pay off. In the autumn of 2003 (within days of World Health Organization scientists suggesting that 160,000 people already die each year from climate change), leaked emails and documents showed that the Bush administration had sought the help of one Exxon-funded think tank – the **Competitive Enterprise Institute** – to try to undermine and dilute the predictions of its own government scientists.

Today, Exxon acknowledges the existence of human-induced climate change but claims that "significant work is still needed to better understand the risks and possible consequences". The company has pledged $100 million towards the Stanford-based Global Climate and Energy Project, whose research runs the gamut of renewables and low-carbon fuels. But this is less than 0.3% of its staggering 2005 profits ($35 billion) and hasn't been enough to persuade campaigners such as Greenpeace to call off their high-profile consumer boycott of the company. Find out more via:

Exxon/Esso www.esso.co.uk
StopEsso www.stopesso.com

Until recently, Esso seemed relatively unconcerned about being seen as a global villain, but some other big oil companies have spent millions trying to redefine themselves as trailblazers of corporate social responsibility. **BP** has very much led this trend – swapping its shield logo for a green and yellow flower and deciding that its initials now stand for "Beyond Petroleum". **Shell** has followed close behind with numerous CSR initiatives, keen to bury associations with Ken Saro-Wiwa and other anti-Shell campaigners who were executed in Nigeria in the mid-1990s.

Both companies still spend much of their time involved in highly controversial projects. Since "going green", for example, BP has been condemned by leading groups such as Amnesty International for trying to create a "human-rights-free corridor" as part of its **Baku–Tbilisi–Ceyhan** pipeline. It's also been slammed by the World Wildlife Fund in relation to drilling in **Alaska**, and even named as an offender in the UK in the government's *Spotlight on Business and Environment Performance*. Shell, meanwhile, stands accused of failing to deal with problems faced by people living near its facilities (for example, in Friends of the Earth's *Other Shell Report 2002*) and was embarrassed by a recent scandal in which executives lied to shareholders over the size of the company's oil reserves.

Clearly, then, there is still a gap between the rhetoric and reality of these companies. But despite the high-budget greenwashing, there are signs of improvement. Both companies have started to be more transparent in their payments to third-world governments (though BP is accused of secrecy in its Baku project). Alongside all the criticism, both have gained occasional and previously unimaginable praise from groups ranging from Human Rights Watch to Greenpeace. They have drawn up codes of conduct relating to human rights and the environment, which, even if they are not always put into practice, at the very least make them much easier targets when they misbehave. BP has also pledged to end donations to any "political activity or party" (it previously gave large sums to US presidential candidates), reduced its operational greenhouse-gas emissions to pre-1990 levels (something which many thought would be impossible), expanded its solar power business (still a tiny part of the company, but

a big boost to solar power's credibility nonetheless) and encourages drivers to offset their carbon emissions via its Target Neutral scheme (see www.targetneutral. com). For its part, Shell is investing in hydrogen-generation projects in Iceland, among other schemes.

With all this in mind, there *is* a case for favouring BP and to a lesser extent Shell while being aware that they're still far from perfect. After all, most of the alternatives – such as **Total** (on the "dirty list" at www. burmacampaign.org.uk) and **Q8** (owned by the oppressive government of Kuwait) – are just as bad, but not as good.

Rick Mills

1000, many diesel engines will run perfectly well on standard cooking oil. And the result may be even greener than biodiesel, since veg oil requires less energy-intensive processing. As long as you declare what you're doing and pay the relevant tax, it's perfectly legal, too.

At the time of writing, you can expect to pay around 70p per litre – including 25p in tax – for vegetable oil, making it cheaper than normal petrol and diesel. Still, be aware that many car manufacturers claim it can be bad for the engine. For more information about using cooking oil to stop the planet frying, including conversion quotes and a list of which cars are suitable, see Daniel Blackburn's site:

Veg Oil Motoring www.vegoilmotoring.com

Cutting back on cars

Efficient vehicles and low-carbon fuels are all well and good, but perhaps the best way to reduce the environmental impact of our driving is simply to drive less. If you want to get shot of your car but don't want to rely solely on public transport, consider looking into car sharing and car clubs. This is not only environmentally sound, but may also make sense financially (it is said that if you factor in the time it takes to earn the money to buy, run, insure, tax and maintain your own vehicle, the typical driver achieves an average speed roughly equivalent to walking).

Either for a regular commute or a one-off drive, **car sharing** is based on the simple rationale that one car carrying, say, three people is three times less polluting, congesting and expensive than three cars carrying one person each. Although the UK has been much slower to grasp this fact than much of continental Europe, the car-sharing movement is taking off. The Internet has also helped, providing the ideal way for people to find and organize sharing. Whether you're looking for passengers or a ride, visit:

Freewheelers www.freewheelers.co.uk
Liftshare www.liftshare.com
National Car Share www.nationalcarshare.co.uk

Car clubs or **car pools** are something else entirely. You don't actually own a car but have access to a communal one situated within a few minutes' walk of your house. Beside a possible joining fee and/or small monthly charge, you only pay for the hours or mileage you use. City Car Club, for example, which operates in London and various other cities, costs around £4 per hour. See:

City Car Club www.citycarclub.co.uk ▷ 01484 483 061

To find your nearest car clubs, see:

Car Plus www.carclubs.org.uk ▷ 0113 234 9299

LPG

LPG (**Liquid Petroleum Gas**) is basically **propane**, as used in camping stoves and standalone gas heaters. A byproduct of oil refining and natural gas extraction, it's a fossil fuel but it has lower greenhouse-gas emissions than petrol and also results in fewer poisonous fumes. Most petrol-powered cars can be converted to run either solely on LPG or on both LPG and petrol, the result being a car that emits about the same amount of CO_2 per mile as an equivalent diesel car.

Conversion to LPG usually costs a few thousand pounds, but once it's done you can get cheap fuel and, in London, exemption from the congestion charge.

Air travel
Exactly how bad is it?

An ethical flight is something of a castle in the air. Combine their high greenhouse-gas emissions – per passenger, per mile – with the fact that they allow us to travel such vast distances and you have a recipe for environmental disaster.

Despite the relatively tiny number of people who regularly fly, aviation accounts for 3–4% of the total human impact on the climate, according to the Intergovernmental Panel on Climate Change. That's around the same as the whole of Africa. And that figure is on the up thanks to the ever-growing number of flights. The number of air passengers flying into and out of the UK is expected to nearly treble by 2030 – to around 500 million. This rapid growth threatens to offset the cuts in greenhouse emissions being made in other sectors.

The reason air travel is so bad for the climate is not just that aeroplanes release a great deal of greenhouse gases into the atmosphere – it's the fact that they do so in the upper troposphere and lower stratosphere, where their effect is compounded. The contrails (vapour trails) that planes create are another factor. The science surrounding this topic is not yet rock solid, but researchers believe that contrails add to the greenhouse effect – especially at night, when their tendency to stop heat escaping from the Earth isn't offset by their tendency to reflect incoming sunlight.

All told, the impact of a flight is thought to be around three times greater than the CO_2 emissions would suggest. So two seats on a return trip from London to San Francisco produces the equivalent impact of at least five tonnes of CO_2 – almost as much as the average UK household's yearly output, or 20,000 miles in an averagely efficient car.

Fuel-cell and other less harmful planes may eventually emerge. But they won't replace current fleets any time soon, since passenger planes stay in use for decades. In the meantime, the only way governments could reduce air travel's impact is by cutting down on passenger numbers by making the price of a ticket reflect the environmental costs – for example by making airlines pay tax on their **aviation fuel**, which is currently duty-free. (If the fuel was taxed at the same rate as petrol, a long-haul flight would cost each passenger around £500 more.) But governments are loath to take

Boeing and bombing

As if the environmental impact of flying wasn't enough, there is the added concern that most passenger aircraft are produced by arms manufacturers. A growing number of consumers are opting for ethical banks, very often specifically because they want to be sure that their savings aren't invested in arms companies. But, for anyone who travels by air, it's not so easy to completely separate your wallet from the budget sheets of "defence" firms. Next time you fly, have a look to see who produced your airborne home for the next few hours. With very few exceptions, it will be either **Boeing** or **Airbus**.

Boeing is one of the world's largest arms companies, whose annual turnover of around $50 billion is in no small part generated from selling military equipment to all kinds of governments, including those with very poor human rights records. According to an investigative report in *Mother Jones* magazine (www.motherjones. com), recent Boeing sales include warplanes to Indonesia, Israel, Kuwait and Saudi Arabia; attack helicopters to Egypt; and missiles to Turkey.

Boeing is even "unethical" according to the low moral codes of the arms industry: in late 2003 its chairman, Phil Condit, resigned after, as the Associated Press put it, "months of ethical controversies over the aggressive methods it used to obtain lucrative defense contracts". It's also a major political donor in the US. According to figures from Open Secrets (www.opensecrets.org), it guaranteed itself a sympathetic president in 2000 by giving nearly a million dollars to both the main parties.

Airbus, meanwhile, is owned by British Aerospace and other major European arms manufacturers. All in all, the tie between commercial aircraft and military equipment is so entrenched that – as Noam Chomsky has written – many passenger planes are actually modified bombers. There's not much that consumers can do about this link, but if you feel particularly strongly about the arms industry it may tip the balance and make you decide to choose another form of transport whenever possible.

It's not just how far they fly – it's how high they fly and the vapour trails they create. A plane's overall effect on climate change is around three times worse than its CO_2 output would suggest.
Photo: Corbis

such steps, not least because aviation, being by its nature international, isn't included in the national targets for emissions cuts specified in the Kyoto Protocol. This is significant: officially, the UK's greenhouse emissions fell by 4% between 1990 and 2004. But factor in shipping and aviation and the net result is a *rise* of 1%.

What individuals can do

For anyone concerned about global warming, cutting back on air travel is an obvious goal. This might mean giving up flying altogether, or it might mean taking fewer flights and making up for it by staying longer each time. It might also mean favouring destinations that are closer to home. Short flights tend to be around 25% worse, per passenger per mile, than long-haul flights (because they have more empty seats and because taking off and landing burns more fuel than cruising) but overall it's still far worse to travel longer distances.

Another approach is to consider alternative ways of travelling. With more than two people on the same itinerary, it can even be more climate-friendly to drive than to fly – especially for short distances such as trips from the UK to northern Europe. Better still are **trains and boats**, which are typically responsible for many times fewer emissions per person per mile than either cars or planes. To find out how to travel from London to almost anywhere in the world by rail and sea, visit:

The Man in Seat 61 www.seat61.com

If you do choose to fly, consider offsetting the emissions (see p.13) and try to favour daytime flights due to the issue of contrails already discussed. You may also want to think about which airline you choose. They all lobby for fewer rather than more restrictions on air travel, but some of the big US firms – including **American Airlines** and **United Airlines** (UAL Corp) – are more active political donors, according to data from www.opensecrets.org. And **Japan** and **Austrian Airlines** are on boycott lists at the time of writing for continuing to operate in Burma.

Finally, you might want to consider buying flights via **North South Travel** (see p.313), who donate their profits to charitable projects in Africa, Asia and Latin America.

FlightPledge

FlightPledge Union is a website at which you can register your intent not to fly for environmental reasons. The objective is "to sign up as many people as possible, firstly to reduce the number of aircraft movements, and secondly to show the government that there is a large number of people who are willing to voluntarily limit their flying and make an individual gesture to reduce their personal impact on the environment". You can either choose the gold pledge (no non-emergency flight in the next year) or the silver pledge (no more than two short-haul or one long-haul).

Flight Pledge www.flightpledge.org.uk

Holidays
Responsible tourism

The most obvious – and arguably most important – ethical consideration involved in choosing a holiday is the greenhouse emissions of the plane, car or train that will transport you to your destination. As we've seen, even a short-haul flight has a large carbon footprint. However, our holidays raise other issues besides climate change, such as the social and environmental effects they have on the countries we visit, and the ethical credentials of the travel companies we support. These concerns are the focus of this chapter.

Regularly described as the **world's biggest employer**, even the world's biggest industry, the tourism sector provides more than 200 million jobs and accounts for more than 10% of global GDP. Despite a brief downturn after the September 11 terrorist attacks in 2001, the industry just keeps on growing. According to the World Travel and Tourism Council, the number of international trips made each year now exceeds 700 million; by 2010 that's expected to be a billion; by 2020 a billion and a half. The range of popular destinations also continues to broaden, with journeys to **developing countries** – from Bhutan to Botswana – accounting for an increasing chunk of the total. However, while the growth of the travel industry and its economic importance are not in dispute, its overall costs and benefits are hotly contested.

Tourism has the potential to be good for all parties. Tourists get to enjoy themselves and/or increase their knowledge of the world and its people. And the residents of host countries get jobs and money. This can be especially important in developing countries, where tourists are often the main source of foreign currency – or even, in cases such as the Maldives, the majority of national income.

The very poorest countries sometimes stand to benefit the most. A 2001 report from the United Nations Conference on Trade and Development pointed out that "International tourism is one of the few economic sectors through which LDCs [Least Developed Countries] have managed to increase their participation in the global economy. It can be an engine of employment creation, poverty eradication, ensuring gender equality, and protection of the natural and cultural heritage."

Few, however, would claim this ideal exchange of benefits is an accurate characterization of most modern tourism. Indeed, it's pretty clear that holiday-makers of all kinds can unwittingly cause social and environmental damage (even excluding the impact of actually getting to the destination). Most obviously, while tourism may have the potential to facilitate mutual understanding, in many cases the visitors are unwelcome, imposing or simply in the way – unaware of local customs and manners, unable to speak the language and taking up in-demand places on public transport. In poor countries, furthermore, tourists can create resentment by flaunting a degree of leisure time and wealth completely out of reach for most of their hosts.

But more serious still are the issues discussed below: the control of land and resources, environmental damage and the possibility that tourists may be propping up oppressive governments. To make things more complicated, all these problems tend to be more acute in precisely those poor regions which have the most to benefit from tourist money.

Land and water

From Peru to the Philippines, there have been many cases of marginalized people being forced – legally, physically or practically – off their **land** to make way for tourist development. Sometimes this has happened to make way for modern beach complexes and other resort-style developments. Tourism Concern, which campaigns for a more ethical travel sector, has reported many such incidents including, a few years ago, that of "a British-controlled company, which was planning a £2.8 billion tourist enclave on the Nungwi peninsula of Zanzibar". Apparently, "the development was to be the biggest in East Africa, with luxury hotels, golf courses and an airport. Shockingly, the plan failed to mention the peninsula's 20,000 residents. Local people hadn't had a say…"

This kind of flagrant disregard for the rights of local people has arguably been an even bigger problem in areas popular for **nature travel**, since areas set aside for conservation and wildlife purposes have often been linked to the displacement of indigenous groups. The famous conservationist Bernhard Grzimek once commented that for a national park to be effective "no men, not even native ones, should live inside its borders", and such views have been responsible for the eviction or even murder of indigenous groups in parks ranging from the California's Yosemite and Tanzania's Serengeti to, more recently, Botswana's Kalahari and Tanzania's Mkomazi. Critics of nature travel claim that common tourist expectations – that locals should live a visually exciting "tribal" existence or not be there at all – are a major factor in initiating or maintaining such human clearances.

Just as serious is the appropriation of resources such as water, which is scarce in many of the hot destinations beloved by Western tourists. A single inefficient hotel – especially one with a swimming pool – can require more water than a whole town. And golf courses can require up to a million litres a day in some climates (as well as more agrochemicals than even the most intensive farmland). Yet they're now relatively common resort features in even the driest countries.

In poor countries, it's possible that the water demands of rich travellers can speed up the development of reliable water infrastructures that will benefit residents. But it's also possible that hotels can buy a monopoly over, or unsustainable access to, the water, emptying groundwater aquifers and causing serious long-term damage. This can also be an issue in relatively wealthy countries. As *Ergo* magazine recently reported, Mallorca's water table has plunged ninety metres in just twenty years.

Environmental damage

Travel can provide the perfect incentive for countries to look after their environments. If tourists are coming to see beautiful landscapes of wildlife, these very "features" become valuable assets worth protecting. And in countries where few other employment opportunities exist, the travel sector can create jobs that offer an alternative to ecologically damaging work such as small-scale mining or tree-felling.

In many cases, however, short-term financial gain wins over long-term ecological protection. From coastal Spain to Goa, whole areas have had their biodiversity decimated by large-scale tourist development. Cruise ships dump sewage straight into the ocean (see www.stopcruisepollution. com). And in countries that lack decent waste disposal, tourist waste – from sun-lotion bottles and food wrappers to toilet paper – may end up in rivers that both people and wildlife depend on.

Even where tourism does encourage conservation – such as in game reserves – it needs to be carefully managed. If not, the tourists and their guides may cause harm to the very animals they have come to see. As Philip Seddon of New Zealand's University of Otago in Dunedin recently told *New Scientist*: "Transmission of disease to wildlife, or subtle changes to wildlife health through disturbance of daily routines or increased stress levels, while not apparent to a casual observer, may translate to lowered survival and breeding."

Who gets the money?

It goes without saying that the real or potential problems described above have to be balanced against the enjoyment of the tourists and the economic benefits gained by the people in the visited countries – both of which can be enormous. However, in many cases, the cash tourists spend exits the country as soon as it leaves their pockets, heading straight into the bank accounts of foreign travel firms.

With package holidays, this economic "leakage" is often as high as four-fifths of the total money spent during a holiday, or even more for pay-up-front **all-inclusive deals**, where tourists get to consume as much as they like as long as they stay in the hotel complex (and hence give their custom to no one else). In these cases, the main economic beneficiaries are not the residents but a surprisingly small number of multinational companies. As with every other area of business, tourism has undergone massive consolidation in the last decade, with big firms snapping each other up across Europe. In the UK, just a handful of companies now account for nearly all package holidays. These include German giants such as **World of TUI** – whose fleet of businesses include Thomson Holidays, Lunn Poly, Travel House and Britannia Airways – and **Thomas Cook AG**, which owns, among other things, JMC, Thomas Cook Holidays and Club 18–30. Other big players are First Choice and My Travel Group.

The money spent by **independent travellers** is less likely to disappear overseas. In India, for example, where non-package travel is the most

The mixed blessings of ecotourism

The most widely known area of travel to claim to have a socially responsible angle is **ecotourism**, which in the last decade or so has grown from a niche market into a major sector, embraced both by tourism industry bodies and by the UN, who named 2002 the International Year of Ecotourism, complete with a World Ecotourism Summit in Quebec. But what exactly *is* ecotourism?

According to the International Ecotourism Society (www.ecotourism.org), the term refers to "responsible travel to natural areas that conserves the environment and sustains the well-being of local people". Or, as the World Conservation Union put it, ecotourism describes "environmentally responsible travel ... to relatively undisturbed natural areas ... that promotes conservation, has low negative visitor impact [and] provides for beneficially active socioeconomic involvement of local populations."

Advocates of ecotourism claim that the sector has contributed a great deal both to conservation and to the economic empowerment of people in remote regions. However, the term has been tarnished by criticism from a range of commentators.

One issue is that ecotourism has no legally binding definition, which means there's nothing to stop an unscrupulous travel agent from slapping the label on any nature-focused holiday, regardless of the damage it may cause. As EcoTravel.com puts it: "An 'eco-lodge' may dump untreated sewage in a river, and still call itself 'eco' simply because it is located in a natural setting."

Another issue is that, in all tourism sectors, what starts as a trickle of travellers can often end up as a flood. So there's a risk that adventurous ecotourists could open

popular type, around half of total tourist spending is thought to stay in the country. Independent travellers can also choose to favour small businesses, from where money is more likely to trickle down through the local economy – and which also tend to pose smaller environmental burdens. However, there's no escaping the fact that the independent traveller is very often the harbinger of the foreign-owned resort. As tourism academic Brian Wheeller has written, "In the rush to escape the mass tourist [the] individual traveller is forever seeking the new, the exotic, the unspoilt – the vulnerable. Inevitably, however, they are inexorably paving the way … the sensitive traveller is the perpetrator of the global spread, the vanguard of the package tour".

Perhaps more of a concern than money *not* benefiting the country in which we spend it is the possibility that it may stay in the country and line the pockets of an oppressive or corrupt government. The most obvious and extreme example of this is Burma, where the military regime has been partly funded by tourism (see box overleaf). But there are many less clear-

up the world's most fragile environments to unsustainable tourism. According to a recent report by Conservation International and the environmental wing of the UN, in the 1990s alone, leisure travel to the world's "biodiversity hotspots" (those areas with richly diverse but delicate ecologies) more than doubled, with rises of more than 300% in Brazil, Nicaragua and El Salvador, 500% in South Africa and 2000% in Laos and Cambodia.

Some NGOs, such as Malaysia's Third World Network and Thailand's Tourism Information Monitoring, have gone so far as to say that ecotourism's viability is "another myth that needs to be exploded", and that it "will destroy more biodiversity and harm even more local communities". Such blanket criticism is somewhat unfair, since there are many examples of well-managed ecologically focused tourist developments that have served to protect the environment and benefited local people. But what's clear is that the term "ecotourism" does not in itself guarantee any particular ethical standards. The tips for finding an ethical travel operator detailed on p.146 apply to this sector of tourism just like every other.

Even with a perfect holiday company, however, there's ultimately a glaring contradiction inherent in flying halfway around the world to look at sensitive environments. For instance, a report by the University of Queensland Centre for Marine Studies suggests that Australia's Great Barrier Reef will lose 95% of its living coral by 2050. The cause is global warming, driven by carbon-intensive activities such as, say, flying from London to Sydney.

The Burma travel boycott

The Asian state of Myanmar, still more widely known as Burma, has been living under a brutal military regime since the early 1960s. This junta has murdered and tortured tens of thousands of innocent people, imposed slave labour on countless children and adults, spent vast sums on arms while the population live in poverty, and imprisoned political opponents such as Nobel laureate Aung San Suu Kyi, who won free elections in 1990 by a landslide, but was never allowed to take office. Despite all this, Burma – which, like neighbouring Thailand, is a place of remarkable ancient history and natural beauty – still has an active tourism industry. The human rights abuses are mostly hidden from travellers since the government has a direct financial interest in maintaining the flow of visitors: it owns most of the tourism infrastructure and obliges each person who enters to buy more than £100 of local currency, providing valuable foreign reserves.

Unsurprisingly, Aung San Suu Kyi and others have called on foreigners to stop visiting the country, and the British government has appealed to UK travel companies to remove Burma from their list of destinations. Some have refused and, accordingly, groups such as the Burma Campaign UK are encouraging us to boycott not just Burma itself but also these companies, along with all the others still on their "Dirty List". At the time of writing, travel-related firms listed include Japan Airlines and Austrian Airlines; tour operators such as Andrew Brock Travel, EastTravel, Explorers Tours, Mekong Travel and Visit Vietnam; and publishers Lonely Planet, Insight Guides, Frommer's and Let's Go (Pan Macmillan).

Some of these firms seem simply uninterested in the ethical implications of working in Burma, ignoring the political situation in their literature or even using it as a kind of selling point: "decades of social and economic isolation have preserved many traditional features which have been lost in other Asian countries" boasts the EastTravel website. Others acknowledge the issues but claim that tourism may help rather than worsen the problem. Lonely Planet, for example, haven't stopped publishing their Burma guide since it would mean "betraying the very principle upon which our company is based: namely that travel CAN make a difference". Burma campaigners describe this view as naive, anti-democratic and irresponsible.

For more information, see:

Burma Campaign UK www.burmacampaign.org.uk

cut cases. Should we avoid travel to China on the grounds of its government's appalling human rights record and its occupation of Tibet (where, incidentally, it is endeavouring to replace Tibetan tourist guides with Chinese ones, in order to keep visitors from getting too many answers about the regime)? What about Russia for its activities in Chechnya, or Indonesia for its actions in Papua?

Browse recent news reports by country at Amnesty International (available online at www.amnesty.org/library) and you might wonder exactly

A Kikuyu dressed as a Masai selling trinkets to tourists on the east coast of Kenya – preservation of local culture, economic opportunity or patronizing "human zoo"?
Photo: Adrian Arbib

how many countries you can visit with a clear conscience. Human rights abuses abound in many favourite destinations, from Cuba ("hasty and unfair trials" of dissident leaders) to the Maldives ("systematic repression of peaceful political activists").

Whether visiting countries with oppressive governments will exacerbate or lessen human rights abuses is debatable. If a government is keen to promote tourism, it may be less likely to commit day-to-day abuses with foreigners around, or it may be sensitive to complaints from tourists who have witnessed any mistreatment. Foreign visitors may also provide income for people who would otherwise be at the financial mercy of the state, and they may also raise awareness of issues back at home. According to George Monbiot, travelling can even be a disincentive to war: "the people of powerful nations might be reluctant to permit their leaders to destroy the countries they have visited".

As with choosing whether to buy or boycott products from specific foreign countries – discussed on p.40 – there are no easy thumbs-up or thumbs-down lists of where and how it's "ethical" to travel. You have to do your own research and make your own rules. You might, for example, decide to avoid big travel companies when travelling in countries whose governments you consider to be problematic, since the bigger firms are more likely to have links to those in power. Or you might decide only to travel to countries with participatory democracies since, with any other system, the people you're imposing yourself upon might not have had the opportunity to vote for or against tourism development.

"Ethical tourism"

The issues raised above – and the global-warming impact of our flights – shouldn't necessarily make us stay at home. After all, a recent report from the International Labour Organization states that, in the post-9/11 tourism downturn, around 6.5 million jobs are likely to have been lost, mostly in poor countries. But such issues should feature in our decisions of where to go, what we do when we get there and, in the case of non-independent travel, what kind of tourism companies we support.

Certain volunteering projects aside, there's no point in deluding ourselves that we're saving the world by going on holiday; but if tourists and travel companies act with an eye on social justice and environmental sustainability, there's no reason why the destination countries can't reap more of the benefits and bear fewer of the costs. This is the rationale behind the ethical initiatives which are increasingly cropping up in the travel industry. You can now even do an MSc in "Responsible Tourism Management" (find out more at this magnificently long domain name: www.theinternationalcentreforresponsibletourism.org).

Self-declared ethical travel took off primarily with **ecotourism** – a loose term for nature travel with a responsible edge (see p.308). But all areas of the travel sector are increasingly being asked to consider their social and environmental impact. This has been in part due to pressure from groups such as Tourism Concern (www.tourismconcern.org.uk), though a number of surveys suggest that it also reflects the fact that the travelling public are concerned, though certainly not preoccupied, with the problems.

Research by anti-poverty group Tearfund, for example, found that more than half of holidaymakers would prefer to book a holiday with a company that had a written code covering working conditions, the environment and the support of local charities. But only when people start asking these kinds of questions in travel agents will pressure for a truly ethical tourism industry be felt.

Finding an ethical holiday

As in any sector, a travel company genuinely committed to acting ethically is very likely to tell you about it. If the promotional literature or website doesn't touch on things discussed above, you can be pretty sure they haven't been considered at a very high level. However, that doesn't mean that every company claiming ethical credentials is for real, so read their claims carefully and ask questions.

Here are a few pointers of where you can go to find ethically minded travel companies, and some of the various award schemes and initiatives that you may come across when shopping around for a trip.

Flights and travel companies

North South Travel

www.northsouthtravel.co.uk ▷ 01245 608 291

Like many other agents, North South Travel offers discount airfares to destinations around the world. Uniquely, however, when you buy a flight from this company the profits are ploughed into a charity – the NST Development Trust – which contributes to "grassroots projects" in developing countries. These range from poverty relief and healthcare projects to recycling and shipping bicycles to poor countries. North South has been running since 1981.

ResponsibleTravel.com

www.responsibletravel.com

Backed by the Body Shop's Anita Roddick, ResponsibleTravel.com sells trips and tours from 270 separate travel firms, covering everything from European skiing and tropical beach holidays to Asian jungle treks. But, unlike other travel agents, it selects its partner firms not just in terms of their service but also by their ethical credentials. In order to have its holidays sold on the site, a travel operator needs to fulfil a series of criteria relating to codes of conduct, use of local suppliers, the provision of advice on the social and political situations in each destination, and advice to staff and customers on reducing the negative impacts they make. This scrutiny can't be exhaustive, of course, but ResponsibleTravel.com turn away five companies for each one admitted.

AITO

www.aito.co.uk ▷ 0870 751 8080

AITO – the Association of Independent Tour Operators – is the industry body for small, specialist travel companies. It has been an advocate of more ethical tourism for at least a decade and a half, and all members are required to sign up to its Responsible Tourism Guidelines. Recently it has also implemented its own Responsible Tourism Awards and developed a scheme in which members can qualify for two stars by carrying out an environmental review and establishing a comprehensive responsible tourism policy, and then three stars by "engaging in specific RT initiatives or projects". You can browse the members, or go straight to those with two and three stars, on their website; alternatively, call the number above for a brochure.

EcoTravel.com

www.ecotravel.com

This searchable directory lists "tour operators, lodges, private guides, non-profit organizations and ancillary travel services" with a progressive outlook. There's no "screening" as such, but each listing includes the company's response to an "EcoResponsibility Survey", which asks them to detail their policies and philosophy, and the way in which their practices preserve the environment and benefit the local community.

Fair Trade in Tourism South Africa

www.fairtourismsa.org.za ▷ 00 27 12 342 8307/8

The concept of "fair trade" tourism is a relatively new one, and there are no global standards to define exactly what it means. Still, this groundbreaking South African initiative could be the start of something bigger. The idea is to ensure that "the people whose land, natural resources, labour, knowledge and culture are used for tourism activities, actually benefit from tourism". This is done by certifying travel establishments that fulfil criteria relating to six areas: democracy, respect, reliability, transparency,

sustainability, and, most importantly, "fair share", which means that "all participants involved in a tourism activity should get their fair share of the income, in direct proportion to their contribution to the activity". The Sabi Sabi Game Reserve and the Stormsriver Adventures Co. are among the seven establishments certified at the time of writing. You'll find links to each at the above website.

Responsible tourism awards

BA Tourism for Tomorrow

www.ba.com ▷ 0870 850 9850

British Airways have been running the Tourism for Tomorrow Awards, to "recognise and encourage sustainable tourism initiatives across the globe", since 1992. BA admit that they can't run a complete "health check" on the entrants – which include tour and hotel companies of any type and size – so the awards recognise "better" rather than "best" practice. Still, they've been welcomed by the likes of Tourism Concern. You can find information about past winners on the BA website.

World Legacy Awards

www.wlaward.org

This award scheme – which so far has only been run in 2002 and 2004 – is overseen by *National Geographic Traveler* magazine and Conservation International, with the aim of promoting "environmentally, culturally, and socially responsible tourism practices across a wider spectrum of the tourism industry". You can find details of, and links to, winners and finalists on their website. The 2004 top prizes went to AL Maha Desert Resort in Dubai, the Gunung Rinjani region of Indonesia, Anangu Tours in Australia, and the Casuarina Beach Club in Barbados.

Green travel labels

EU Eco-label

www.eco-label-tourism.com

You may recognize the European Union's little flower logo from energy-efficient washing machines and the like (see p.83). Recently the scheme has been extended to take in tourism accommodation. Anyone "from a large hotel chain to a small farmhouse" can apply, and the flower is awarded to those who meet criteria such as the use of renewable energy sources and measures to reduce waste as well as less obvious things such as offering organic food and using low-emissions paints and cleaning chemicals. Since the scheme is very young, you're unlikely to come across many accredited hotels for at least a year or two.

The Green Globe 21

www.greenglobe21.com ▷ 020 7838 9400

The Green Globe 21 environmental certification standard (the number refers to the Agenda 21 Sustainable Development Principles from the 1992 Rio Earth Summit) was established by the World Travel and Tourism Council, a coalition largely made up of CEOs from major hotel chains, large travel companies and airlines. As such, while it's undoubtedly raising the profile of the environmental and social impact of tourism, it's sometimes been accused of having more to do with advertising and greenwash than achieving real results. But it's certainly worth knowing about their three-tier membership policy – an "ABC Pathway" referring to Affiliation, Benchmarking and finally Certification. Only level "C" companies that have been externally audited can use the logo with a tick on it; "A" and "B" companies, who have had no external assessment, can use the logo, just without the tick.

Confused?

The mixture of issues, schemes, logos, claims and groups described above can make the world of ethical travel seem pretty impenetrable. For this reason, and to encourage global good standards, some groups have called for the establishment of a Sustainable Tourism Stewardship Council – much like the Forest Stewardship Council for wood or the Marine Stewardship Council for fish. An extensive 2003 report by the Rainforest Alliance concluded that this was a realistic goal, and although the scheme is still in its conceptual stages, it may emerge in the next few years. For more information see:

Sustainable Tourism Stewardship Council www.stscouncil.org

Find out more

Throughout the text of this book, we've included Web addresses and phone numbers that will help you find out more about specific issues and products, from political donations to fairly traded rugs. But there are also scores of publications – online and on paper – that will lead you to information that's either more general (such as news and views about ethical consumerism) or more specific (such as in-depth profiles of the behaviour of individual companies). What follows is a short selection of the best sites, magazines and books in both these categories.

Researching companies online

If you want to find out about the ethical standards of a particular company, there are a number of excellent websites to turn to. Following is a list of the best.

Business & Human Rights Resource Centre

www.business-humanrights.org

An amazing resource, this website – run "in partnership with Amnesty International Business Groups and leading academic establishments" – is an index of practically everything on the Web that relates to the effect of companies upon human rights (including environmental damage). Updated hourly, it points to articles and stories published by newspapers, companies, NGOs and academics alike, and the clear, easy-to-navigate structure makes it simple to view all the links that relate to any one of 1600 individual companies (or to specific industries or issues). All in all, a fantastic free service.

Corporate Critic

www.corporatecritic.org

Corporate Critic is the company ethics database maintained by ECRA, the research association behind *Ethical Consumer* magazine. It contains data on more than 50,000 companies. The in-depth analysis is designed for professional researchers, with a price tag of £120–150 per month for access. But you can do a free search on any listed company and view its overall ethical ranking out of twenty.

Ethiscore

www.ethiscore.org

This online ethical shopping guide is a consumer-focused version of Corporate Critic (see above). It's £15 per year to access and offers easy-to-use lists comparing the various brands in each product area. Each brand receives an overall "Ethiscore" of 1–20, with some background on how that number is arrived at.

Gooshing

www.gooshing.co.uk

Put together by the folks who produce the *Good Shopping Guide* (see p.321), Gooshing aims to make online ethical shopping simple by letting you search for a product, compare the ethics of the various brands and click through to buy from third-party websites. In some categories nearly all the products listed seem to get three or four stars, making it difficult to base decisions on the results, but there are handy lists of ethical suppliers of fish, meat, etc.

IdealsWork

www.idealswork.com

"What companies do. What to do about it" is the strapline of this American site that rates companies up to five stars on everything from labour issues and nuclear energy to women's issues and addictive products. Simply choose a product category and your ethical criteria, and a set of comparative ratings will appear, including the option to send the companies a message (and, for US browsers, to buy products online).

ResponsibleShopper

www.responsibleshopper.com

Run by Co-op America, this site includes hundreds of companies along with a list of their brands and advice on what they've been "praised for" and "criticised for", along with links to the original sources. It's not comprehensive, and it has a US-focus, but it's still very useful.

Going deeper

For a more comprehensive guide to examining the dark underbelly of corporate behaviour, visit the **CorporateWatch** website and, within the Resources section, you'll find a few pages titled "DIY Guide: How to Research Companies". This gives tips on everything from finding out about corporate structure to digging the dirt on a firm's financial analysts and shareholders. The same site also provides profiles on a range of big companies. These tend towards the harshly, and occasionally fanatically, anti-corporate, but they're well researched and well written.

CorporateWatch www.corporatewatch.org.uk

For more tips and reports from across the Atlantic, see **CorpWatch** and **PR Watch**:

CorpWatch www.corpwatch.org
PR Watch www.prwatch.org

Magazines

There are many magazines that are relevant to the issues discussed in this book – from the *Economist* to the *Ecologist*. But with the departure of *Ergo*, there are only two titles focusing specifically on ethical living:

Ethical Consumer

www.ethicalconsumer.org ▷ 0161 226 2929 ▷ Published every two months ▷ £3.75 per issue or £21 annual subscription

Ethical Consumer describes itself as "the UK's leading alternative consumer magazine". Each issue features a number of in-depth "buyers' guides", focusing on specific product areas – anything from TVs to fruit juices. The various brands are compared on a *Which*-style table, with columns for oppressive regimes, factory farming, political donations, etc. There are also features and regulars such as Boycott Updates and Money News (which keeps tabs on ethical investment funds). Subscription is "risk free" – if you don't like the first issue you're sent, simply cancel your order and your money will be refunded.

New Consumer

www.newconsumer.org ▷ 0141 335 9050 ▷ Published every two months ▷ £3 per issue or £15 annual subscription

Set up by *Big Issue* co-founder Mel Young, *New Consumer* launched as a "fair trade magazine", though has subsequently broadened the remit to cover ethical living in general. Published six times a year, it's as much a shopping catalogue as it is a magazine, with full-colour pages crammed with photos of the latest and greatest fairly traded clothes, gifts, toys, ornaments and more, along with prices and where-to-buy information – a better way to shop than browsing the often second-rate websites of fair trade suppliers. Elsewhere there are features, news and light-hearted columns on gardening, finance, shopping and more.

Books

There isn't space here for a complete bibliography – and anyhow many of the subjects touched on in this book are better covered in magazines, journals and websites than in books. But here are a few particularly relevant recent titles that have been referred to in the text.

Ethical consumerism guides

Ethical Travel Guide, Polly Pattullo and Orely Minell (Earthscan, 2006, £12.99, ISBN 1853838373)
Discusses the issues and then lists hundreds of "alternative", "eco" and "green" holidays.

The Good Fish Guide, Bernadette Clarke (Marine Conservation Society, 2002, £10, ISBN 1857503422)
A scarily comprehensive guide to eating water-borne species ethically. Get it from www.mcsuk.org

The Good Shopping Guide (Ethical Marketing Group, 2005, £12.95, ISBN 0955290708)
Published annually since 2003, this colourful, user-friendly guide covers everything from batteries to breakfast cereal to banks. Each product area gets a discussion of the issues and then a table comparing the main brands, each of which are ranked in three categories: good, evil and those in between. The research is provided by *Ethical Consumer* magazine.

The Good Wood Guide (FoE, 2002, £7.50, ISBN 1857503422)
A complete guide to buying ethical wood, with a directory of timber types and background issues.

Context & issues

Ethical Tourism: Who Benefits (Hodder Arnold, 2002, £5.99, ISBN 034085734X)
Four essays on the the pros and cons of "eco" and "responsible" travel.

Green Alternatives to Globalisation, Michael Woodin & Caroline Lucas (Pluto, 2004, £11.99, ISBN 0745319327)
The most recent localization manifesto, co-authored by a Green MEP.

The Little Earth Book, James Bruges (Alastair Sawday, 2004, £6.99, ISBN 1901970523)
Pithy, fact-filled mini-essays on everything from water to soil.

The Little Food Book, Craig Sams (Alastair Sawday, 2003, £6.99, ISBN 1901970329)
Small but juicy look at the whole subject of food, taking in subsidies, sugar, obesity, organics and more.

No Logo, Naomi Klein (Flamingo, 2001, £8.99, ISBN 0006530400)
The book that put branding, world trade, globalization and sweatshops into the public eye.

Not On The Label, Felicity Lawrence (Penguin, 2004, £7.99, ISBN 0141015667)
An investigative tour of the food industry, from gangmasters and pesticides to the coffee crisis.

Open World, Philippe Legrain (Abacus, 2002, £7.99, ISBN 034911529X)
A readable defence of globalization,

covering poverty, sweatshops, trade rules, brands and big business.

The Rough Guide to Climate Change, Bob Henson (Rough Guides, 2006, £9.99, ISBN 1843537117)

A comprehensive overview of climate change science and proposed solutions, both international and individual.

Shopped, Joanna Blythman (Fourth Estate, 2004, £12.99, ISBN 0007158033)

The Food We Eat, Joanna Blythman (Penguin, 1998, £6.99, ISBN 0140273662)

A gourmand takes a stand against supermarkets, factory farming and the UK's dying food culture.

Something New Under the Sun, John McNeill (Penguin, 2004, £10.99, ISBN 0140295097)

A scholarly yet readable "environmental history" of the last century.

So Shall We Reap, Colin Tudge (Penguin, 2004, £8.99, ISBN 0141009500)

An intelligent plea for sustainable agriculture, including the potential limitations of organic farming.

Index